100 FUNNY
IRISH RUGBY
MOMENTS

Paud

100 FUNNY
IRISH RUGBY
MOMENTS

JOHN SCALLY

BLACK & WHITE PUBLISHING

First published in the UK in 2022 by
Black & White Publishing Ltd
Nautical House, 104 Commercial Street, Edinburgh EH6 6NF

A division of Bonnier Books UK
4th Floor, Victoria House, Bloomsbury Square, London, WC1B 4DA
Owned by Bonnier Books
Sveavägen 56, Stockholm, Sweden

This book is a work of non-fiction, based on the recollections of the author
and interviews conducted by the author. The author has stated to the publishers
that the contents of this book are true to the best of their knowledge.

A CIP catalogue record for this book is available from the British Library.

ISBN: 978 1 78530 408 8

3 5 7 9 10 8 6 4 2

Typeset by Data Connection
Printed and bound in Great Britain by Clays Ltd, Elcograf S.p.A.

www.blackandwhitepublishing.com

To Mick Quinn
The Perfect Ten
An Irish international like no other.

CONTENTS

FOREWORD

by Tony Ward

When I read the newspaper every day I am exposed to all the troubles of the nation and the world. There are times when it seems like there is nothing but bad news. I am acutely aware of the many difficulties so many people face today.

In these troubled times we live in, it is nice to take time to reflect on happier things. Who was it said laughter is the best medicine? I am not sure, but whoever did would have loved this book.

I was so lucky to play for Munster and Ireland. I remember great days like that magical day in 1978 when Munster beat the All Blacks and winning my first cap for Ireland. Even more than the memories of the games I am so fortunate that I have a treasure trove of great memories about the great personalities I played with and against.

To take one example, I was so lucky that when I began my career with Munster and Ireland, it coincided with that of the one and only Moss Keane. Moss was a great player, but perhaps the greatest character in the history of Irish rugby. It is fair to say that playing with Moss was a . . . unique experience! His preparation for big games was certainly unorthodox. I can still see him getting his nutrition by eating raw eggs. It was not a sight I particularly enjoyed! Mind you, it never seemed to do him any harm.

In fact, there was a concoction Moss, Willie Duggan, Mike Gibson, Fergus Slattery and the more seasoned players used to make before matches. I can't remember all the ingredients but central to it were raw eggs, honey and rum. It was gross, but if it worked for the legends then this rookie needed no convincing. I took it once only on the morning of my first match against Scotland, and (because I was so nervous) I convinced myself that I was tipsy with just hours to kick-off. True story. One hundred per cent true, and it was in a massive bowl in the team/meal room for anyone who so desired to dip into when he wanted. Once bitten, twice shy, and never ever repeated, I can assure you!

Few personalities in Irish sport were so loved. This book is a celebration of all the great characters like Moss, Peter Clohessy, Ronan O'Gara and so many more of the last one hundred years.

Books are the quietest and most constant of friends, and I am sure this book will be a quiet and constant friend to many readers for years to come and will be a welcome and worthy addition to the ever-growing anthology on the lore of Irish rugby.

We all need from time to time to find a feel-good factor, and this book provides us with it in abundance. It is a must for rugby fans and indeed for anyone who needs a good belly laugh. This fascinating, witty compilation will delight all those addicted to the sport played by women and men with odd-shaped balls!

Tony Ward

INTRODUCTION

Welcome to the rugby house of fun.

This is a story of a lot of pointy balls.

Actually, it's a hundred of them.

This book was written to fight the stress of buying and selling a house. The problem with my old house was not that I could hear all the noise from my neighbours; the real problem was that the walls were so thin, I could hear their inner doubts.

My last book was to ghostwrite the autobiography of a witch. To be honest my main role was the spell checking.

I am often asked why I decided to become an editor. Well, to cut a long story short . . .

My lack of fitness has also been an issue. Things have got so bad that I have been enlisted in a fitness protection programme.

Much of our memory is dictated by nostalgia. As a boy, one of my heroes was Tony Ward. It has been a great thrill to become friends with him for the last thirty years. His friendship has been very important to boosting my self-confidence. If there was a low self-esteem Olympics I would win the . . . bronze medal.

The only problem with Tony is that he thinks a cup of tea is the answer for everything. That explains why he did so badly when he went on *Mastermind*.

Tony likes to take everything with a pinch of salt. It works brilliantly for him as a pundit. It means he makes a terrible cup of coffee.

It is his only blemish apart from the time when he was a student and he lost his job in the candle factory. He refused to work wick ends.

As a student in Limerick, Tony Ward had a part-time job as a chef in a confectionery. He was fired for no raisin.

He does continue to surprise me like when he rang me recently from Dublin airport when he was due to head off for his holiday and said, 'You know that small table beside my hall door?'

I replied, 'Of course I do. It's lovely.'

'Well I wish I brought it with me.'

'In the name of God, why?'

'My passport was on it.'

Most rugby fans of a more mature vintage will remember that Tony owned a sports shop in Limerick. However, what is less well known is that he had a less successful venture as an entrepreneur. He started a cold air balloon shop. It never took off.

Tony recently set up a new business which involves hugging celebrities. He is the majority Cherholder.

I do worry though about Tony's musical knowledge. He claims his favourite singer is Vinyl Richie.

Since meeting Tony I have the opportunity to meet the great and the good of Irish rugby as well as some of the giants of rugby on the international stage such as Ray Gravell and Bill McLaren. This book is the product of thirty years of very enjoyable conversations.

As a general rule I would say that most rugby players of the past were great talkers and very au fait with all the rugby gossip as anybody, though they have neither viciousness nor bitterness. They love a good yarn but are never unduly bothered about trifles like veracity. If the truth has to be adapted to suit the story, they tend to have no problems with it. As we say in the West of Ireland, they regularly 'say more than their prayers'. Whenever I hear Emily Dickinson line 'tell all the truth but tell it slant', I think of them.

I got a revealing insight into rugby's place in Irish life when my local priest, Fr Seán, decided to hold a pre-marriage course on the day of the Ireland–Wales Six Nations match. He couldn't understand why so many of the men, and some of the women, spent their time looking under the tables while they were supposed to be listening to the lectures. It was only afterwards that someone explained they were checking for updates on the match on their mobile phones.

My agenda in this book is a simple one: to entertain. If you want the truth, the whole truth and nothing but the truth this is not the book for you!

The stories in the book are based on the truth – with varying degrees of looseness. Only the facts have been changed! I am taking a very liberal understanding of 'moment' for this book.

Discretion prevents me from naming the prominent former international who has a Cocker Spaniel called 'Black and Tan' as his colouring is black and tan. His (the dog's) favourite song is Leonard Cohen's version of 'Kevin Barry' sung in the National Stadium in 1972. Alan Partridge would have approved.

Likewise I refuse to name the current Irish international who brought his girlfriend to an orchard for her birthday. Turns out that is not the Apple watch she wanted.

Sadly I am also honour-bound not to reveal the name of the former Irish international who came home from a rugby trip four days late and was greeted by his angry wife, who after venting her outrage said as he tried to defend himself, 'One more word from you and I'm going home to my mother.'

He shouted in response, 'Taxi!'

For legal reasons I cannot disclose the name of the wife of the Irish rugby legend who I asked how she was coping with the retirement of her husband from his lucrative job. She shook her head ruefully and said in a tone of weary resignation, 'Retirement means twice the amount of time with my husband but only half the income.'

The critic Vivian Mercier famously reviewed *Waiting for Godot* as a play in which 'Nothing happens twice'. As these pages illustrate, the story of Irish rugby is very different.

1

THE GIRL ON THE TRAIN

Ollie Campbell Takes the Luas

He was a national treasure with a great love for one of Ireland's greatest rugby heroes.

Before finding fame as a writer, Samuel Beckett found acclaim on the playing fields of Trinity College both as a rugby player and cricketer. As a Trinity graduate myself, I do have to take exception to his claim that 'the students of Trinity College are the cream of Irish society as they are rich and thick.'

I have to protest in the strongest possible terms. We are not all rich.

The poet John Montague (1929–2016) paid a tribute to one of Ireland's greatest writers, the Nobel Prize for Literature winner Samuel Beckett, on the occasion of his death in 1989. He recalled how a journalist, visiting the writer in Paris, casually mentioned he used to play rugby with Ollie Campbell. Beckett claimed that Campbell was 'a genius' and then selected an all-time fifteen of Irish writers. He picked James Joyce at scrum-half, despite his poor eyesight: 'Very crafty. Very nippy. He might surprise you when the light is fading.'

When Montague wondered how the literary genius knew so much about Campbell given he never watched television, Beckett conceded: 'Only for the games. And only when the Irish play.'

Beckett only retained two items in his Paris home to remind him of Ireland. One is said to be a picture of the Halfpenny Bridge and the second was a picture of Ollie Campbell playing for Ireland. It is perhaps the ultimate compliment to Campbell. For younger readers who never saw him play, just see confirmation of his genius by watching the 1982 edition of *Reeling in the Years* as he kicked, tackled and passed Ireland to its first Triple Crown in thirty-three years. He twice toured with the Lions in 1979 and 1983 before recurring hamstring injuries forced his premature retirement in 1984 when he was just hitting his prime.

HAVE YOURSELF A BERRY MERRY CHRISTMAS

Last year Ollie took the Luas to visit the Dundrum Shopping Centre to do his Christmas shopping. He thought he would avoid the crowds, so he went early on a Monday morning. Not used to the Luas, he was shocked to find that the tram was already almost packed.

He found a place to stand. He looked around to see his fellow passengers.

Then his heart almost stopped.

Sitting on one of the seats, opposite him was the most beautiful woman he had ever seen. She reminded him of the classic beauty of Audrey Hepburn in *Breakfast at Tiffany's*.

As he is the least likely man that rugby has ever produced to breathe in the fumes of toxic male masculinity, Ollie did something that was completely out of character.

He smiled at her.

His heart started to accelerate a little because she smiled back at him.

Then his innate modesty kicked in and he looked away.

But after a few minutes he found himself, as if drawn by a magnet, sneaking a look at her again.

His heart started to pound because this time – she smiled at him.

He smiled back.

Then an unexpected development.

She got up and walked towards him.

Ollie noticed three things about her.

She had the most lustrous long hair. She was clearly very healthy.

She had a stunning figure.

But as she got closer, he noticed her most striking feature.

She had the biggest pair of . . .

Ocean-blue eyes he had ever seen.

It was as if she had been moulded by a sculptor with a unique capacity to achieve perfection.

Then when she was little more than a foot away, she spoke to him.

By now Ollie's heartbeat felt it was about to explode.

Her voice was like musical honey.

To his dying day and probably longer, Ollie will never forget her seven immortal words:

'Would you like to take my seat?'

2

THE SPY WHO DIDN'T LOVE HIM

Michael Cheika Gets a Text

Most of us at school learned Robert Frost's poem about two roads diverging in a wood. Then the protagonist chose the road not taken. He would be happy with his choice as that was the one that made all the difference.

Ross McCarron is perhaps the most famous rugby version of such a story. As he was making his mark in the Leinster squad, he turned down a senior Leinster contract at the age of twenty-three in 2008. At that time Leinster were on the cusp of becoming the superpower of European rugby. McCarron opted instead to finish his degree and seek a job in the real world.

However, McCarron's time in Leinster is best remembered for his tempestuous relationship with the coach Michael Cheika. It is probably fair to say that Cheika favoured some of his players with a 'tough love' approach and McCarron was one of those players.

Sailing down the river of memories, McCarron reflected on his most famous incident with his coach at a time when he was peeved with the treatment he was getting.

'I'm thinking: "F**k this. I'm supposed to be playing a game tomorrow. I don't want all of the confidence knocked out of me." I jumped in the car with a few lads to grab some lunch. When they were buying grub, I sent an expletive-ridden text to my girlfriend, venting about Cheika.

'It was a brutal text message – "This guy is an eejit, I absolutely hate him, etc." I was on an old Nokia, which prompted me to send the text to my most recent contact: Michael Cheika. And I pressed OK by mistake. I will never forget the feeling. My heart dropped to the bottom of my stomach.

'When the lads came back, they said that I was as white as a sheet. I told them what I had done and one of them — I won't say who — asks me, "Where's Cheika now?" He was training with the seniors. Then he says, "Where's his phone?"'

Fortunately in a scene that involved all the tension of a John le Carré novel, McCarron managed to sneak in to Cheika's inner sanctum and delete the text before the coach could read it.

Not before his blood pressure rocketed sky high.

TONE-R DOWN

Carwyn Rees James was a Welsh rugby union player and coach. He won two Welsh international caps but is most famous for his coaching achievements with Llanelli, the 1971 British Lions and the Barbarians, with all of whom he beat the All Blacks. He was once asked to coach Wales. He replied, 'It would be the honour of my life. But I would do it only on one condition.'

'What's that?'

'That I would have sole charge of selection.'

In the era when rugby committees ruled supreme the offer was quickly withdrawn and a universally recognised coaching genius never coached his own country. Michael Cheika would have appreciated James's independent spirit. At Leinster, though, he was his own man, as many of the players found to their cost. Felipe Contepomi credits Cheika with changing the culture in Leinster: 'Culture is something that you can destroy overnight, but it takes a long time to build. You have to work on it every day and get everybody to buy in. You get people to change, then the behaviour becomes a habit and eventually it changes into a culture. Cheika was great for some players like me, but maybe he was not for everyone.'

However, Cheika did have a benign attitude to Devin Toner. He called him 'Inkjet' because you put ink into the toner of a printer.

ROCKY

In the 2008–9 season the key player for Leinster in many ways was Rocky Elsom. He was man of the match in the majority of games. He was Michael Cheika's pet. Cheika of course did also blood new players in Rocky's position like Kevin McLaughlin, who would go on to play eight times for Ireland.

The only time the players saw Cheika panic was one morning before training: news spread like wildfire that there was a crash in Donnybrook and that Rocky Elsom was involved. When he heard the news, the blood drained from Cheika's face. Then a text came in and one of the players blurted out, 'Don't worry, it's not Rocky. It's only Kevin McLaughlin!'

3

SIMPLY THE BEST?

Captain Sleeping Beauty

It was like a scene from a slapstick comedy.

The English flanker James Haskell recalls how Rory Best and Iain Henderson, who were both Ireland and Ulster teammates at the time, were inseparable on the Lions tour of New Zealand in 2017. He called them 'Shrek' and 'Donkey' on that trip. They were always cracking jokes, although he could only understand about half of what they were saying. He honestly thought Henderson was speaking Irish for the first few days because of his strong Ulster accent.

Haskell's philosophy is: 'There are a few basic rules to live by as a rugby player. Never trust a teammate who doesn't attend team socials, never trust a teammate who doesn't front up in a contact session and never trust a man who showers with his pants on.' He claims that both Henderson and Best 'had hollow legs' when it came to holding their drink and recalls how he was having breakfast one morning when the two Irish forwards came stumbling in.

It was eight in the morning after the final Test, where the Lions claimed a draw to tie the series, and Haskell was convinced to have a drink with them, which ended up turning into an epic all-day session.

He believes that while Best is incredibly clever, he never met a man who could drink so much without falling over. He claims that Henderson was in a similar category.

He recalls Best and Henderson wandering in a 'merry state'. Best asked him, 'Want a drink, Hask?' Although he didn't, his two colleagues persuaded him to have a cider with his eggs on toast.

The terrifically talented threesome barely moved from that table for the next fifteen hours. They just sat there from 8.30 a.m. to 10 p.m. that night, talking, laughing and drinking – a lot.

Things escalated though when some drinking games were introduced. One was called 'Toothpicks', which involved sticking toothpicks in their faces. Another was called 'drink', which involved necking whatever drink they had in front of them whenever Best said, 'Drink'.

After a few hours, they all had beer boxes on their heads, with holes cut out for eyes and faces drawn on them. After about seven hours, they noticed that Best was starting to drift off. Haskell said, 'Come on, old fella. Let's have a little lie-down.'

He wheeled in a hospital bed, put Best on it and tucked him in so that he looked like a corpse – arms folded across his chest, like he had been read the Last Rites, blanket up to his chin, his bald head poking out the top.

Then Haskell got a brainwave, though with the benefit of hindsight he now thinks of it otherwise. He said, 'Why don't we wheel him outside and leave him on the street?' They pushed him through the hotel, all still with boxes on their heads, sniggering like children and shushing each other, so that they were making even more noise than normal while telling each other to quieten down.

When they got him outside, Haskell said, 'Why don't we push him down that hill?' The Lions' hotel was right on top of a massive hill in Auckland that sloped down for miles to the sea.

Haskell kicked the back of his bed and off he went. Initially they all thought this was one of the funniest things they had ever seen – Best, a pale corpse, gently rolling down a hill in a hospital bed. The problem was that as the hill became steeper, the bed picked up speed and panic set in.

Four or five of the greatest rugby players in the Northern Hemisphere were chasing Best in this bed, with beer boxes on their heads, shouting and screaming, as people in suits wandered past on their way home from work.

For a short time, they thought they had killed the Irish captain. Happily, though, a fatality was averted when a fortuitous bend in the road sent Best swerving into a bus stop, scattering commuters and depositing the Irish captain onto the pavement.

People were screaming because they thought he was a runaway corpse that had rolled out the back of some under-taker's ambulance.

PARTY CENTRAL

Peter O'Mahony and Bundee Aki went viral in July 2022 for the gusto of their celebrations after Ireland won their first test series down under against the All Blacks. The New Zealanders were in awe of O'Mahony's toughness – claiming that covid-19 has now got a vaccine against Peter O'Mahony.

They also state that O'Mahony ordered a steak when he went to the restaurant for a celebratory meal. The steak did what it was told.

Sadly, later that night a cobra bit O'Mahony's leg. After a week of excruciating pain, the cobra tragically died.

4

WHEN PAULIE MET PRINCE WILLIAM

Paul O'Connell Remembers Eight Hundred
Years of Oppression

Forsan et haec olim meminisse iuvabit.
Perhaps one day it will be a joy to remember
these things too.

(Virgil's *Aeneid*)

Even during the bleakest days of the Coronavirus crisis there were moments of humour. In 2021 a large number of the French contingent tested positive after they beat the Irish in Dublin in the Six Nations. The assumption in France was that they caught it in Ireland. One Irish WAG though poured cold water on the idea, 'They couldn't have got it here. The Irish team are incapable of passing anything on.'

The Irish attack and their attack coach, Mike Catt, was the focus of much criticism afterwards. One fan said, 'Our attack is useless. Even our attack coach is called Catt.'

Crimeline did a feature afterwards on a missing item – the Irish offload.

Another fan remarked, 'We obviously were preparing for the virus long before everyone else. Our defenders were never closer than two metres to anyone. Our winger never caught anything. Our forwards never passed anything on. And of course our committee members were always washing their hands for everything.'

The mood music changed dramatically though in the final game of the 2021 Six Nations when Ireland comprehensively beat England. The Finance Minister Paschal Donohue claimed that Ireland's first half against England was the best forty minutes of the year. Much of the credit for Ireland's improvement was attributed to the fact that rugby legend Paul O'Connell joined the coaching ticket.

The hardest man in the history of rugby has to be Wayne 'Buck' Shelford. The All Black forward and former captain was playing against France in what became known as the 'Battle of Nantes'. First, he lost three teeth after he was kicked in the face at a ruck. Then he was knocked out cold by a blow to the head. To cap it all, he had his scrotum ripped open, leaving one of his testicles hanging free. Buck recalled to ESPN, 'It bloody well hurt at the time, so I just chucked the old proverbial Jesus water down the shorts to make it feel better. That didn't do a lot, so we just played on. I went off the field with twenty minutes to go not really knowing where I was, let alone what day it was. As history shows, we lost the game, and it was not until I got changed that I realised that my scrotum had been torn, and that the testicle was hanging a good four or five inches out of the scrotum. It was all put into place and stitched up nicely.'

Limerick's favourite son Paul O'Connell must push him a close second. In the first Lions Test in 2013 he broke his arm but did not come off. After the match prop Ben Alexander spoke for all when he said, 'He's just broken his arm. But he got up and packed those last few scrums.'

Paulie was asked to stay on despite his injury because of his motivational powers. He told the squad: 'This is your shot at forever – don't let the opportunity pass you by.'

NOT HANGING ON THE TELEPHONE

Paulie's stature as a player was confirmed in 2009 when he was selected as captain of the Lions team to tour in South Africa. It is indicative of Irish players' people skills as much as their capabilities on the pitch that ten Irish players have been chosen to captain the Lions, compared to four each for England, Scotland and Wales. He was unlucky in many respects. The Second Test on the 2009 Lions tour is most remembered for an incident when Schalk Burger gouged the Lions winger Luke Fitzgerald in the very first minute and incredibly escaped just with a yellow card.

To compound the Lions' misery, Ronan O'Gara missed a tackle on Jaque Fourie to gift the hosts a late try. Four minutes into injury time, with the game tied, O'Gara was deemed to have taken out Fourie in the air. The Boks nailed the kick from their own half to give them a 28–25 win.

There was an initial hurdle to be jumped at the start of the tour. The coach Ian McGeechan was trying to ring O'Connell to tell him he was going to captain the Lions. It was much more difficult than he expected. Paul had been shielding his call from UK numbers. It took Sir Ian three attempts before Paulie accepted the call!

PRAGMATISM

On that tour someone suggested playing a game in outer space, but Paulie had to point out there just would not be any atmosphere.

A TALE OF TWO FATHERS

Paulie's Twitter page contains this story:

Two fathers are watching a youth game.

'Which one is your son?'

'Why?'

'I wanted to tell him how bad he is.'

'You can't say that, he's only a kid. How would you like it if I said that to your son?'

'Well, you've done it all game.'

'Why who's your son?'

'The ref.'

ALL CREATURES GREAT AND SMALL

Paulie is such a loved character that when his dog got sick and had to stay in the surgery for a few days the vet gave him a courtesy cat.

TIGHT FIT

Given his imposing frame as a student, Paul worked as a security guard. His most memorable encounter was with a woman with a ladder in her tights. She was a serious shoplifter.

NO CALAMITY JANE

After Paulie's appointment as Irish forwards coach, the fortunes of the Irish team improved dramatically in 2021, culminating in a 28–20 victory over the All Blacks. Such was the dominance of the Irish win that Rob Kearney's cousin, President Joe Biden, Face-Timed the Irish players and management to congratulate them.

The star of the game was Ireland's Calen Doris. Even before his try he had been the best player on the pitch, with twenty-four combined tackles and carries. One headline summed it up the next morning: 'Doris Day.'

Credit for the victory must also go to Eddie O'Sullivan. Before the match Eddie had issued a war cry to the team – a unique version of bottoms up: 'It simply boils down to the fact that they have as many bones in their arse as we have.'

THE OLD ENEMY

O'Connell has a keen awareness of the nuances of Irish history, including its 800 tears of oppression by our closest neighbours. During the 2005 Lions Tour, Prince William (a keen rugby fan) visited the squad to wish Clive Woodard and his players the best of luck. When he met the Munster contingent the prince was anxious to let them know he was very au fait with the stories of Thomond Park and the global reputation of rugby in Limerick.

A decade earlier Prince Charles had visited in Ireland, and famously in 2011 the queen would visit the country and thrill the nation by speaking in Irish. In the post-Good Friday Agreement environment and the growing spirit of rapprochement between the countries, O'Connell decided to invite William to come and watch a game in Thomond Park.

The prince demurred, saying that there would a lot of logistical headaches to be overcome if he was to visit. Quick as a flash Paulie replied, 'Some of your ancestors had no problem coming over to Ireland.'

WEDDED BLISS

Paul O'Connell's wedding in 2013 was memorable. During the ceremony, which was held in France, Paul was bewildered to spot a few uninvited lads make their way into the chapel:

'The cathedral is kind of a tourist attraction in the area, so there's lots of people in the place and there was a guy sitting really close to our guests with no top on and wearing Bermudas.

I said to the priest, "Look, we're nearly getting ready to kick off now, when do you clear out the church?"

'He said no, the doors are always open, they're never closed.

'So everyone stayed in for the thing, there was all sorts of random people taking photos, just randomers, but there was a guy in a Connacht polo shirt and Connacht Bermudas.'

HIP-PY

George North was rooming with Paul O'Connell ahead of the 2013 Lions tour of Australia.

North was just twenty-one at the time and in awe of the fact that he was about to meet a giant of the game.

'I was in camp in Cardiff, the rooming list comes up and I was sharing with Paul O'Connell. I walk in and I see Paulie's bags on the floor and I'm like, wow. I've not really spoken to Paul before apart from after a game briefly.

'I'm thinking, oh my god what do I say to this man now. A legend, let's face it, of the game, and that's not a word I like to bat around, but he is, as you well know, a hero.

'So I'm sat there on my bed, waiting for him to come out, thinking do I stand up and shake his hand? Do I hug him? But he's just out of the shower it's a bit weird now . . .

'So then basically while all this is going on I can start hearing him singing a song. And in his broad Irish accent he starts singing Shakira. You know that one, the "Hips Don't Lie". "Oh baby when you talk like that!" In the most Irish accent ever. And then he goes "Shakira", and at that point I absolutely burst out laughing.

'And when he came out then I thought . . . oh he's normal.'

SCARED SHI*LESS

Since he retired Paulie has become a cultural icon because of his singing ability! The genius of Mario Rosenstock has created a new national treasure as part of the Gift Grub slot on Ireland's most popular morning radio programme 'The Ian Dempsey Breakfast Show'. Ian is to Irish morning radio what Brian O'Driscoll was to Irish rugby. Super Mario has created a super group with his impersonations of O'Connell, Ronan O'Gara and Alan Quinlan called 'The F.O.G.'s'. The name comes from O'Connell's famous exhortation 'Put the fear of God into them.' They bring a 'unique' re-imagining of some classic songs which regularly send social media into meltdown, such is their popularity.

One of their highlights came in advance of Ireland's Six Nations game against Wales in 2021. The F.O.G.'s creatively re-interpreted the Miley Cyrus smash hit 'Wrecking Ball' into 'Wrecking Wales'. Paulie proudly proclaims that he came in with his rugby ball and then 'scared the sh**e out of them all'.

DO YOU THINK I AM SEXY?

It is not universally known but Ronan O'Gara once had a quickie with Rob Kearney.

Some context may be necessary at this point.

O'Gara doubles up on Gift Grub as the presenter of 'Radio Rog', a deliciously devilish exploration of the world of rugby. On one occasion Radio Rog invites Rob Kearney into the studio after the former fullback launched a new fitness app. Kearney begins one of the quickie exercises with the immortal instruction: 'Gently sit your right buttock on top of the orange.'

5

BYE BRAVEHEART

Willie Duggan's Funeral

Only he could have pulled it off.

Willie Duggan's funeral would have been expected to have been a desperately sad occasion. Instead it was an occasion of much laughter. The fact that Willie had insisted that the event be a party and that nobody was to wear black was the catalyst for the unique atmosphere.

In 2017 the sixty-seven-year-old died suddenly at his home in Dunmore, County Kilkenny. Willie was capped 41 times by Ireland between 1975 and 1984 and also played all four tests for the Lions during their 1977 tour to New Zealand. The high point of his career came in 1982 when he won the Triple Crown as part of a pack affectionately known as 'Dad's Army' after the famous television series of the time.

Willie was a wit, as was evident in his comment on a diminutive colleague: 'Colin Patterson was the only Irish player to have a full-size photo on his passport.'

The funeral Mass in Kilkenny cathedral deliberately started eighteen minutes late, which was the average time Willie was late for training sessions when he played for Blackrock. Willie often joked that there was a Holy Ghost priest who coached rugby in Blackrock College who famously said, 'The two most important things in life are the grace of God and a quick heel from the loose – though not necessarily in that order!'

In her address during the funeral Mass, directed to her father, Willie's daughter Helena said, 'Growing up, we never knew you were famous, you never told any of us. We just thought you had lots of friends and were just bad at remembering their names.'

Helena noted how he would cry during the epic movies with 'big music', how he would 'stir the pot with all of us' at home and sit back and laugh as chaos followed, how he 'rang every bank manager in the country trying to track down Mam, so she would go out with [him]' and how he bought an engagement ring in New Zealand before she had even agreed to a date.

The chief celebrant Fr Purcell, in his homily, prompted much laughter when he remembered times in Dunmore: 'All the fighting we used do and the arguments and the lies we used tell each other. I don't think I ever left Willie Duggan without having to go and Google some expression or other to see what it meant and let me tell you, sometimes it wasn't pretty.'

He also shared that Willie had made a joke at his expense claiming that he was a priest who had taken up rugby and that he scored a few tries but had not made any conversions yet.

Willie was fascinated with the newly evolving concept of teams warming up on the field before a game, and Donal Lenihan recalled that after observing Ireland's exhausting pre-match routine Willie claimed that, 'I could do the warm-up or play the match but I couldn't do both.'

Hugo MacNeill recalled how Willie had a problem selling an oversized sink. So he contacted a journalist to do a feature on it for the local paper. The journalist said he would be happy to give him a plug.

Sartorial elegance was not Willie's forte. The most common description of him was that 'on and off the field he looked like an unmade bed'.

ANIMAL FARM

When I told Willie that I grew up in a small village in Roscommon he said, 'You could be from a one-horse town if there was a horse in it.'

Willie was very interested in the fact that I was brought up on a farm. He even suggested a new name for my goat. He suggested I call him 'Vincent van Goat'.

He caught me by surprise when he asked me: 'Do you know what gets my goat?'

When I shook my head in defeat he coolly replied, 'Rustlers.'

Willie caught me out perfectly once. He asked me in his most deadpan voice if I knew that Johnny Cash worked in Dublin Zoo. When I expressed shock at this startling revelation he calmly replied, 'Yeah he did. He walked the lion.'

THE INVISIBLE MEN

Moss Keane is one of the all-time greatest characters in Irish rugby and is often associated with his teammate Willie Duggan for the way they played on the pitch and the way they celebrated off it. In victory or defeat, Moss and Willie knew how to party after a game.

Of course Willie and Moss were kindred spirits. Gary Halpin once told me that for a dare Willie and Moss drank a jar each of invisible ink. They both had a bad reaction to it and had to go hospital. They only problem was that they spent hours there – waiting to be seen.

A DANGEROUS HABIT

When Ireland finally won its second Grand Slam in 2009 after sixty-one years Moss Keane said, 'It was a long time between drinks.'

The late, great Phil Bennett recalled: 'Moss and Willie read that drink was bad for you. So they gave up . . . reading.'

LOVE AND MARRIAGE

Willie was once asked his opinion of marriage. 'Rugby is like marriage. The preliminaries are often better than the main event.'

Duggan was told that a young rugby player was taking his chances on the roulette wheel of love and getting married the following day. 'Congratulations, my boy,' said Willie. 'I'm sure you will look back on today as the happiest day of your life.'

'But I'm not getting married until tomorrow,' protested the young player.

'I know,' said Duggan.

Three years later a mutual friend asked Willie how the young player's marriage was. Duggan replied, 'I think his wife has just left him. He's turning cartwheels out on the lawn.'

YOU DON'T BRING ME FLOWERS

Willie had a moment when he realised that his rugby 'activities' off the field more so than on it were causing him to neglect his wife a little. So on his way home from work one evening he bought her a dozen red roses and a big box of chocolates. He was eager to see how she would react to his grand romantic gesture. He walked through the door with a huge grin but was stunned when she burst into tears.

'What's wrong love?' he asked in bemusement.

'I've had the worst day ever. Our youngest son tried to flush a nappy down the toilet. Then the dishwasher stopped working. Then our daughter came home bleeding because she fell on the pavement. And now to cap it all you come home acting so strangely that you must be drunk.'

SPEED

Willie once had a brush with the law. A garda asked him, 'Why are you driving so fast?'

Duggan calmly answered, 'My brakes are faulty and I wanted to get home before I'd have an accident.'

MAGIC MOMENTS

The other Irish player whose name Willie's is inescapably inter-twined with was his backrow colleague Fergus Slattery. Slatts shared Willie's favourite story.

Will Carling interviewed Slattery before Ireland played England in Twickenham. He asked Slatts if Ireland prepared differently for taking on the old enemy in Twickenham. Slatts first informed him that it was not such a big deal for Ireland to play there because half the crowd were Irish since they all came down from Cheltenham Festival.

Slattery took Carling by surprise, though, by saying that the special quality Ireland brought to playing England was 'MAGIC'.

When Carling was bemused by this Slatts explained: 'Before the game the team gets together and picks some little boll***s like Will Ca . . . like Austin Healey for special treatment. In the first minute we kick the ball 60 feet in the air over the head of the little boll***s. The ball starts to drop 50 feet, 40 feet, 30 feet and then at 20 feet its action stations. One of our prop forwards is 30 yards away and shouts at the top of his voice,

"REFFFFFFFFFFFFFFFFF". The startled ref turns around and sees the prop with his togs around his ankles howling in pain. As he turns around the Irish team take the opportunity to give the designated boll***s an almighty thumping. And that is MAGIC.'

6

THE STRIFE OF BRIAN

Brian O'Driscoll Makes a Mistake

When I went fishing, the only thing I caught was the flu.

A rare few have the Midas touch.

There is a team of crackpot scientists in a basement in Trinity College whose sole job it is to investigate whether there were strange astrological phenomena at work in the alignment of the stars on the day Brian O'Driscoll was born. Irish rugby has never known such a creature. So far they have concluded that there was a unique alignment of the stars on that occasion.

So elusive was Barry John that it was said of him that if he ran through a field of daffodils nobody would ever know. O'Driscoll was Ireland's equivalent.

'They call him God. Well I reckon he's a much better player than that.'

Thus spoke Stuart Barnes during the Sky Sports commentary of one of the all-time great tries. In his first Test for the Lions in 2001 Brian O'Driscoll left the World Champions, Australia, looking as slow as growing grass as he ran half the field and scythed through their defence to score one of the greatest individual tries ever seen, the very signature of genius. Following his vintage displays for the Lions, Brian continued his dizzying ascent to become one of the very biggest names in world rugby.

THE FRUIT OF WISDOM

Bod was once dared by Gordon D'Arcy to say something unusual in a press conference. The rugby media were a bit taken aback when, in the middle of a press conference, O'Driscoll observed, 'Knowledge is knowing a tomato is a fruit but wisdom is knowing not to put it into a fruit salad.'

SOCIAL MEDIA

The 2019 World Cup was a great disappointment for Irish rugby fans. It had one moment of comedy, though. Brian O'Driscoll was recording a video message for his many fans on social media. He was not the only former rugby player to be doing so, with Jamie Heaslip also particularly active.

The only problem was that Brian forgot to turn the sound on. So Bod was waxing away eloquently about rugby but nobody could hear him.

His social media was flooded with messages letting him know that he was not wired for sound.

One WAG commented, though, 'I'd much rather watch this and not be able to hear anything than have to listen to Jamie f**king Heaslip!'

CINEMA PARADISO

As a student, O'Driscoll was watching a film when he decided to pause it and take a break to make some coffee and get some custard cream biscuits. He immediately lost his job as a cinema projectionist.

UNSTEADY EDDIE

The year 2020 saw a dip in the team's fortunes, which troubled Drico, but he found two moments of amusement. English coach Eddie Jones taunted Ireland ahead of their Autumn Nations Cup match at Twickenham, calling them 'the United Nations of rugby'. Andy Farrell's starting XV contained five players, Bundee Aki, James Lowe, Jamison Gibson-Park, CJ Stander and Quinn Roux, who were all born in the Southern Hemisphere.

As Ireland struggled in that game, O'Driscoll was fretting over our fiddly carry-on in the centre of the pitch, but laughed at Donal Lenihan's cri de cœur in the RTÉ commentary: "DON'T BE FLUTING AROUND THE MIDDLE OF THE FIELD!"

FINDING JOY

In 2021 Drico found himself back in the media spotlight again. The new series of *Reeling in the Years* premiered with a programme on the events of 2010, opening with the classic footage of the man slipping on the ice on RTÉ News. Prominent in the programme was the social event of the year: the wedding of Ireland's answer to Kate Middleton and Prince William, actress Amy Huberman and her husband, Brian O'Driscoll.

Amy tweeted: 'Nothing makes you feel old quite like being in bed at 8.30 p.m. on a Sunday evening. Except being in bed at 8.30 p.m. on a Sunday evening and your mother texting you to say you were on *Reeling in the Years*.'

Later she went on to tweet: 'Just about recovered from being on *Reeling in the Years*. But I don't think I will ever recover from the fact it's been eleven years since that fella slipped on the ice.'

The next morning, Amy took to Instagram to poke fun at her other half, posting a picture of Brian along with the caption: 'Oh my God there's that other old person from *Reeling in the Years*! #spotted #fangirling'

The couple got married on 2 July 2010. Their tenth wedding anniversary was marked by Amy in an Instagram post captioned: 'Happy 10 year anniversary to the best husband I've ever been married to. Can't believe it's been ten years, it feels soooooooooo much longer.'

EVERY GIRL IS CRAZY ABOUT A SHARPLY DRESSED MAN

During the Covid lockdown Amy has also shared a snap of Brian with the caption: 'Honestly the urge to yell upstairs "DID YOU PUT A RED SOCK IN THE WHITE WASH?!" is overwhelming.'

She also shared a sneaky snap of the door into the room in which Brian was working and captioned it: 'I have so many questions about attack and defence and game strategies etc. Obvs. But my burning question has to be IS HE WEARING THE SLIPPERS AGAIN BEHIND THIS DOOR?!?'

The post referred to when Amy revealed Brian's work from home attire on Valentine's Day was slippers and shorts teamed with a stylish shirt.

BY ROYAL APPOINTMENT

Amy attended Prince William and Kate Middleton's wedding and had to use some very unfortunate documentation as proof of address. 'Because there's so much security, they were like, you need two bills in your name to the exact address that the invitation had been sent to. The only bills that I could find in my name were for the bin collection and for a rat problem that we'd had in our garden!'

Huberman had to attend the wedding solo because her husband was playing a rugby match. She added: 'There were three stages to that wedding and I was gone after that first stage and I met my friend who has an apartment in London. We went to her apartment after and the bathroom had the vantage point of Buckingham Palace so we were standing on her loo looking out the toilet to watch the rest of it.'

A MISCARRIAGE OF JUSTICE?

In America, they are called 'Monday Morning Quarterbacks'. Those who have all the answers on how the weekend's game should have been won after they have been played.

Munster rugby fans have not always appreciated O'Driscoll in the same way as their Leinster counterparts. In 2020 RTÉ broadcast a special Comic Relief programme to raise money for charities badly impacted by the public health crisis. Amy and Brian took on Roscommon-born actor Chris O'Dowd and his wife, writer Dawn O'Porter, in a lip sync battle.

Although Amy and Brian's stunning rendition of Johnny Logan's classic 'Hold Me Now' won out on the night over Chris and Dawn's version of John Prine's 'In Spite Of Ourselves', Munster fans claimed that the O'Dowd-O'Porters had been robbed.

BOND GIRL

In June 2021 Bod spent an evening with a Bond girl. Amy was filming a TV series with Jane Seymour, who starred in *Live and Let Die*, and Drico invited her to the family home for a barbecue. O'Driscoll had sourced the finest meat in Dublin and done a stellar job cooking it – only to discover that she was a vegetarian!

DANNY BOY

Danny O'Reilly, lead singer of The Coronas, sang at Brian and Amy's wedding. Joe Schmidt is also a fan of O'Reilly's. He invited Danny to sing for the Irish rugby squad at the 2019 rugby World Cup in Japan. Having had a few glasses of lemonade – or perhaps one too many of something stronger – after Ireland's opening victory over Scotland, O'Reilly sent Schmidt an encouraging text in the middle of the night. The only problem was that he forgot Joe didn't speak Irish. Instead of telling him that a good beginning was a good start, O'Reilly texted the Irish version: 'Tús maith leath na hoibre.'

7

SEX ON FIRE

Johnny Sexton Gets Engaged

More eminent minds than mine have written many great books on love.

What have they concluded?

No idea. I haven't read any of them.

Nobody has driven high standards in Leinster more than Johnny Sexton. He succeeded Felipe Contepomi as Leinster's out-half when the Argentinean (educated by the Irish Christian brothers) left for Stade Français. The conventional wisdom is that Contepomi had a bitter rivalry with Ronan O'Gara when he played with Leinster. The Argentinean legend offers a different perspective:

'I am not friends with Rog but I had great respect for him when he was a player and now for what he has achieved as a coach. My most bitter rivalry back then was with Denis Leamy. Denis always tackled you with such ferocity. He personified the passion which Munster played with, which I admired so much. When Denis was a coach at Leinster he brought that absolute passion and one hundred per cent commitment to Leinster and I have such a respect for him.'

Contepomi laughs at the funniest moment of his career:

'I had a bit of a nightmare at fly-half for Stade Français in the Top 14 against Toulouse in 2011. It is funny now but at the time it was anything but funny. I got a bad knock in the head and was concussed, but they put stiches on my head and a scrum cap over it and sent me on the field when it was the last place I should have been. For the last play of the game we were 6 points down and needed a converted try to win the game. In my concussed state, though, I thought we were only 2 points down. I was someone who always tried to run the ball and only ever scored four drop-goals in my career for that reason. On that occasion I struck the ball perfectly and scored what I thought was a brilliant and winning drop-goal. I ran down the pitch punching the air but on YouTube there are brilliant images of our coaching staff, who are in total shock. The bewildered looks on their faces are priceless.'

IT'S HARD TO BE HUMBLE

'Sex on fire.'

This was the headline in a newspaper after Ireland's compre-hensive victory over Wales in the Six Nations in 2022. Happily it was not gushing about Johnny Sexton's talents in the bedroom but on the playing fields.

When Sexton got engaged to his childhood sweetheart Laura, he texted his family to let them know the good news. If he was expecting messages of effusive congratulations and goodwill in response, he was in for a disappointment. Instead he got a terse comment back which simply stated: 'About time.'

WHEN HE KISSED THE TEACHER

Jimmy Carter never won an argument with his wife. He thought he had once but he discovered that the argument had only been paused.

As Laura is a teacher, she has taught Sexton many important lessons, including: what is the difference between a cat and a comma? A cat has claws at the end of his paws, whereas a comma is a pause at the end of a clause.

ROMANTIC GESTURE

Sexton decided to take Laura away for a well-deserved break during his summer holidays. He rang up to book a hotel. He was thrown when the receptionist said, 'Best Western.'

Johnny panicked and blurted out, '*The Unforgiven* by Clint Eastwood.'

LOST

On their holiday they watched a live performance by the Bermuda Philharmonic Orchestra on television. All was going well until the musician with the triangle disappeared.

JE NE REGRETTE RIEN

When he moved to Paris, Sexton was excited about the opportunity to sample the world-famous French cuisine. He brought his wife to a posh restaurant. He was intrigued to see 'Edith Piaf Burger' on the menu. After eating it he said, 'I bet that is the one thing she did regret.'

DADDY'S GIRL

Johnny is now a devoted father. His little daughter came to him all excited, shrieking, 'Daddy! Daddy! Guess how old I'll be in October!'

Playing along, he laughed, 'Oh I don't know, princess, why don't you tell me?'

She gave him a huge smile and held up four fingers . . .

Three hours later she still would not tell the gardai where she got them from.

TV STAR

Nicknames are part of the rugby landscape. Brent Pope was called 'Somewhat Surprisingly'. At one stage he was voted one of Ireland's hottest men with the likes of Colin Farrell. When the RTÉ personality was reading out the list she completed it by saying . . . 'and, somewhat surprisingly, Brent Pope.'

In the Leinster set-up, James Lowe has been responsible for a number of nicknames like rechristening Jack Conan 'Moanin' Conan'.

Robbie Henshaw is called 'Old Man Bob Henshaw' because he plays the accordion, fiddle, guitar and piano.

Fellow Irish international Iain Henderson is known as 'the Llama' since former Ireland lock Donncha O'Callaghan saw the bearded Ulsterman at a training camp tucking into a bowl of cereal at breakfast.

Johnny Sexton has a reputation as a perfectionist, so when his very high standards are not met, he can get a little grumpy. Hence his nickname is 'the Rat'. His teammates find it hilarious that he is the star of a TV ad with the slogan 'going the extra smile'.

Sexton's long-running partner at half-back for Ireland, Conor Murray is known as 'Bieber' a gift from the Irish squad on their 2012 tour to New Zealand. There is a debate whether he likes the pop idol or just shared the boyish good looks.

Conor Murray asked Sexton, 'You know what really makes me smile?'

'No.'

'Facial muscles.'

SHINY HAPPY PEOPLE

Not all Munster fans love Johnny. After seeing his TV ad, a Munster rugby fan said to Sexton, 'Even people who are good for nothing have the capacity to bring a smile to your face, for instance when you push them down the stairs.'

NO THANK YOU FOR THE MUSIC

Craig Casey won great plaudits when he made his debut for Ireland against Italy in 2021. Johnny Sexton went so far as to compare him to Jonny Wilkinson. Neil Francis, though, went against the tide and said he should never be capped again. In fairness this was nothing to do with Casey's performance on the pitch but because footage emerged of him singing 'Careless Whisper' in the dressing room afterwards.

A SHARP POINT

The thirty-six-year-young out-half Johnny Sexton won his 100th cap, kicked 11 points and scored his 15th Ireland try as his side beat Japan 60–5. After the match the Japan captain Pieter Labuschagne presented him with a samurai sword. One of his Irish teammates told me afterwards it was the perfect gift for the perfect ten. When I asked why he replied, 'Johnny always likes to play on the edge.'

SEXTON'S SUB

Some years ago I invited Johnny Sexton to be the special guest at a charity event that I was organising. He wrote a gracious letter to me to explain that because of his busy schedule he was unable to attend. Joe Schmidt kindly agreed to be the guest speaker and was riveting to listen to. He was a little late because he had a rugby referee's retirement function to attend. It was a good send-off.

Joe shared a story of when Willie Duggan had invited Moss Keane to speak at a black-tie event in Kilkenny. The only problem was that Moss completely forgot about it.

Unfazed, Willie got up to speak to the five hundred guests and brought the house down with his short speech: 'Ladies and gentlemen, it is customary to say on these occasions that the special guest needs no introduction. Well that was never truer than tonight. Our guest needs absolutely no introduction. The f**ker hasn't shown up!'

8

OUT OF SOUTH AFRICA

CJ Stander Signs for Munster

He has that heavy quiet which commands.

In 2021 CJ Stander sensationally announced that he was retiring from a rugby career that included 51 caps for Ireland and over a hundred and fifty appearances for Munster. He was just thirty-one years old. He wanted to return to his native South Africa where his wife Jean-Marié and two-year-old daughter Everli were waiting for him.

However, he stressed that he would never forget how the Irish people looked after him when he first arrived in the country with just a thousand euro to his name. He laughs, though, at the unnecessary hardship he inflicted on himself:

'I had never flown by myself, it was always with a team, and I almost got lost in Amsterdam, tried to leave the airport building. I had very little English and I was struggling. I could have asked the family (for money) but I had just got a fiancée and I knew I wanted to be my own man coming over.

'The manager at Munster drove me from Cork down to Limerick and put me in the Castletroy Hotel. I only had a thousand euro and I knew I needed to get a house as my fiancée, my wife now, Jean-Marié, was coming over in a few weeks and I wanted to be set up and I wanted to save money.

'So I went across to the local shop and bought eggs, a dozen I think, and noodles. The cheapest things I could find and I could understand; only things I could see that I knew.

'I went back to the hotel room, cooked the eggs in the kettle, poured the noodles with warm water over them and that was my dinner for five days. But after training I was putting away three or four plates of food and the lads were saying, "This guy can really put away some food but he's going to blow up."

'I walked down to reception on my last day at the hotel after a lovely stay and the lady said, "Did you enjoy the facilities at the pool and the spa"? And I said, "I don't want to pay for it", and she said it was complimentary!

'And there was this unbelievable restaurant, I had seen guys having steaks and so on, and then I was asked did I enjoy the complimentary breakfast, lunch and dinner. I nearly fainted. I could have been eating like a king but instead I was living on eggs and noodles.

'When I told the Munster lads, they thought it was hilarious. They laughed hysterically but I just wanted to cry!'

LATE NO SHOW

In Ireland we are not big on ceremony or reverence. We don't like players or personalities to get too big for their boots. This was best illustrated in the 1970s when someone said to Gay Byrne, 'There are no real stars in Ireland. You are the nearest thing we have to it, but you are not there yet.'

After the announcement of his retirement it was widely reported that CJ was due to be a guest on the *Late, Late Show*. Despite the Ireland and Munster star being teased as part of the line-up throughout the week, there was not even a mention of the sporting legend once the programme went live on air. The rugby star was due to join Ryan Turbidy in studio for a chat about his incredible career and plans for retirement. (He did appear on the show weeks later.) When Ryan failed to mention him or give an explanation to why Stander was not on the show as expected, people took to social media to speculate about what was going on.

In Munster rugby circles, rumours centred around the fact that there was also a country music special scheduled for the show. The story emerged that CJ had been kidnapped with Daniel O'Donnell and both were going to be shot. Before they were shot, they were asked for one last request before they died.

Wee Daniel said, 'I would like to listen to "Achy Breaky Heart" a hundred times in a row.'

Then CJ was asked for his final request. He replied, 'Please, shoot me first.'

9

THE HUMBLING OF THE GREAT O'REILLY

Tony O'Reilly Visits Cardiff Arms Park

Henry Kissinger said of him he was the only Rembrandt in the world of business. Tony O'Reilly is a legend of rugby for both Ireland and the Lions, and a legend of business. He remains the record try scorer for the Lions with an astonishing 38 tries.

O'Reilly turned nineteen on the 1955 Lions tour. Before the tour it was stated that he would be the boy amongst men. Such was his brilliance on the tour that his teammates said, 'He is a man among boys.'

That Lions team were known as 'the entertainers'. Because there was so much spirit between both sides, it was said that there was no need to have a referee in any of the games.

As a student in Belvedere, O'Reilly learned the phrase *Sic transit gloria mundi* ('Thus passes worldly glory'). He also learned a form of the phrase that appeared in Thomas à Kempis's spiritual classic *The Imitation of Christ* (1418): *O quam cito transit gloria mundi* ('How quickly the glory of the world passes away').

O'Reilly was to recall that phrase when he brought his wife for her first visit to Cardiff Arms Park to see Wales play Ireland in 2005. As he walked to the stadium, he overheard two men who were talking; one was older, one younger. The older man said, 'There's the boyo.'

The young man looked clearly baffled and said, 'Who is he?'

'Well he used to be Tony O'Reilly.'

O'Reilly immediately thought of John Milton's line: 'Fame is the last infirmity of the rational mind.'

After that affront to his dignity O'Reilly felt obliged to bring out his 'A game' and shared some of his classic stories. The first one concerned a beautiful young woman who spots an Irish rugby immortal in a bar. Their conversation unfolded as follows:

'Are you Moss Keane?'

'I am.'

'The rugby player?'

'Yes.'

'What height are you?'

'Six foot five and a half.'

The woman looked wistfully at Moss's manly charms and asked, 'Are you in proportion?'

'No.'

Her face was as sad as a flooded meadow. But the sparkle in her eye returned when Moss added, 'If I was in proportion, I would be nine foot tall.'

ON YOUR MARX

When asked about his hero, O'Reilly said that his role model in business was Groucho Marx, who said that the two most important attributes were honesty and sincerity, and if you can fake them you could do anything.

DOING IT BY THE BOOK

Suspecting that his audience were of a literary sensibility, O'Reilly decided to tell the story of the Christmas party he threw for Brendan Behan. He decided to share some of Behan's classic lines:

'It's not that the Irish are cynical. It's rather that they have a wonderful lack of respect for everything and everybody.'

'I am a drinker with writing problems.'

'There is no such thing as bad publicity, except your own obituary.'

'The big difference between sex for money and sex for free is that sex for money usually costs a lot less.'

'I have never seen a situation so dismal that a policeman couldn't make it worse.'

'One drink is too many for me and a thousand not enough.'

'New York is my Lourdes, where I go for spiritual refreshment . . . a place where you're least likely to be bitten by a wild goat.'

'If it was raining soup, the Irish would go out with forks.'

'Critics are like eunuchs in a harem: they know how it's done, they've seen it done every day, but they're unable to do it themselves.'

'It is a good deed to forget a poor joke.'

'The Hebrews and the Gaels have much in common. Both are exotic enough to be interesting and foreign enough to be alarming.'

'The Irish are a very popular race – with themselves.'

'The number of people who buy books in Ireland would not keep me in drink for the duration of the Sunday opening time.'

'I enjoy smoking expensive cigars made in Cuba by Castro. You can feel radical and bourgeois at the same time.'

O'Reilly introduced his guest of honour to the great and the good of Irish society in America and they all told him how well they were doing. Brendan promised to let everyone who knew them know how well they were doing as soon as he returned to Ireland because, given the national passion for begrudgery, 'it will put them in bad form for Christmas'.

Behan also shared his experiences of going to a clinic in Cork: he liked the relaxed environment because the patients drank, the doctors drank and the nurses drank. Behan claimed that nobody was ever cured but the time just flew.

DRINK, DRINK, DRINK

O'Reilly also told the story of the time Behan turned up on a chat show on Canadian television totally drunk. The presenter was very unimpressed and asked him why he was so inebriated. Behan replied, 'Well a few weeks ago I was sitting in a pub in Dublin and I saw a sign on a beer mat which said: "Drink Canada Dry." So when I came over here I said I'd give it a go!'

THE DEAD CENTRE

Is this real life?

Or is this fantasy?

O'Reilly's final remark was in the strange but true category. Fanagans Funeral Directors are sponsors of Old Belvedere RFC. Their advertising board in Anglesea Road is perfectly positioned on the dead ball line.

DOYLER

O'Reilly delights in the story of the unorthodox interview procedure that led to former Irish coach Mick Doyle being accepted to study at Cambridge University. The myth goes that the young Doyler walked into the interview room and was thrown a rugby ball, which he duly caught.

'You're in,' the impressed academic is reported to have exclaimed.

BIG MONEY

Cliff Morgan told me a great story about Tony O'Reilly. It began when I asked him about his first broadcasting experience. Wales had just beaten Ireland 14–3 in Dublin on their way to the Triple Crown and Grand Slam when BBC radio commentator Sammy Walker asked the great man what he remembered about the match.

'My father losing his teeth,' said Cliff. 'When Ken Jones scored our second try, Dad was so excited that his dentures flew out of his mouth into the crowd and he hasn't seen them since.'

Some years later, Morgan was recounting the tale to Tony O'Reilly, who played twenty-nine times for his country before becoming a mega-rich international businessman and head of the Heinz empire. O'Reilly, who was renowned for his great wit, feigned surprise at the news.

'Your father's, were they?' he said. 'That's amazing. I know the guy in Cork who's still wearing them.'

On another occasion, O'Reilly had to make a brief trip to a Dublin hospital after being involved in a minor traffic accident. With medical treatment in Ireland charged on a sliding scale according to income, the nurse who was filling in the details on his behalf asked, 'Mr O'Reilly, do you earn more than 10,000 punts (pounds)?'

Quipped Tony: 'Now that depends on whether you are talking about the hour or the day.'

10

LIFTING A FINGER

Gary Halpin Shocks the All Blacks

To be forgotten is to die twice.

He will not be forgotten.

A heavy cloud of sadness fell over me in February 2021 with the shocking news of the death of Gary Halpin. He played for Ireland in both the 1991 and 1995 World Cups, winning 11 caps. The prop played for Leinster, Harlequins and London Irish during his club career.

SIDESTEP

I met Gary once for a late lunch. He was so hungry that he joked he was tempted to eat the breast of a low-flying bird. His great love was for his family, though he told me in mock seriousness, 'I don't like the way my kids are always quick to blame other people. They get that from their mum.'

He had a riddle for me:

Q: What do you get when you cross rugby with Halloween?
A: A drop-ghoul.

The high point of Gary's rugby career was when he famously scored a try against New Zealand at the 1995 Rugby World Cup. He was almost as famous for his soundbite about the game: 'People forget that I sidestepped Jonah Lomu three times in that game. The only problem was that I didn't have the ball at the time. He did.'

SIGN LANGUAGE

More infamously, he gave the All Blacks the finger as a celebration after *that* try:

'There are worse things you can do in life. But it was a really stupid thing to do. It wasn't a conscious thing. There was a frustration there. [Seán] Fitzpatrick is a bit of a wind-up merchant and you don't get too many chances to stab the dragon.

'He had said a few things about us which were disrespectful, about how the Irish are always full of fire and passion to begin with, and then they run out of gas. Thing is, he was probably right!'

Famously, Andy 'Art is What You Can Get Away With' Warhol suggested everyone in the future would be famous for fifteen minutes and the try had that effect on Gary:

'It was really funny in the aftermath of that game, Andy Warhol's thing came through for me, I got my fifteen seconds. I'd spent the rest of that summer in Africa, my wife Carol and I, we went touring. I literally got a "Daktari" Jeep and toured as far as Lusaka in Zambia and we were all over Zimbabwe as well, stayed on a tobacco farm at one point. The great thing was that while I was there, I was thinking we have a rivalry with England, but, man, these South Africans have a rivalry with New Zealand like you wouldn't believe!

'So everywhere I went that summer it was "this is the guy who gave the finger to the All Blacks". I couldn't get out of bars, everyone wanted to meet me and buy me a drink. It was pretty good chaos!'

BOOT CAMP

During his time with Harlequins, Gary Halpin went on a 'boot camp', which was run by former soldiers with military zeal. The squad were flogged to death, hungry, wet and tired late one night and totally demoralised. Then Gary let out an almighty roar. When he was asked what was wrong, he said, 'I bit my lip when I was eating my (fictious) cheeseburger.' The squad collapsed into laughter and it was just the boost they needed.

OPEN DOOR POLICY

Gary was a big believer in the philosophy 'when a door closes another opens.' It caused him great problems, though, when it happened to his first car.

AN ANNOUNCEMENT

Gary's other claim to fame came in 1996, playing in a Pilkington Cup semi-final for London Irish against Leicester when he got a distraction:

'We were being coached by Clive Woodward, so he was up against his former club. Sunbury was packed – it had a capacity of maybe six or seven thousand and wasn't really up to these big occasions. I'd arrived late and the parking was so tight. I had this big Volvo estate, so I'd parked illegally if truth be told. Because of the time I assumed there would be nobody coming in behind me.

'We started pretty well. We were winning when it happened, so it was a really crucial stage in the game. I think there had just been a minor injury, so there was a bit of a lull in the crowd. We were given a scrum, and just before we got started there was this announcement over the tannoy – an ambulance needed to get through and a car was in the way. I just caught the words "green Volvo", and I froze. That was my car.

'I remember Graham Rowntree was giving me a funny look, because he could see I was somewhat bemused. So I said to Graham: "Could you just hold on for a minute there?" And off I went. I remember Dean Richards sticking his head up from the scrum and saying: "For f**k's sake what's going on now?"

'I ran over to the touchline. The manager was up in the stands, and I had to tell him to get my keys from the dressing room and get the car moved. So I was shouting up at him, and he couldn't hear. He was just going: "What? What?" In the end I had to shout up: "It's my bloody car!"'

KNOW YOUR SPORT

Gary loved how conspiracy theorists have had a field day with the 1995 Rugby World Cup final. They claim that mysterious waitress, Susie, poisoned the food of the All Blacks team. The game was the subject of a memorable answer on the popular TV programme *A Question of Sport*. Asked who won the final, Phil 'Tuffers' Tufnell replied:

'I know the answer to that one. I'm sure that was the President Nelson Mandela final in South Africa, at the end of apartheid. Didn't Mandela come on the pitch with the blond fella, you know their captain ... Francois ... Francois Pienaar. Yeah, that's right. Oh it was the All Blacks wasn't it? That Lomu guy? He scored 4 tries, ran over everyone, didn't he?

'It was the All Blacks. Yeah Jonah Lomu won it that year with the All Blacks. No, wait a minute, didn't the All Blacks get food poisoned? Yes, that's right and South Africa won and Nelson Mandela, wearing Pienaar's number seven jersey, presented him with the trophy. Yeah, that's right. And the jumbo jet buzzed the top of the stadium.'

'So,' asked Sue Barker patiently, 'have you got a final answer for us?'

To hysterical laughter in the studio, Tuffers replied: 'I have, Sue. Australia. I've just had this sudden flash of inspiration. The Wobblies won it that year.'

11

POWER TO THE PEOPLE

Jim Glennon Enters Politics

The year 2022 began with a media storm when tennis star Novak Djokovic went to war with the Australian government over his non-vaccination status before the Australian Open at the height of a global pandemic. The saga spawned some good jokes.

Q. Why did Novak Djokovic struggle in Australia?
A: He missed two shots.
Q: Why did Djokovic use his Mastercard to pay for his flight to Australia?
A: His Visa didn't work.

Personally I didn't understand what all the *racket* was about. *Serves* him right.

Closer to home and rugby and politics have also amused. Having won 6 caps in the pack for Ireland, Jim Glennon also made his mark on the political stage in the noughties. After initially serving in the Senate, he was elected to the Dáil in 2002 as a Fianna Fáil TD for Dublin North. Not surprisingly, Glennon sought advice from 'the godfather' in the constituency, former Taoiseach Charlie Haughey.

Charlie was happy to share memories of his sporting career. He won a county medal with Parnells in 1945 – a noteworthy year for him because he also achieved notoriety then for allegedly burning the Union Jack outside Trinity College. On the pitch he was known for his fiery temperament. He was suspended for a year for striking a linesman. His brother Jock won an All-Ireland medal in 1958 when Dublin beat Derry, the county of birth to both his parents.

Charles Haughey was a keen horseman, though he did have a few famous falls in his career. He was once alleged to have said that he chose black and blue as his colours because he was black and blue so often following riding mishaps. He laughed when quizzed about the veracity of that remark. 'I think you'd have to take that as apocryphal!'

When Glennon asked him what advice he had for him, Haughey answered immediately, 'Life is too short to be drinking bad wine!'

POWER TO ALL OUR FRIENDS

Charlie then told Glennon a story:

While walking down the street one day, a head of state is tragically hit by a car and dies. His soul arrives in Heaven and is met by St Peter at the entrance.

"Welcome to Heaven," says St Peter. "Before you settle in, it seems there is a problem. We seldom see a high official around these parts, you see, so we're not sure what to do with you."

"No problem, just let me in," says the politician.

"Well, I'd like to but I have orders from higher up. What'll we do is have you spend one day in Hell and one in Heaven. Then you can choose where to spend eternity."

"Really, I've made up in my mind. I want to be in Heaven," says the head of state.

"I'm sorry but we have our rules."

And with that, St Peter escorts him to the elevator and he goes down, down, down to Hell. The doors opened and he found himself in the middle of a golf course. In the distance is a club and standing in front of it are all his friends and the politicians who had worked with him. Everyone is very happy and in evening dress. They greet him, hug him and reminisce about the good times they had while getting rich at the expense of the people. They play a friendly game of golf and then dine on lobster. Also present is the Devil, who really is a very friendly guy who has a good time dancing and telling jokes. They are having such a good time that, before he realises it, it is time to go. Everyone gives him a big hug and waves while the elevator rises. The elevator goes up, up, up and reopens in Heaven, where St Peter is waiting for him.

"Now it's time to visit Heaven."

So twenty-four hours pass with the head of state joining a large number of contented souls moving from cloud to cloud, playing the harp and singing. Before he realises it, the twenty-four hours have gone by and St Peter returns.

"Well then, you've spent a day in Hell and another in Heaven. Now choose your eternal destination."

He reflects for a minute, then the head of state answers, "Well, I would never have expected it. I mean Heaven has been delightful, but I think I would be better off in Hell."

So St Peter escorts him to the elevator and he goes down, down, down to Hell. The doors of the elevator open and he is in the middle of a barren land covered with garbage. He sees all his friends, dressed in rags, picking up the trash and putting it in bags. The Devil comes over to him and lays his arm on his neck.

"I don't understand," stammers the head of state. "Yesterday I was here and everyone was on the golf course and we ate lobster and caviar and danced and had a great time. Now it is a wasteland full of garbage and my friends look miserable."

The Devil looks at him, smiles and says, "Yesterday we were campaigning. Today you voted for us!"

CHEQUE THIS OUT

Charlie regularly engaged in what Donald Trump calls 'plausible hyperbole'. Glennon recommended one of his tradesmen friends when Charlie needed some work done on his mansion in Kinsealy. His friend travelled to the estate early one Saturday morning and rang the doorbell. Mrs Haughey answered and then called her husband to deal with the situation. When he arrived at the front door Charlie looked at the man and said, 'You should know that in the circumstances you should have gone to the back entrance.'

The man apologised profusely and duly went around to the back door.

Charlie was waiting for him and guided him to the cellar where the work was needed. At the end of the day when the job was done Haughey was called to inspect the work. He expressed satisfaction and said, 'I suppose you want to be paid.'

Charlie went away to find his cheque book and returned with a cheque. The man was dismayed at how small the figure was but felt too intimidated to complain.

That night Glennon rang the Taoiseach to express his friend's dissatisfaction. Charlie listened to the complaint, cleared his throat theatrically and said, 'The signature on that cheque is worth much, much more than any money.'

Then he hung up.

SEX APPEAL

As a man who lived life to the full, Charlie Haughey found a kindred spirit in former Irish rugby coach Mick Doyle. When

Doyler wrote his autobiography, Haughey was the only man to approach to launch it. But when he rang the Taoiseach, Charlie had misgivings and asked, 'Is it just about rugby?'

'No. It is 20% rugby and 80% sex.'

'You got the balance just right.'

After describing in considerable detail some of his (s)exploits when he appeared on *The Late Show*, Gay Byrne commented, 'I thought this was a book about rugby'.

Doyler won twenty consecutive caps for Ireland (three with his brother Tom) and toured with the Lions to South Africa in 1968. He once bemoaned the lack of bite in the Irish pack and recounted a story from his own playing career when he was leader of the forwards. One of his colleagues had shipped an underhand blow and Doyler angrily called his warriors together as the victim was receiving treatment.

'Right lads, listen up,' said Doyler. 'Whoever did this, I want the f**ker "got" in the next ten minutes.'

The ref was passing by and overheard him.

"You've got five, Mick," he said.

FROM RAGS TO RHAPSODY

Doyler steered Leinster to five consecutive Interprovincial Championships between 1979 and 1984, and he became Irish coach in 1984. His philosophy was 'give it a lash'. England coach Dick Greenwood responded by saying that Irish rugby would need a 'brain transplant' if this new approach was to work. Before the first Five Nations game against Scotland, Doyler instructed the players: 'Boys, I want you to run the ball and if it doesn't work, I still want you to run it.'

In 1985 Ireland won the Triple Crown against England in Lansdowne Road before a banner in the crowd stating 'Dr Doyle's transplant clinic'.

12

TOP OF THE BILL

Ireland v Scotland 1978

Growing up, I believed in the Fab Four.

I still think those four sports broadcasters were peerless: Micheál O'Hehir for Gaelic games; Dan Maskell for tennis; Peter O'Sullevan 'the voice of racing'; and Bill McLaren 'the voice of rugby'.

I count myself blessed among sports fans to have met up with both Peter and Bill. They say you should never meet your heroes. I have had a few experiences which make me see the wisdom in this adage but meeting Peter and Bill was the very opposite. Both were gentlemen to their fingertips and time flew by in their company because they were such entertaining conversationalists and both had a great sense of humour.

I thought of Bill in March 2022 on the day Ireland beat his beloved Scotland to win the Triple Crown. A few hours earlier, after thirty-six straight losses, Italy finally won a Six Nations game following a sensational finish to their clash with Wales at the Principality Stadium in Cardiff. Ange Capuozzo, in his first ever start for Italy, produced a thrilling run in the last minute to create the winning try in a 22–21 score. Moments earlier Josh Adams had been selected for the player of match award. But the gracious winger gave his award to Capuozzo. Bill would have seen the gesture as the embodiment of all that is good in the game he loved so well.

In January 1978 Tony Ward won his first cap for Ireland against Scotland in the theatre of dreams that was Lansdowne Road. It was the thrill of a lifetime, especially as Ireland won. There was huge pride for Ward in wearing the green jersey for the first time but the added bonus was that it gave him the opportunity to meet Bill McLaren, who was and will always be the world's best rugby commentator ever.

Bill was old school. He believed in sportsmanship – shaking hands, thanking the ref and respect. He loved the characters in the game with a passion. Ollie Campbell told me that just the mention of Bill McLaren's name brings great memories rushing back. His unique descriptions and authoritative voice added so much excitement, intrigue and enthrallment to his unforgettable commentaries for the BBC.

WORDS TO THE WISE
Above all the master is best remembered for his classic quotes such as:

'The All Blacks that day looked like great prophets of doom.'

'I've seen bigger legs hanging out of a crow's nest.'

'Safe as houses; warm as toast.' (After a Gavin Hastings clearance kick.)

'Wade Dooley the big Blackpool policeman standing like a lighthouse at the back of the line-out.'

'I look at Colin Meads and see a great big sheep farmer who carried the ball in his hands as though it was an orange pip.'

As Scott and Craig waited to join the fray on the touchline: 'There's the Quinnell brothers, two well-nourished individuals.'

Referring to one of the French front row as 'having a face like a carpenter's bag o'chisels.'

'Big Vleis Visagie – born when meat was cheap!'

On Andre Venter: 'He's no oil painting, but look at him working the blind side like a pop-up toaster!'

On Os du Randt: 'There he goes – South Africa's rhino!'

On Scott Gibbs: 'When he hits you, you think the roof has just fallen in.'

On the late, great Phil Bennett: 'They say down at Stradey that if ever you catch him you get to make a wish.'

On Gerald Davies: 'His sidestep was marvellous – like a shaft of lightning.'

On England's twinkle toes Jason Robinson: 'Billy Whizz'

On Gavin Hastings as he prepared to kick at goal: 'He hoists his breeks, does a little shammy shammy . . .'

On the goal-kicking style of the Scottish Captain Peter Brown: 'It's similar to a cow kicking over a milk pail.'

On missing a kick: 'That one was a bit inebriated – just like one of my golf shots.'; On missing a kick that fell short: 'He's kicked that like a bag o' rice.'

After Scotland's Renwick missed a kick and clearly mouthed 'Effing Hell' Bill chirped: 'I think he's muttering a few naughty Hawick words'. (Note 'words' was pronounced 'wurr-eds'.)

On the difficulty of kicking in poor conditions: 'Gaining purrrrchase on the slippery turrrrf.'

'He strikes the ball with clinical precision, as you would expect from a member of the Royal College of Surgeons.'

On Mark Andrews and Doddie Weir contesting a line-out: 'They both go up like two pieces of white bread in a pop-up toaster.'

On Hennie Bekker: 'South Africa's roving lighthouse.'

On French forward Cristian Califano: 'Built like a bicycle shed.'

'And there's Beaumont in that English scrum looking like a man who enjoys his food . . .'

On Jonah Lomu: 'It's like trying to tackle a snooker table!'

On Scotland's towering Doddie Weir running with the ball: 'Like a run-away giraffe.'

On Ireland's Simon Geoghegan: 'He's like Bambi on speed.'

On New Zealand's Grant Batty: 'He plays like a runaway bullet.'

'The balls as slippery as a wet trout.'

'I tell ye, that ball's like a bar of soap down there.' (After a ball was knocked on.)

LOVE AT FIRST SIGHT

Tony Ward knew immediately that McLaren had taken a shine to him because when they first met after the Irish training session Bill shared his beloved Hill's Hawick Balls with him. These boiled sweets were minty and buttery at the same time and come in a wonderfully retro tin.

When Ward asked Bill what was the best thing in his view about his years of commentary at rugby matches, McLaren replied: 'I've hardly ever had to pay to get in.'

Bill had a wonderful way of painting pictures with words and that was evident in his commentary of Ward's debut match. When Ward kicked a superb defensive kick into touch, McLaren said, 'He kicked that ball like it were three pounds o' haggis.' As Ward launched his first, Garryowen, the ace commentator, said, 'My goodness, that wee ball's gone so high there'll be snow on it when it comes down.' After his second one Bill said, 'That's a real howitzer of a Garryowen.'

McLaren, though, was even more impressed by Ward's running and evasive skills: 'He could sidestep three men in a telephone box'; 'He's like a slippery salmon'; 'He's like a whirling tsetse fly!'; 'He's like a demented ferret up a wee drainpipe'; and 'He's as quick as a trout up a burn.'

With reference to Moss Keane he described him as 'eighteen and half stone of prime Irish beef on the hoof; I don't know about the opposition but he frightens the living daylights out of me.' Then when Moss took off on a characteristic run Bill said, 'He's like a raging bull with a bad head.' He described Fergus Slattery's rucking as 'burrowing like a giant mole'.

Bill played down an incident when there was fisticuffs: 'A little bit of argy-bargy there . . . Those props are as cunning as a bag o' weasels.' When Willie Duggan's toughness was on display Bill said, 'You wouldn't want to meet him in a dark alleyway!'

The decisive score on Ward's debut was a Stewart McKinney try for Ireland. McLaren said in response, 'They will be dancing in the streets of Dungannon tonight. He can smell a try like a forest animal.'

BUM DEAL

I asked Ward to select the all-time greatest Bill McLaren commentary. He picked a game between England and South Africa in 1994. Big Victor Ubogu had his shorts ripped to shreds in a frantic ruck and, as he bent down to change them right in front of the camera, his big bum filled the screen. Bill's dulcet tones calmly commented: 'A splendid rear-view there!'

IMMORTALITY

For Tony Ward, 1978 was an unforgettable year. Not only did he first play for Ireland but he also starred in Munster's famous victory over the All Blacks. The Munster team were coached by 'the Grey Fox', the late Tom Kiernan. When he retired from international rugby in 1973, he held the Irish for most caps (54), most points (158) and most games as captain (24). As a Lion he twice toured South Africa. In 1968 he captained the Lions despite having initially declined to tour due to his job as an accountant. In the first Test he kicked 17 points and by the end he had scored 35 of the Lions' Test points – another record.

Against the All Blacks Martin Walsh, a Dubliner who was one of the touch judges in Thomond Park. With three minutes remaining on referee Norris White's watch, Walsh was officiating a line-out on halfway when he heard a voice behind shouting, 'Martin, Martin . . .' When he turned around he saw Kiernan, no longer able to sit in the stand as the final whistle loomed.

'If he asks you what time is left, tell him it's all up,' exhorted Kiernan.

'As if I wouldn't,' retorted Walsh.

13

NOT ON BENDED KNEE

Con Houlihan Is Injured

When I was a boy the publication that captivated my attention to the greatest extent was *The Evening Press:* because of both Joe Sherwood's regular feature 'In the Soup' and the column written by the peerless Con Houlihan.

I especially remember when Con wrote about a famous Scotland–Ireland game in which a marauding Moss Keane scored a try despite the best efforts of the Scottish defence. Con's verdict was that 'a rolling Scot gathers no Moss.'

The Castleisland legend once described a new Irish international who was out of his depth: 'He was as confused looking as a Kerry man in Paris.'

Con's favourite Dublin pub was Mulligans. Spotting a fellow journalist sitting sadly at the end of the bar in Mulligans, Houlihan said: 'There he is, poor fella, forgotten but not gone.'

Although he witnessed many brutal and violent incidents on the rugby field there was only one unforgivable crime for him: 'It is my belief that anybody who misuses the apostrophe is capable of anything.'

I once shared a meal of sorts with Con. He was less than impressed with the fare on offer and quoted John B. Keane on a Kerry man describing fat rashers to me 'There wasn't as much lean in them as you'd draw with a solitary stroke of a red biro.'

When I asked him why he was drinking brandy and milk, he matter-of-factly explained: 'The brandy takes the shting [sic] out of the milk.'

He surprised me again when he told me that he had something in common with the Queen Mother. He read his favourite paper *The Sporting Life* drinking brandy and milk, just like the Queen Mother at eight every morning would get her copy of the same publication brought to her bed accompanied by a large measure of gin and a bottle of tonic water.

QUOTE UNQUOTE

Con enjoyed a good rugby quote. His favourites included:

'Paris hasn't witnessed anything this ugly since Charles Laughton started ringing the bells on top of Notre Dame Cathedral.' (Martin Johnson, after England KO France from WC07.)

'There'll be tears and beers in Temple Bar and Cork after this abject failure.' (*The New Zealand Herald*, after Ireland's dismal 2007 World Cup.)

'It goes to show that Dermot MacMurrough was wrong to invite Strongbow in in 1171 or whatever it was.' (George Hook, after Ireland beat rugby world champions England in Twickenham in 2004.)

'American football is rugby after a visit from a health and safety inspector.' (Anonymous)

'The Empire Strikes Back.' (Nike advert in *The Telegraph* after England beat Australia in the 2003 World Cup final.)

'When they ran on to the field it was like watching a tribe of white orcs on steroids.' (Michael Laws, New Zealand sports columnist, describing the English rugby team.)

PARISIAN WALKAWAYS

Con loved his biannual trips to Paris to see Ireland play France. At one stage he went with sports-writing colleague David Faiers. On the eve of the big game, the two were enjoying a long, liquid session in the French capital when, after a disagreement, they abruptly decided to finish up and go their separate ways. To his horror and great surprise the towering figure of Con was the victim of a mugging on his way back to the hotel, losing his money, his passport and, most terrifying of all under the circumstances, his match ticket.

The following afternoon and, with only minutes to go before the kick-off, there remained a vacant seat in the press box where Con was supposed to be. At that juncture, Faiers was approached by a stadium official who said that there was a 'Monsieur Oolahan' outside who claimed to be a member of the Irish press corps. Would Mr Faiers provide a description of his colleague so they might permit him access to the game? 'Of course,' Faiers replied, with a big smile. 'Monsieur Houlihan is a small, dapper (Con was a giant and perhaps the most sartorially challenged man in Christendom and beyond) gentleman . . .'

After a minute, though, he remembered there was honour amongst sportswriters as well as among thieves and Con was finally let in.

THE POETRY PROGRAMME

Another time Con went to Mulligans for a liquid lunch to see that a poet of his acquaintance was waiting for him. The poet asked Con if he was familiar with the Russian poet Alexander Vvedensky, who died on a prison train in 1941. (He has since acquired a new English-language audience since Pussy Riot's Nadezhda Tolokonnikova quoted Vvedensky at her trial in August 2012.)

Con's reply was that Alexander Vvedensky was born in St Petersburg in 1904 and as a young adult became part of Leningrad's Futurist movement. Much of his work has been lost and destroyed and what remains, mostly published posthumously, is not very accessible. Con quoted from one of the poems: 'The only thing that is positive to the end is meaninglessness.' He then quoted from 'God May Be Around' (1931):

> A star of meaninglessness shines,
> it alone is fathomless.
> A dead gentleman runs in
> and silently removes time.

It was immediately obvious that his friend was less than happy with Con's familiarity.

'Well, Con, what would you say to a bit of horse-trading — the collected works in pristine condition in exchange for two tickets for Ireland's rugby international with England. What do you say, Con?'

After a short pause, Con replied: 'That is not horse-trading, that is ass-trading.'

BENDING THE KNEE

Con looked back on his own rugby-playing career with typical self-deprecation: 'I was never capped for Ireland but I was once knee-capped playing for Castleisland.'

I'LL SEE YOU IN CHURCH

Another Irish media personality with an interest in rugby is Pat Kenny. His rugby knowledge and his understanding of religious experiences are not always as good as they might be. In the mid-noughties the Golden Boy (known for his use of fake tan) of Welsh rugby was Gavin Henson. He was involved in a high-profile relationship with singer Charlotte Church at the time. Pat was unaware that Henson spilled the beans about his passionate pre-match romps with Charlotte and added that the couple send each other saucy mobile phone pictures: 'There's no rule in rugby which says you can't have sex the night before a game and it's hard not to with Charlotte. We love each other. I've never seen a person who looks as good as Charlotte. She's beautiful both physically and as a person.'

After Ireland played Wales, Pat Kenny generated one of the most awkward moments in the history of Irish radio when, during a conversation with Des Cahill, he read out a text about 'Gav the Chav': 'Is it true that Gavin Henson goes into Church after every game? I don't understand Des, is Henson religious?'

BACK AND TAN

Brian O'Driscoll shared a room with Henson on the 2005 Lions tour. Henson could take up to three hours in the bathroom to ensure that he was looking his best before matches, according to O'Driscoll. Henson's philosophy was: 'If you look good, you play good.' Former Wales scrum-half Dwayne Peel claimed that Henson started 'washing and showering with Evian. So he's buying bottled water and bathing in that.' Henson was most famous for his perpetual tan. Hence Drico's belief that if tanning is ever introduced as an Olympic Sport Henson will be a certainty for the bronze medal.

14

WHEN FERGIE HELPED BELVO

Alex Ferguson Befriends Rugby School

Sir Alex Ferguson is well known as a racing fan but less so as a rugby fan. Nonetheless he has helped out Old Belvedere rugby club. This is because of his friendship with Fr Joseph Dargan S.J., who held many positions of responsibility in the Society of Jesus in Ireland, most notably that of provincial, or head, of the Irish Jesuits from 1980 to 1986. Fr Joe also spent almost ten years as rector of Belvedere. He was one of the pioneers of that school's social diversity scheme, which was set up to enable boys from less well-off backgrounds to attend.

In 2009 he persuaded Manchester United Manager Alex Ferguson to answer questions on his glorious career at a special fundraising dinner at the Croke Park Conference Centre. Tickets for the event were to support the school's scholarship scheme for disadvantaged pupils. About ten per cent of Belvedere's pupils enter via the scholarship scheme, a much higher percentage than in other fee-paying schools.

In his speech Fergie shared some fascinating insights, including his view that the most stressful hour of the week for him was the one before kick-off because he had to leave the players to themselves; if he did not it, would tell them that he did not trust them.

Fr Joe was at a table for dinner with Sir Alex and organised a 'guess the length of the speeches' competition. At the end of the night the clear winner was Fr Joe himself.

He never told anyone he was giving the final speech!

Fr Joe brought the house down with these six stories about Fergie. Many were inspired by his long-running rivalry with Arsène Wenger.

ELEMENTARY

After years of wrangling, a PR executive suggested that Sir Alex and Arsène Wenger should go on a camping trip in the interest of enhancing the image of their respective clubs. And so they did. The two men set up their tent and fell asleep. Some hours later, Ferguson woke up his new friend.

'Wenger, look up at the sky and tell me what you see.'

'I see millions of stars.'

'What does that tell you?'

Wenger pondered for a minute. 'Astronomically speaking, it tells me that there are millions of galaxies and potentially billions of planets. Astrologically, it tells me that Saturn is in Leo. Time wise, it appears to be approximately a quarter past three in the morning. Theologically, it's evident the Lord is all-powerful and we are small and insignificant. Meteorologically, it seems that we will have a beautiful day tomorrow. What does it tell you?'

Ferguson is silent for a moment, then he speaks: 'Wenger, you idiot, someone has stolen our tent.'

ACCIDENTAL DISCLOSURE

Alex Ferguson and Arsène Wenger were in a car accident, and it was a bad one. Both cars were totally demolished, but amazingly neither of them was hurt.

After they crawled out of their cars, Ferguson said, 'Wow! Just look at our cars. There's nothing left, but fortunately we are unhurt. This must be a sign from God that we should meet and be friends and live together in peace the rest of our days.'

Wenger replied, 'I agree with you completely; this must be a sign from God!'

Sir Alex added, 'And look at this – here's another miracle. My car is completely demolished, but this bottle of whisky didn't break. Surely God wants us to drink this and celebrate our good fortune.'

Then he handed the bottle to Wenger. Arsène nodded his head in agreement, opened it and took a few big swigs from the bottle, then handed it back to Ferguson, who immediately put the cap back on.

Arsène asked, 'Aren't you having any?'

Sir Alex Ferguson replied, 'No. I think I will just wait for the police . . .'

THE LAST JUDGEMENT

There was a terrific lightning strike and tragically Alex Ferguson and Arsène Wegner died, but before they were allowed into Heaven they were sent to Purgatory.

Fergie was walking along arm in arm with a stunning young woman when he met his old foe.

'Well!' said Arsène. 'I see you're getting your reward up here while you purge your sins.'

'She's not my reward,' said Fergie. 'I'm her punishment.'

HAIR TODAY

Alex Ferguson and Arsène Wenger somehow ended up at the same barber shop. As they sat there, each being worked on by a different barber, not a word was spoken. The barbers were both afraid to start a conversation, for fear it would turn to football. As the barbers finished their work, the one who had Fergie in his chair reached for the aftershave.

Sir Alex was quick to stop him with the words, 'No thanks, my wife will smell that and think I've been in a whorehouse.'

The second barber turned to Wenger and said, 'How about you?'

'Go ahead,' he replied. 'My wife doesn't know what the inside of a whorehouse smells like.'

ALL DONATIONS GRATEFULLY RECEIVED

In 2008, a man on his way home from work was stuck in a traffic jam outside the Emirates Stadium, and he thought to himself, Wow, the traffic seems worse than usual. Nothing's moving.

The man noticed a policeman walking back and forth between the lines of cars, so he rolled down his window and asked, 'Excuse me, what's the problem?'

The officer replied, 'Alex Ferguson just found out that the club owners are planning to cut his budget and he's all depressed. He stopped his car in the middle of the road, and he's threatening to douse himself in petrol and set himself on fire. He says everybody hates him and he doesn't have any more money since he paid for Ronaldo's new contract. I'm walking around taking up a collection for him.'

'Oh, really. How much have you collected so far?'

'Well, people are still siphoning but right now I'd say about three hundred gallons.'

THE HORSE WHISPERER

Alex Ferguson is known for his love of racing despite the protracted controversy about his ownership of the champion horse Rock of Gibraltar.

Once, on a walking holiday, Fergie stopped alongside a field run on a country road to rest for a few minutes. He had just closed his eyes when a horse came to the fence and began to boast about his past.

'Yes sir, I'm a fine horse. I've run in twenty-five races and won over £2 million. I keep my trophies in the barn.'

Fergie computed the value of having a talking horse, found the horse's owner and offered a handsome sum for the animal.

'Aw, you don't want that horse,' said the farmer.

'Yes, I do,' said Fergie, 'and I'll give you £100,000 for that horse.'

Recognising a good deal, the farmer said without hesitation, 'He's yours.'

While he wrote out the cheque, Fergie asked, 'By the way, why wouldn't I want your horse?'

'Because,' said the farmer, 'he's a liar – he hasn't won a race in his life.'

15

THE AMBASSADOR'S BALL

Hugo MacNeill Is Honoured

Trinity College is Ireland's oldest university.

Since 1592 it has made a massive contribution to Irish educational, cultural, social and sporting life.

The college has produced many famous sporting personalities. Few were more colourful than Jonah Barrington, who more than anyone created the squash boom which brought the game from the elite to the masses because of his great rivalry with Geoff Hunt. His victory in the British Open in 1973, squash's equivalent of Wimbledon, was his sixth title in seven years and firmly established him as the world's greatest squash player. However, Barrington's omission from the Trinity hall of fame is perhaps not all that surprising.

After an unhappy time during his teenage years in secondary school, Barrington followed family tradition and went to Trinity in 1958. Ireland's most famous university came as a culture shock to the Englishman. Never was this more evident than on one of the rare occasions when the fun-loving teenager struggled in for a lecture at nine o'clock in the morning. Thirty-two students should have been present but there were only four. However, when the lecturer called the roll all thirty-two names were answered without any puzzlement. Then, half an hour later, when a fifth student arrived, the lecturer was struck dumb in amazement: 'Glory be to God. Is it yourself or your ghost that I'm seeing at the door?'

CROSSDRESSING

Jonah's escapades did not endear him to the college authorities. He had precious little respect for the college rules, as he proved when he brought one of his girlfriends for dinner into the all-male bastion of Commons. Women were absolutely forbidden but he tried to get around the problem by dressing her up like a man. The fact that she had a 36-inch bust made this task rather difficult.

THE FINAL STRAW

That indiscretion was relatively minor by comparison with the incident which led to his expulsion. He attended the end of term celebrations with a bag of flour hidden on his person. The target for this missile was to be a Nigerian friend as he got up to receive his degree. Tragically, his aim was askew and the flour landed on a distinguished, visiting Hungarian academic who had travelled over especially to receive an honorary doctorate. Just at that moment, the heavens opened and the flour became a dense white paste. To temporarily escape the college porters, Barrington was forced to seek refuge in the college chapel.

SEARCHING FOR LOVE

Although he played rugby for Trinity's second team, it was his extra-curricular activities for which he is best remembered. One of his biggest problems was holding down a residence for longer than a week because of his love of 'wine, women and song.' Incidents like tripping over the lavatory seat in a drunken stupor and falling straight through the window naturally did not endear himself to his landlords.

His most spectacular fall was to come in Trinity itself. In the middle of the night he was clambering around on the roof of the ladies' hall of residence with a view to serenading some attractive ladies but, thanks to Mr Guinness, his footing was not very sure and he slid rapidly down the steep roof and disappeared over the edge of the building. Incredibly he escaped without serious injury.

BIG MAC

In 2019 Trinity alumnus Hugo MacNeill was announced as a brand ambassador for Trinity Sport. Nelson Mandela, sometimes described as the President of Humanity, claimed that: 'Sport has the power to change the world; it has the power to change peoples' lives to make them healthier and happier; the power to inspire and the power to unite people in a way that little else can.'

It has a sentiment that MacNeill adheres to. The honour from Trinity recognises his achievements with Ireland, Leinster, the Barbarians, and the British and Irish Lions. It also celebrates his contribution to the 'Peace International' in 1996 between Ireland and the Barbarians, which promoted the positivity of a community living together in peace and pointed to the futility of violence at a critical time in Irish history. Hugo has also become a strong advocate for diversity and inclusion, as he is an ambassador for Trinity Centre for People with Intellectual Disabilities.

In his role as sports ambassador, Hugo had an interesting encounter. He met a young lady who took it on herself to explain the rules of rugby to him:

'The fat lads all run into each other, while the thinner lads stand in a line watching them. Eventually the fat lads get tired and have a lie-down on top of each other. The ball comes out the back of this lie-down and the skinnier lads kick it back and forward to each other for half an hour. Then the fat lads wake up and start running into each other again. From time to time the referee stops play because someone dropped the ball. That's the only thing you are not allowed to do in rugby. Everything else is fine and dandy. Occasionally one group of fat lads pushes the other group over the line and there is some manly hugging, but no kissing like in soccer. After eighty minutes they add up the score and the All Blacks win.'

16

THE O'DRISCOLL REDEMPTION

Drico Gets Arrested

The level of fame experienced by Brian O'Driscoll was on a level never before experienced in Irish rugby.

Denis Hickie and O'Driscoll had a great relationship on and off the field while they played together for Ireland and Leinster.

Prop forwards are generally a more rotund breed than backs – consequently, when you want to insult a back, you say he looks like a prop forward. Tony O'Reilly famously said, 'Prop forwards don't get Valentine cards for religious reasons – God made them ugly!'

Denis Hickie was attending a wedding and saw Bod in the distance, at a time when Drico was carrying a few extra pounds in the bum area and waspishly remarked, 'I didn't know Paul Wallace (prop forward with Ireland and the Lions in South Africa in 1997) was coming to the wedding.'

HAIR TODAY

Hickie and O'Driscoll enjoyed a good-natured rivalry as they yo-yoed in the race to be Ireland's record-breaking try scorer. O'Driscoll grabbed the record off Hickie with his twenty-fourth try for Ireland against Italy in 2004. After the match Drico received a text message from Hickie: 'I suppose I should maybe, perhaps, congratulate you on your new record. Boll****!'

Another occasion for good-natured banter between the two good friends came before the 2003 World Cup when O'Driscoll famously acquired a new blond hairstyle. However, Hickie denies all responsibility for the spate of O'Driscoll blond jokes that swept through the Irish squad during the competition. His teammates spun the yarn that Drico had entered a Robert Redford lookalike contest. He was knocked out in the first round – beaten by a Nigerian.

The jokes began in earnest as the Irish squad boarded the plane to Australia with tickets for the standard class seats. O'Driscoll looked at the seats and then he looked ahead at the first-class seats. Seeing that the first-class seats appeared to be much larger and more comfortable, he moved forward to the last one. The flight attendant checked his ticket and told the Irish star that he was in the wrong place. O'Driscoll replied, 'I'm young, blond and beautiful, and I'm going to sit here all the way to Australia.'

Flustered, the steward went to the cockpit and informed the captain of the problem. The captain went back and told O'Driscoll that he must return to his assigned seat. Again, O'Driscoll answered, 'I'm young, blond and beautiful, and I'm going to sit here all the way to Australia.'

The captain didn't want to cause a commotion and returned to the cockpit to discuss the situation with the co-pilot. The co-pilot said that he had a blond girlfriend, and that he could take care of the problem. He went back and briefly whispered something into O'Driscoll's ear. He immediately got up, said

'Thank you so much', shook hands with the co-pilot, and rushed back to his designated seat. The pilot and flight attendant, who were watching with rapt attention, together asked the co-pilot what he said to the Irish rugby legend.

He replied, 'I just told him that the first-class section wasn't going to Australia.'

Shortly after he arrived in Australia O'Driscoll was invited to be guest of honour at the Blondes Are Not Stupid Convention. The MC said, 'We are all here today to prove to the world that blondes are not stupid. Can I have a volunteer?'

The crowd enthusiastically volunteered the guest from Ireland. The MC asked him, 'What is fifteen plus fifteen?' After twenty seconds O'Driscoll replied, 'Eighteen!'

Obviously everyone was a little disappointed. The twenty thousand blondes started cheering, 'Give him another chance. Give him another chance.'

The MC said, 'Okay, mate as you came all this way I guess we can give you another chance.' So he asked, 'What is five plus five?'

'Twelve.'

The MC let out a dejected sigh – everyone was disheartened but then the twenty thousand blondes began to yell and wave their hands shouting, 'Give him another chance. Give him another chance.'

The MC, unsure whether or not he was doing more harm than good, eventually said, 'Okay, okay. Just one more chance – what is two plus two?'

'Four?'

Throughout the stadium pandemonium broke out as all twenty thousand blondes jumped to their feet, waved their arms, stopped their feet and screamed . . .

'Give him another chance. Give him another chance!'

After all the excitement the Irish star just wanted to escape for a quiet night with a few friends but he faced a new problem:

Q: Why did Brian O'Driscoll take seventeen Irish players to the cinema?

A: Under eighteen not admitted.

DO YOU THINK I'M SEXY?

On legal advice, what Ronan O'Gara said to Bod after he went on *The Late Show* to talk about being voted Ireland's sexiest man cannot be repeated in these pages. Likewise if the exact words Peter Clohessy used when he saw Drico had died his hair blond were printed here, this book would need a triple X rating.

THE WRITE STUFF

The publishing event of the year in Irish rugby circles in 2014 was the launch of Brian O'Driscoll's autobiography. Unfortunately for Brian the book was somewhat overshadowed by the controversies created by both Roy Keane and Kevin Pietersen's books. The *Irish Independent* tried to come to his rescue by its summary of Keano's book: 'Roy has a lot of rows, swears a lot, sees another player eating crisps, has a big beard – and, em, that's about it.'

Drico was moved to tweet: 'I reckon my book is going to read like something from Enid Blyton in comparison to KP & Keano's!!!'

After O'Driscoll published his autobiography much of the press interest was generated by the fact that he had once been arrested in America. Mario Rosenstock did a sketch on the Ian Dempsey breakfast show on Today FM. They changed *The Shawshank Redemption* to *The Bodshank Redemption*. In prison Bod regales his fellow prisoners with tales of his many dealings with

a strange breed of 'hookers' and of the hardest man he knows, Paulie, who goes out to 'take people's heads off'.

In the original film the hero puts up a poster of Rita Hayworth and escapes by digging a hole in the wall behind the picture. In the remake Bod puts up a poster of Ollie Campbell and escapes 'through Ollie Campbell's hole'.

For his part Drico had given a preview of what was to come when interviewed before the book was launched. He was asked if he would get into trouble. He joked, 'I'll be arrested.'

17

LEAVING ON A JET PLANE

O'Gara v Sexton

It is probably safe to assume that Jason McAteer and Roy Keane were never going to be soulmates given the difference in their personalities.

Jason was lounging around the Ireland team hotel when Roy laid into him about being too unfocused.

Jason said, 'I go with the flow.'

Roy gave him a withering look before saying, 'Do you know who else goes with a flow?'

Jason blinked. 'I don't know.'

'Dead fish,' replied Roy scathingly.

At the height of the rivalry between Ronan O'Gara and Johnny Sexton the story went around that there was a terrible plane crash. According to folklore Brian O'Driscoll went up to Sexton and said, 'I've got good news and bad news. Which do you want first?'

'Give us the bad news.'

'A plane has gone down, killing a hundred people.'

'Oh my God, that's awful. What's the good news?'

'Ronan O'Gara was on it.'

A STRETCH IN TIME

For his part O'Gara was sceptical when he was told that Sexton had started doing yoga every day. In his typical deadpan manner Rog replied, 'That's a bit of a stretch.'

COLLEGIALITY

Johnny Sexton's favourite joke is: what do you call those types of people who constantly hang around rugby players, follow them to cool places and generally idolise their every move?

Forwards.

THE PRINCES OF WALES

Such was the Welsh dominance of the Lions third Test team in 2013 that Johnny Sexton joked it was a matter of enormous pride to him to have finally made his Welsh international debut.

DOES TOMMY BOWE KNOW IT'S CHRISTMAS?

In 2021 both O'Gara and Sexton couldn't miss the opportunity to tease their former Irish teammate Tommy Bowe arising from his mishap in his role as presenter on *Ireland AM*. The Monaghan winger's gaffe occurred while co-presenter Clare McKenna was introducing author Seamus O'Reilly, who she explained as part of the intro had ten siblings. This surprised Tommy who gasped in awe 'Ten siblings!' before Clare could finish the rest of her sentence. Then Clare continued to say that they had 'sadly lost their mother' when the author was just five years old. Bowe's cringey moment immediately went viral on social media.

One of O'Gara's riddles was: 'What does Tommy Bowe have for Christmas?'

'A T-Bowne steak.'

18

OUR WILLIE IS BIGGER
THAN YOUR CONDOM

Ireland v France 1985

In sporting terms he is one of a kind. He is famous in the rugby world for playing the bagpipes. Whatever that indefinable quality called charisma is, this guy has it in buckets.

As a player Willie Anderson had many highs and lows: the highs being the 1985 Triple Crown and the night he captained a scrap Irish side to a famous victory over France at Auch in 1988 – Ireland's only victory over France on French territory in over twenty years. His appearances against France were memorable for his epic struggles with the French lock, Jean Condom. Hence the banner that appeared in the crowd in Lansdowne Road at the Ireland–France match in 1985: 'Our Willie is bigger than your Condom.'

THE FUTURE KING AND I
After captaining Ireland to a defeat against England, Willie Anderson was talking to Will Carling at the dinner in the Hilton.

84

It was a very serious atmosphere, so he asked Carling to go downstairs with him for a 'wee drink'. Willie asked him what he wanted and Carling said a gin and tonic, so he ordered two. He nearly dropped dead when the barman charged him ten pounds. When he asked him could he charge it to his room, the barman said no. Then Willie pulled out two Northern Ireland five-pound notes. The barman immediately said he could not take these. He said to Carling he would have to pay for the drinks. When Carling pulled out his wallet, Anderson claims there was a combination to it because Carling was not renowned as a big spender. Although Ireland lost the match, at least Willie had the satisfaction of making the English captain buy him a drink, which was said to be a more difficult task than beating England!

Before Austin Healey, Carling was the England player with an exceptional capacity to rub people up the wrong way. Carling went up to Leicester to play for Harlequins in a league match, in a fixture that was being filmed by *Rugby Special*. After the match Carling was set upon by a Leicester fan who punched him on the chin. It was widely reported afterwards that it was the first time the fan had hit the sh*t.

Carling has a more sociable side. On the Lions' tour in 1993 Carling was rechristened 'O'Carling' when he started drinking Guinness.

THE WILL TO WIN

Anderson enjoys the stories about Carling's former marriage to the TV presenter Julia Smith. After she woke up one morning, Julia said to her husband, 'I just dreamed that you gave me a pearl necklace for our anniversary. What do you think it means?'

'You'll know tonight,' Carling said. That evening he came home with a small package and gave it to his wife. Delighted, she opened it – to find a book entitled *The Meaning of Dreams*.

Some of his critics portray Carling as a bit tight with money. When Anderson is asked if this is a fair perception, he recalls that one WAG suggested that Will's idea of a Christmas treat for his children was to take them to Santa's grave!

One of Anderson's favourite stories about the former English captain goes back to early in his marriage to Julia when, after being away a long time on tour, he thought it would be good to bring her a little gift. 'How about some perfume?' he asked the girl in the cosmetics department.

She showed him a bottle costing £100.

'That's too much,' he said.

The girl then said, 'We do have this smaller bottle for £50.'

'That's still too much,' he said.

The girl bought out a tiny £20 bottle, but even that was too costly for him.

'What I mean is,' he said, 'I'd like to see something really cheap.'

The assistant handed him a mirror.

IT'S THE WAY HE TELLS THEM

In the late eighties Willie Anderson was chosen as Captain of Ireland. The flip side of the coin was that he had to make the speeches at the dinner. A lot of drink is consumed on those occasions and not everyone wants to listen to a speech. One of his earliest dinners as captain was after a Scottish game. During his address he looked down and he could see Kenny Milne with his hand over his mouth trying to hold back the vomit. He could only hope it was from drink and not from listening to his speech.

Willie seemed to have an effect on Scottish players. At another Scottish dinner he was sitting beside Craig Chalmers all night. At the end Chalmers had to be carried away on one of the tables.

Willie cannot be held responsible for all the accidents at Scottish dinners. In 1986 the table on which the Scottish tight-head prop Iain 'The Bear' Milne was leaning at the post-match dinner in Cardiff collapsed. Milne's response was to say, 'Waiter, bring me another table.'

As a forward, Milne did not enjoy the expansive game. In 1988 he was asked if he was happy that the pitch was just right for fast, open, running rugby. Milne's reply was, 'the conditions are bloody awful!'

RUBBING THEIR NOSES IN IT

As Irish captain, Willie Anderson was known for a famous piece of sporting theatre before Ireland played the All Blacks in 1989 when he led the Irish team literally up to the noses of the All Blacks in an effort to intimidate them:

'It was a joint effort between myself and our coach Jimmy Davidson. After the match Wayne Shelford was asked if he was scared. He answered that he was absolutely petrified. When asked why, he replied: "I was terrified that Willie Anderson would kiss me!"'

LEGGING IT

Years later when Ireland played New Zealand in the Bermuda Classic the Irish players knew Willie would have something special planned for the 'haka'. The New Zealanders were led in the haka by their physiotherapist, who was a woman. Willie kept his hands behind his back until they had finished, then he walked up to her and pulled out a big bunch of flowers.

Anderson arranged for his players to theatrically swung over their legs. The All Blacks weren't sure what the Irish were up to until they started singing, 'You put your left leg in and your left leg out . . .' The whole place cracked up.

BIN IT

Welsh icon Jonathan Davies once played in the Hong Kong Sevens. He decided he would go out for a real Chinese meal with Willie Anderson. After they had finished Jonathan said he was going to do a runner. Willie told him not to be crazy because there were six guys at the door with machetes precisely to discourage people from leaving without paying their bill. Jonathan could do the 100 metres in about 10.5. Willie could do it in 16.5, so sprinting off was not a realistic option for him. When Jonathan ran out, Willie carefully considered his options. Eventually he took the decision and paid for both of them. When he went out, he found Jonathan hiding behind a dustbin!

MAMMY'S BOY

Anderson loved the joy of rugby:

'Even when things are at their blackest on tour, from a rugby point of view, there are moments of comedy. After we lost to Australia in the World Cup in 1987 Donal Lenihan rang home. As a result of the time difference the match was shown live on Irish television at 6 a.m. His mother had seen the match and knew the result already. Instead of offering him sympathy she said: "Anyone stupid enough to play rugby at 6 o'clock in the morning deserves to lose!"'

THE NUMBERS GAME

Like David Campese, Anderson believes in having an upbeat attitude to rugby and life, which is typified in the story of the man at his 103rd birthday party who was asked if he planned to be around for his 104th.

'I certainly do,' he replied. 'Statistics show that very few people die between the ages of 103 and 104.'

A RIPE, OLD AGE

In 1985, after Ireland famously beat England to win the triple crown, Willie Anderson's wife, Heather, met the wife of the Nobel Prize winner for Literature Seamus Heaney, which was a big thrill for her as she was an English teacher. A few weeks afterwards they were at the dinner to mark the Triple Crown victory. It was the night of one of Barry McGuigan's big fights and Willie went upstairs to see the contest on the television. Heather was there on her own and was trying to make polite conversation. She was chatting to Ciaran Fitzgerald and made a bit of a faux pas by telling him that she had met James Joyce's wife after the English match. Fitzie turned around and asked Hugo MacNeill what age would Mrs Joyce be. Hugo answered, 'About 150!'

UN-MODEL BEHAVIOUR

Heather is a very creative woman. Their son Jonathan is now a major figure in the world of fashion. For his first fashion show everyone was understandably very nervous. Heather had the perfect solution to ensure that everything would go well. She would recruit help from outside: God. This was to be done by blessing holy water on everyone involved. Heather was only momentarily thrown when she was told that the models would not welcome having holy water splashed over them. Within a few minutes she had come up with an imaginative solution. She put the holy water into the steam iron and used it to iron the models' clothes!

19

GATLAND DROPS O'DRISCOLL

The 2013 Lions Tour

The high point of Brian O'Driscoll's career came when he was chosen to captain the Lions in 2005. On that tour Clive Woodward decided to take Tony Blair's 'spin doctor' Alastair Campbell as the team's press officer. After the infamous spear tackle Drico was replaced by Gareth 'Alfie' Thomas. At one point Tony Blair rang Campbell and wanted to wish Alfie well. When Campbell passed him the phone the Prime Minister said, 'Hi, it's Tony.'

Thomas blurted out, 'Tony who?'

When he saw Campbell's reaction, he immediately became aware of his error and attempted to undo the damage by saying, 'Oh for f**k's sake. I'm so sorry, sir.'

At one point on the tour Donncha O'Callaghan yanked down Campbell's trousers from behind. As he frantically tried to cover up his Burnley FC boxer shorts, he did not notice his mobile phone drop out of his pocket. The English hooker Steve Thompson took it away from him and the entire squad later tried to send a love message to Tony Blair. When they could not find the PM's number, everyone in his address book was sent an 'I love you' message.

IN BOD WE TRUST

O'Driscoll fell into a swimming pool and was fined £25 by the players' court on the Lions tour to South Africa in 2009. Tour Judge Alun-Wyn Jones remarked: 'Brian is a great player but I can confirm he can't walk on water.'

DROPPED

Warren Gatland's sensational decision to drop O'Driscoll on the Lions tour in 2013 was the main talking point. Despite the controversy of being dropped for the final Test, Drico had some sweet moments after the game. He was able to bring his baby daughter Sadie onto the pitch. Then he met James Bond himself when Daniel Craig went into the Lions changing room. The bad pun police were called when someone suggested Drico was in 'Double-O-Heaven.'

Weeks after the tour Drico told Shane Horgan in a TV interview that Warren Gatland would not be on his Christmas card list after he dropped him. O'Driscoll's comments got huge media attention and shortly afterwards he realised that he was going to have to meet Gatland at a function. Not wishing the 'feud' to develop further, O'Driscoll took the wind out his coach's sails by presenting him with a Christmas card even though it was only September.

RADIO GA-GA

After the Lions tour Drico went into a hi-tech electrical store to buy a car radio and the salesman said, 'This is the very latest model. It's voice-activated. You just tell it what you want to listen to and the station changes automatically. There's no need to take your hands off the wheel.'

On the way home O'Driscoll decided to test it. He said 'Classical' and the sound of the BBC orchestra filled the car. He said 'Country' and instantly he was listening to Dolly Parton. Then suddenly a pedestrian stepped off the pavement in front of him, causing him to swerve violently and shout at him, 'F**king idiot.' Then the radio changed to a documentary on Warren Gatland.

REVENGE IS SWEET

Gatland's decision to drop Drico immediately put the focus on Ireland's next game against Wales. Ireland's call was answered resoundingly with a 26-3 win. *The Sunday Independent* had the best take on it with their headline: 'Wales left to sink up Schmidt creek.'

SNAKES ALIVE

On the 2001 Lions tour to Australia four of the squad – Rob Howley, Derek Quinnell, Daffyd James and Brian O'Driscoll – were at a zoo and were being shown a snake. The snake handler explained: 'This is a 25ft Asian Python. This type of snake is capable of eating goats and lambs, and is reputed to have eaten humans as well.' The four brave Lions were ready to beat a hasty retreat when a photographer who was working with the Lions came up: 'Right lads, let's have a picture, all four of you holding the snake! No getting out of it, you're all doing it.'

Realising that they had to have their photo taken, Quinnell immediately rushed forward and grabbed hold of the snake's tail. Howley and O'Driscoll copped on immediately and stepped smartly forward. Daffyd James couldn't fathom why his three friends were suddenly keen to embrace this huge great snake. Then, too late, he twigged what was going on. O'Driscoll and Howley had grabbed the middle section of the snake, and there was only one place left for James in the photo. He had to hold the python by its head, flicking tongue and gleaming eyes. The photo showed three happy Lions and one looking absolutely terrified!

GROANER

After the tour Jonny Wilkinson described O'Driscoll as 'the Monica Seles of table tennis. You've never heard grunting like it.'

THE LIFE OF BRIAN

O'Driscoll has been in thrall to the game of rugby for as long as he can remember. It helps that his father, Frank, played for Ireland and that his cousins Barry and John also played for their country. Ours is an age wedded to an almost mystical concept of celebrity. Brian's mother, Geraldine, is all too aware of this. The France game in 2000, when he scored the 3 tries, changed everything for Brian and indeed for his family. Geraldine first realised that when she was introduced to someone after the match and they said, 'This is Geraldine O'Driscoll. She used to be Frank O'Driscoll's wife. Now she's Brian O'Driscoll's mother!'

The game was on a Sunday and shortly after the match Frank and Geraldine had to rush for the train to be home for work the next day. One of their daughters was in Australia in the time and she rang them on the mobile. She said, 'Mum, after Brian's 3 tries I'm now a minor celebrity here!'

Geraldine most noticed just how famous Brian had become the following Halloween. She knew there would be lots of kids calling to the house trick or treating. She put piles of sweets on the table and left Brian in charge of them. When she came, back she was shocked to find all the sweets still there and to see a bundle of pieces of paper lying beside the sweets. She asked Brian what had happened and he replied, 'The doorbell hasn't stopped ringing all evening but none of the kids want the sweets. They just want my autograph!'

HOLY SMOKES

Everybody loves as winner. In 2001 the Irish rugby team got an audience with the Pope when they travelled to Rome to play Italy. Injury forced O'Driscoll to miss the trip. Pope John Paul II was said to be still eagerly awaiting his audience with Brian O'Driscoll on his death bed.

HOL-Y MOSES

As a keen golfer Brian enjoys the story of the two Mexican detectives who were investigating the murder of Juan Gonzalez.

'How was he killed?' asked one detective.

'With a golf gun,' the other detective replied.

'A golf gun?! What the heck is a golf gun?'

'I'm not certain, but it sure made a hole in Juan!'

POSH

Such are his commercial opportunities that his colleagues joke that Drico can afford to live in an area that is so posh, the fire-brigade is ex-directory.

RUCK AND ROLLERS

Brian O'Driscoll faced God at the throne of Heaven with Ronan O'Gara and Tommy Bowe. God said to them, 'Before granting you a place at my side, I must ask for your beliefs.'

Rog stared God directly in the eye and said, 'I believe rugby is the meaning of life. Nothing else has brought so much joy to so many. I have devoted my life to spreading the gospel of rugby.'

God was moved by his passion and eloquence, and said, 'You are a man of true faith. Sit by me at my right hand.'

He then turned to Monaghan's most famous rugby son. 'Now, my child, tell me what you believe in?'

Bowe answered, 'I believe courage, bravery, loyalty, teamwork, dedication and commitment are the soul of life, and I dedicated my career to living up to those ideals.'

God replied, 'You have spoken well, my child. Sit by me at my left hand.'

Then he turned to Bod. 'And you, Mr O'Driscoll, what is that you believe?'

Drico gave him a withering look and replied, 'I believe that you are sitting in my chair.'

20

BLESS ME FATHER

Paul O'Connell Goes to Confession

None of the Munster players took the field with fear but such was the force of Paul O'Connell that when he walked on the pitch it was fear itself that was afraid!

His innate modesty was also revealed when he was asked by this writer if he had any interest in a career in the media after rugby: 'I don't think I have the boyish good lucks for a career as a TV pundit!'

THESE MISS YOU NIGHTS

Paul O'Connell was walking down the streets of Limerick when he met a beautiful, blond woman who was in great distress. He asked her to tell him what was wrong: 'Oh, it's terrible. My husband is spending all our savings going to see Munster playing. He thinks about Munster all the time. He likes me but he loves Munster. I gave him an ultimatum: It's Munster or me.'

Paul replied, 'Well that seems perfectly reasonable. I'm sure he will see sense. But why are you crying?'

'I'm going to miss him.'

ABSOLUTION

One of the stories told about O'Connell goes back to the aftermath of Ireland's triumph over South Africa in autumn 2004. Before the game the Springboks coach Jake White became the bête noir of Irish rugby when he publicly stated that Brian O'Driscoll was the only Irish player who would get into the Springbok side, although he reluctantly conceded that the second rows, Paul O'Connell and Malcolm O'Kelly, would be contenders.

According to legend, O'Connell went to confession a month after the game and confessed to the priest, 'I lost my temper and said some bad words to one of my opponents.'

'Ahhh, that's a terrible thing for an Irish international to be doing,' the priest said. He took a piece of chalk and drew a mark across the sleeve of his coat.

'That's not all, Father. I got mad and punched one of my opponents.'

'Saints preserve us!' the priest said, making another chalk mark.

'There's more. As I got out of a ruck, I kicked two of the other team's players in the . . . in a sensitive area.'

'Oh, Jesus, Mary and Joseph!' the priest wailed, making two more chalk marks on his sleeve. 'Who in the world were we playing when you did these awful things?'

'South Africa.'

'Ah, well,' said the priest, wiping his sleeve, 'boys will be boys.'

GRAND SLAM

In 2009 Ireland won a long overdue Grand Slam. Paul retains a strong affection for the coach Declan Kidney:

'My favourite story about him, though, goes back to 2000 before I joined the Munster squad. On the way to the Heineken Cup final against Northampton, Munster had to play Saracens away. Saracens were a club without a tradition and they brought in marketing people to tell them how to bring in the crowds. One of the things they did was to play the Rocky music whenever there was a fight or a row; when the team came onto the pitch they played the *A Team* music; when the opposition came on they played "The Teddy Bear's Picnic"; when the Saracens placekicker faced up to a penalty the crowd put on fez hats and had a little routine to guide the ball over the bar and the tee came on in a remote-controlled car. To play against Saracens you have to face a lot of distractions. Before Munster played them, the Munster squad were watching a Saracens match as part of their video analysis. With about two minutes to go on the video Declan turned on a ghetto blaster and had the *A Team* music blaring, put on his fez hat and started playing with the remote control and the lights. After a minute or so Declan turned off the television, took off his hat, turned off the ghetto blaster and asked: "What happened in the last sixty seconds of the Saracens game?"

'Nobody knew because they had all been watching him.

'Point made.'

21

THE MIGHTY QUINN

Mick Quinn Plays for Ireland

The first time we met in 1995 he shook me warmly . . .

By the throat.

I had told him in a tone that I thought left no room for argument that Ireland's two great number tens of the modern era were Tony Ward and Ollie Campbell.

He assured me that not only was he better than both of them – he was better than both of them put together!

He has since paid me a unique compliment.

He assures me that nobody misquotes him better than me. It is not that he holds a grudge. He just finds it difficult to let go of his resentment.

He is a romantic at heart. He proposed to his wife at the halfway line in Lansdowne Road. Nonetheless I was surprised when he told me that his great ambition is to write a best-selling novel. It will be called *Fifty Shades of Gravy*. When I asked him why, he explained that he wanted to write a saucy book.

He is a true legend of Irish rugby, albeit in a different way than Brian O'Driscoll.

SUPERQUINN

'Mine has been an eventful career.'

This is Mick Quinn's summation of his life in rugby which brought him 10 caps for Ireland at out-half:

'I get on great with Tony Ward, even though he was the main impediment to my international career. In his biography he jokes that if it wasn't for Ollie Campbell he would have got 40 caps. When I read that I rang him up and said if it wasn't for him, Mike Gibson, Barry McGann, Ollie and Paul Dean I would have won 80 caps!'

For his part Barry McGann jokes: 'I got Mick Quinn his ten caps for Ireland because I was his only competition and I wasn't up to much at the time!'

AGAINST THE HEAD

One of Quinn's most endearing qualities is also being able to tell stories against himself:

'After one international match a young autograph hunter said to me: "Can I have your autograph please, Johnny?" I didn't have the heart to tell him he had got the wrong man so I just signed it. "To Bert. Best wishes, Johnny Moloney." As he was leaving he looked up and said to me: "How do you keep playing with Mick Quinn? He plays like sh*t!"'

COMPETITION

Quinn relished his rivalry with both Ward and Campbell:

'Wardy's great champion was Ned Van Esbeck of *The Irish Times*. Whenever I kicked a great penalty it was just a great penalty but when Wardy kicked one it was "a wonder strike from the master craftsman". Whenever I was kicking exceptionally well I would shout up at Ned and ask him whether or not Wardy could have bettered that.

'There was a time I got one up on Ollie. I am good friends with Chris De Burgh and was with him in Rome for the World Cup quarter-final in 1990 when Ireland lost to Italy. It was incredible to see the way all the Italians mobbed Chris before the game but we went into the middle of the crowd just as ordinary fans. I saw some of the U2 guys up in the stands with their bodyguards away from the riff-raff but Chris wasn't like that. After the match Jack Charlton and the players went on the team bus but the Irish fans were still in the stadium yelling for Jack. I ran out and asked him to come back out on the pitch, which he did. I walked out behind him and when I looked up there was Ollie in the stands. So I waved at him knowing full well he would be wondering to himself how that so-and-so Quinn managed to get on the pitch with Jack Charlton!'

BARE NECESSITIES

Quinn's career brought some revealing moments:

'One of the highlights of my career was winning the three-in-a-row of Leinster Cups in 1981 with Lansdowne. We beat Old Belvedere in the final and it was nice to put one over on Ollie Campbell on the pitch. After the match the team bus was bringing us on to the victory celebrations. I suggested to the boys we should "lob a moon" or display our bums out the window to the people of Dublin. This proposal was enthusiastically agreed to. When we were on display I turned around and saw there was a car travelling alongside the bus. To my horror the occupants were my father, mother and sister. My mother told me afterwards that she had recognised my bum because it hadn't changed since the time she used to change my nappies! I told her I found that hard to believe.'

DOZY

Quinn's rise to the top was meteoric:

'After I left school I joined Lansdowne. In my first year I played for the third team. The next season I was on the first team and playing for Ireland when I was only twenty. I don't remember much about the build-up for my debut except that I fell asleep during Willie John McBride's team-talk! Ray McLoughlin told me that I was a cheeky bugger.'

NUMBER ONE

'It was pay for play with a difference. I had to pay for my jersey. We beat France 6–4 for my first cap. The player who scored their try was killed by lightning sometime later. The great J.P. Romeau missed the conversion. As it was my first cap there was no way I was going to part with my jersey but I really wanted Romeau's. I went back into the dressing room and asked Ray McLoughlin for his number one jersey. You have to remember that he was a very successful businessman, who headed up the James Crean company – so he was not short of a few bob. He sold me his jersey for £10. I rushed out and swapped jerseys with Romeau. I was thrilled with myself when I returned but suddenly the French man came into our dressing room. With his dreadful English, and my awful French, communication was a problem but it didn't take me long to see that the problem was that he wanted a number 10 jersey. I used sign language and said to him: "Zero fello offo!"'

22

NO ORDINARY JOE

Joe Schmidt Has Problems

'*Let them be ashamed and brought to confusion,
who seek to destroy my life.*'

(*Psalm 40*)

Since my first meeting with Joe Schmidt I have been clinically diagnosed as an A.R.S.E.

A Rabid Schmidt Enthusiast.

In conversation with this writer in 2018 Joe Schmidt revealed the two biggest hazards of his job: 'One is injuries to players and the other is that Mick Quinn is always taking the p**s out of me.'

THE SWEETEST FEELING

Last time I met Joe I said to him, 'I started my diet today . . . I had eggs for breakfast.'

'Scrambled or boiled?' he asked me.

'No. Cadbury's.'

Joe Schmidt has a weakness. In fact he has two, as he revealed to me. His more recurring weakness is that he is a bad sleeper:

'It doesn't bother me. If I am awake at 4 a.m. I will just get up and do something. We had Rog (Ronan O'Gara) with us for a week on our summer tour a few years ago and he told me that I had a lot of energy. I do. I am like a battery that is on full power but I know the day will eventually come when the power goes down. Until that day comes, though, I am going to continue flat out!'

His other confession was: 'I have a terrible diet.'

When I expressed extreme scepticism about this fact to him based on his waistline, I asked for evidence. He answered in a guilty voice, 'I ate some chocolate biscuits this afternoon.'

He jokes that when he is eating too much rubbish his wife Kellie will go into full Dolly Parton mode and start humming non-stop: *Joe-Lean, Joe-Lean.*

Kellie will sometimes try to hide all the chocolate bars from him. Hence she is known as 'the Guardian of the Galaxy'.

SIMPLY THE BETTER

Given his teaching background it is no surprise that Schmidt took a keen interest in the Irish education system. Hence one of his favourite stories is about the time a fee-paying rugby school on the southside of Dublin challenged a northside Christian Brothers school to play a game of hurling. The date was arranged and the Christian Brothers boys decided to adopt a gentlemanly stance and send the college a telegram which read: 'May the best team win.'

The southsiders sent a telegram in reply: 'May the better team win.'

MODESTY PERSONIFIED

At the height of his fame managing Ireland, Schmidt met former Irish international Neil Francis. A group of workmen saw them and burst into spontaneous applause. Francis put up his hand and said, 'Ah shucks lads. Don't be clapping for me. This man here deserves a bit of credit as well.'

23

TIME GENTLEMEN PLEASE

Ireland Win the 2018 Grand Slam

There was almost a giddy sense of anticipation about the impending drama.

It was like a flash of lightning in the summer sky before a terrible thunderstorm.

It seemed to be all that anybody was talking about. Could we do it?

Irish rugby's greatest year was 2018 winning the Grand Slam, winning the summer tour to Australia and beating the All Blacks at home for the first time. Their success was reflected at the official awards ceremony that year:

World Team of the Year: Ireland

World Player of the Year: Johnny Sexton

World Coach of the Year: Joe Schmidt

Schmidt not only led Ireland to the Grand Slam, he did so while integrating Jacob Stockdale, James Ryan, Bundee Aki, Chris Farrell, Andrew Porter, Joey Carbery, Jordan Larmour and Dan Leavy into the first team.

The Welsh coach Warren Gatland had tried to play mind games before their showdown but the Irish coach did not bite. 'I tried to make a joke about it to Gats afterwards but he did not laugh.'

CELEBRATION

The weather ensured that not only was the Grand Slam home-coming scheduled for Lansdowne Road cancelled, but the players were late in leaving London as Joe Schmidt recalls, 'We got delayed four times because of the "Son of the Beast", and I'm not talking about Billy Vunipola!

'At 10 a.m., everyone had finished breakfast and it was very sedate, slightly hungover but very sedate. Then we got news that we had been delayed forty-five minutes. We said, "Lads, chill out and have another coffee." We got to about 10.30 when we saw the first pints starting to be shared! We thought, that's okay we'll get out of here in fifteen minutes. Delayed another forty-five minutes . . . cocktails! Cocktails – times have really changed.'

24

THE SCUMMY IRISH

Eddie Is Not Steady

Days before the 2018 Grand Slam decider, a major controversy erupted. English coach Eddie Jones and the Rugby Football Union both issued apologies after video footage emerged of the England head coach referring to 'the scummy Irish' and Wales as a 'little sh*t place' during a speech the previous year. Jones said he was 'very sorry' for remarks he conceded were inexcusable.

Jones had made the comments the previous July during a talk on leadership for the truck manufacturing company Fuso, the Japanese sister company of the England team sponsor Mitsubishi, but they only came to light that week. Jones had said, 'We've played 23 Tests and we've only lost one Test to the scummy Irish. I'm still dirty about that game, but we'll get that back, don't worry. We've got them next year at home so don't worry, we'll get that back.'

Joe Schmidt, though, was unfazed by the noise:

'I was not going to get distracted by anything Eddie said. I know Eddie of old and the idea of him saying controversial things is nothing new at this stage. I am very thankful to Eddie, though. Eddie had tried to play it clever and had extended the dead ball line by two metres behind the goalposts thinking it would suit England. That is where the luck came in because without those extra two metres Jacob Stockdale would not have scored his try. It was a delicious irony which I loved – but Eddie not so much.

'There was another irony. Because they changed the lines, they had to change the colour of those lines – but the referee was colour-blind! You could not make it up!'

Schmidt's attention to detail is legendary but there was one thing he had not bargained for:

'Everybody remembers that we beat England in Twickenham on Saint Patrick's Day but what some people forget is that it was played during an unseasonal snowstorm both here and in England. It was Artic cold and there was a vicious wind. Our forwards coach Simon Easterby had prepared our line-out calls and had them on a table in our dugout before the game on three sheets of paper, and this huge gust of wind came and blew two of them into the English dugout, which meant that the English had most of our line-out calls – except the short ones. So we used our short ones for most of the game and in the weather conditions it was the right strategy, so that was a case of something that might seem to be a big disadvantage for us working in our favour.'

25

NO SMOKING

Joe Lays Down the Law

Joe Schmidt had not intended to be a rugby coach.

When Schmidt was twenty-four, he opted to take a year over-seas. He and his wife, Kellie, moved to Mullingar. He played for the local club and was persuaded to do some coaching at Wilson's Hospital School. That year Wilson's Hospital made the A final of the Schools Cup for the first time. They won, and scored 5 tries, 'throwing the ball around'. Schmidt can still remember the names of the lads who got them. His brief to the players was the stuff of legend, including the instruction to one aspiring star: 'Don't smoke in the showers.'

LOQUACIOUS
Joe Schmidt was keen that the team would be aware of important issues in society:

'I think it is important that the Irish team has a social conscience. The second year I coached Ireland I wanted to do something substantial at our Christmas gathering. I spoke to the team captain at the time, Paul O'Connell. He agreed to my suggestion that we should visit the Capuchin Centre and see their great work for needy and homeless people at first hand. We spent three hours there and I know it was a very positive experience for all of us.

'The first year we had our Christmas camp we had a Kris Kindle. We put Rala (Patrick O'Reilly, the team's baggage manager) in charge of it. The only problem was that he talked so long it felt like we were there till New Year's Day! Rala is a great character but brevity is not his forte. He did his own book and I asked him how many words he would need. He said 70,000 words. I said that was a lot of words and asked him how many were his. He answered: "130,000."'

TUMMYSOME

One of Schmidt's legacies to the Irish team is that he is responsible for one of Tadhg Furlong's nicknames, Rikishi. The Irish tighthead explains: 'My belly gets a good flash on national television. It came up in the video review, Joe Schmidt said, "Oh, here comes WWF . . ." Not even WWE so, WWF. We're going back a few years. And of course the lads jumped on the bandwagon and started calling me Rikishi, the big fat wrestler!'

However, Joe is not responsible for Furlong's two other nicknames: Ear Lingus and Shrek.

GET SMART

Given his success with Ireland, Schmidt gets a lot of invitations to speak at events. Early in his time as Leinster coach Schmidt was invited to speak at a function for Garryowen rugby club. The climatic part of his speech involved him making a joke about a Limerick fan and a smartphone. The punch line was: 'You mean somebody from Limerick has a smartphone!'

The Garryowen fans clapped politely and he escaped with his life. It might have been a different story if he had made the joke in front of a Young Munster audience!

THE YOUNG ONE?

Joe is a master of self-deprecation: 'I've reached the age where people don't ask me any more how old I am. They ask me if I've had carbon dating.'

A LITTLE OF WHAT YOU FANCY BUS YOU GOOD

The rugby gods have a sense of humour. Ahead of New Zealand's first Test in 2022 against Ireland, All Blacks head coach Ian Foster, forwards coach John Plumtree and defence coach Scott McLeod all tested positive for Covid-19, forcing them into isolation. Who did they draft in to replace them? Joe Schmidt.

One Irish fan was dismayed: 'It's been a terrible day. First Joe Schmidt becomes All Blacks coach. Then Joe was knocked down by a bus. Then I lost my job as a bus driver.'

26

LEINSTER'S INSPIRATIONAL SPEECH

Leinster v Northampton

Testicular fortitude was called for as never before.

Johnny Sexton was not found wanting.

Some games leave you scratching your head. The 2011 Heineken Cup was one of them. There have, statistically, been bigger second-half comebacks in rugby union but there have been none in which a team has undergone the extreme makeover which propelled Leinster to a second European title in three years. Lazarus was in all likelihood a Leinster man.

Leinster tailed 22–6 at half-time. Cometh the hour. Cometh Jonathan Sexton.

It is given to few half-time speeches to attain instant immortality. Sexton's was one of them. He invoked the memory of Liverpool's famous 2005 European Cup comeback against Milan in Istanbul. Joe Schmidt told his players they would be remembered forever if they regrouped and dug deep. For someone like Brian O'Driscoll this was a call to arms. 'When you say "go to the well, boys", he's 200 feet down,' said Schmidt. 'He can dig pretty deep when the going gets tough.'

For Joe it was a vindication of the culture he had created in Leinster. He liked to keep the lads entertained, and one of the odder games he had was not to celebrate for scoring tries. His rationale being that they were paid to score tries, and a postman does not celebrate when he delivers a letter! Initially he brought it into training and then quickly extended into matches. But the lads had great fun when a player celebrated scoring a try as he would be doing laps for the rest of the training match while everyone else got on with playing the game. Any chat at all to Schmidt when he was reffing a game, e.g. 'That was a knock-on' or 'He celebrated' resulted in immediate removal from the game for the offender and the starting of laps!

Discipline was absolutely key to Schmidt's modus operandi. His motto is: if you cannot be disciplined in training, how could you expect to be disciplined on the field of play? The one time he overlooked the try celebrations was when Mike Ross scored his one and only try: 'He never even scored a try as a kid, so I was happy to let that one pass!'

Schmidt is very proud of the fact that Leinster won the fair play award two out of the three years he was in charge – and it was an after-match citing and ban for one player late in the season that cost them three from three.

They had a system of internal fines and penalties for misdemeanours, where the players imposed penalties on each other for indiscretions, however small. Once a week they all gathered to dish out the punishments. Eoin Reddan was the administrator and called out the offenders. They rolled a massive dice, and whatever number they rolled decided the punishment. The players thought the worst one was a €250 fine, and they went crazy with excitement whenever someone got this. Schmidt believed that they showed they were really a bunch of big kids!

The other one they hated getting was 'suits for two weeks', i.e. every day for training they had to arrive in a suit, shirt and tie, and after training they had to put them all back on.

Schmidt was conscious of the weight of expectation before the game.

'Everyone expected Leinster to beat Northampton in the Heineken Cup that year but at half-time it was looking very bleak for us.'

With the benefit of distance Schmidt is happy to shed new light on the half-time events. He laughs when it is suggested that there must have been a lot of bad language used.

He joked, 'Unlike Munster we didn't actually swear in Leinster. But once I became Irish coach and was dealing with the Munster lads, I had to learn the swear words so they could understand me!'

Schmidt usually left the pre-match team talks to his players. All his work was done by then, though he might issue a few reminders to players on an individual basis.

He shares the accolades that were given to Sexton but not in the conventional narrative that has emerged about the game: 'Johnny's speech was good but in my memory it was Jenno (Shane Jennings) who gave the most forceful speech. The thing about Johnny, though, was that he delivered on the pitch immediately after half-time and that is what really mattered.'

However, Schmidt has a third name to add to the equation about the half-time speeches: 'Everyone knows about Johnny's half-time speech but Jamie Heaslip also made a very impassioned short speech. It was twenty, or twenty-two, or twenty-four words long. I can't remember exactly what was said but I know it was an even number of words, because every second word was the same!'

27

LOWE POINT

Leinster Do the Double

Keith Earls has insightfully remarked that Joe Schmidt did not rule by fear but by excellence.

If you go to the library every day you will eventually read a book. Jack McGrath believes there is an analogy there for Leinster rugby:

'Culture is also crucial in Leinster. When I was starting off I saw Joe Schmidt creating a new culture. Joe spoke about the habits that would lead us on to excellence and that we would learn the habits of winners. He absolutely drilled those habits into us. I think some of Joe's legacy lives on in Leinster and that is part of the reason we won the double.'

FATHER OF THE BRIDE

For Jack McGrath, though, his biggest match came off the field when he married Sinead Corcoran, daughter of much loved RTÉ commentator, Michael. As he is such a big fan of Munster, Today FM's *Gift Grub* did a hilarious sketch of Michael's father of the bride speech – which was in essence how could she marry a Leinster player when she could have married a Munster player – even a 'blow-in' like Joey Carbery.

McGrath believes that personalities were key to Leinster's Champions Cup and League double in 2018:

'I am very serious about my game. When things are not going well I am very hard on myself and get very serious. A lot of the lads are the same and then the likes of Johnny (Sexton) are not exactly a bundle of laughs when we lose or when we make mistakes. That is why you needed a few personalities in the camp who were more extroverted. Fergus McFadden always was like that. When you were beating yourself up about a match you lost or a mistake you made Fergus was always there with a laugh or a joke and that gives everyone a lift.

'Once James Lowe came into the squad things kicked up a whole new level in that respect. He is not one to get down and he is able to lighten the mood when things get too serious. He is very chilled and is a welcome counterbalance to the other personalities in the group and that light touch amidst all the seriousness helps create that winning culture.'

Felipe Contepomi is another fan of Lowe's. 'There are a lot of characters in the Leinster squad like Dan Leavy but James Lowe is the biggest character. He certainly does things differently!'

An indication of Lowe's personality came before Leinster's match with Wasps in October 2018. Somebody tried to break into his car. To the amusement of the gardai, when he reported the incident Lowe asked that, when they found the culprit, he could be left alone with him for ten minutes!

28

CIVIL WAR

Campbell v Ward

We may not be able to choose the music life plays for us. What we can choose, though, is how we dance to it.

People use different techniques to motivate players. At Italia '90 Ireland were facing Romania in a penalty shoot-out. Tony Cascarino was wavering about taking a penalty until Ray Houghton went up to him and said, 'Are you a man or a mouse?' Then Andy Townsend shouted at him, 'Pass the cheese.' Cascarino laughed. He agreed to take the penalty and, critically, he scored it.

Ireland's first sporting civil war was not between Roy Keane and Mick McCarthy in Saipan but in 1979 when the country was split between whether Tony Ward or Ollie Campbell should be the Irish rugby number 10. While he was the European Player of the Year the Irish selectors caused a sensation by dropping Ward on the tour to Australia. Campbell stepped up to the plate brilliantly but the Ward supporters were not placated.

A few months later Leinster travelled to play Munster in the interprovincial series. Leinster were captained by the former Irish scrum-half John Robbie. This was the time when the captain really called the shots. Robbie was determined to beat Munster but knew that their hosts planned to bully and intimidate them. Robbie was the last to speak before the Leinster team took the field. Before doing so he pulled Campbell aside and told him to ignore what he was about to say. After giving, in the GAA vernacular, a 'tyranny of speech' and telling each of the players individually what he expected of them, he finally turned to Campbell and said, 'Ollie Campbell, you are the best number 10 in Ireland. There's no question about that. But are you a winner? I am not sure.' He left it like that. Those words were like an electric shock to Campbell. He played like a man possessed and guided Leinster to victory. It was a brilliant example of player management on Robbie's part.

For three years a fierce debate raged: who should wear Ireland's number 10 jersey – Tony Ward or Ollie Campbell? Campbell recalls the experience with wry amusement: 'Tony Ward, a great friend to this day, had just been voted European Player of the Year for the second year in a row but to everyone's amazement (not least mine) I was selected for the Tests.

'"Ward Out, Campbell In" took precedence over the announcement that the Pope would be visiting Ireland later that year on the front page of the now defunct *Irish Press*. Ever since that tour our coach Noel "Noisy" Murphy has reminded me that had we not won the series (2–0) he would probably now be an Australian citizen! The names of Tony Ward and Ollie Campbell have been inextricably linked ever since, too.'

Campbell thought he had finally resolved the Tony Ward issue with a series of stunning performances that ensured Ireland broke a thirty-three-year famine and won the Triple Crown in 1982. A few weeks later Ollie was leaving Westport one morning when he picked up a lady of mature years who was visiting a friend in Castlebar Hospital. After an initial flurry of small talk the conversation unfolded as follows:

Her: 'And what sports do you play? Do you play Gaelic?'

Ollie (as modestly as possible): 'No, I play rugby?'

Long silence.

Her: 'Do you know there's one thing I'll never understand about rugby?'

Ollie (with all due modesty): 'What? I might be able to help.'

Short silence.

Her: 'The only thing I don't understand about rugby is why Tony Ward is not on the Irish team!'

ME AND JIMMY MAGEE

Years later Campbell was invited to be the guest speaker at a huge charity event where Jimmy Magee was the MC. Before the event Jimmy asked Campbell what he planned to say. Ollie recounted the Westport story in full for Jimmy's benefit and was thrilled with Magee's reaction to it. He was much less pleased, though, when Jimmy introduced him at the event by telling that exact story just as Campbell was standing up to make his great speech!

BIG VICTORY

Campbell came from a rugby family: 'My mum and dad, although they didn't even know each other at the time, were both in Ravenhill in March 1948 when Ireland won their first Grand Slam. I was born six years later and was weaned on the exploits of that team, particularly the immortal Jackie Kyle.'

His favourite Leinster memory came playing against Tony Ward: 'In the late seventies and early eighties we were playing thrilling, running rugby. We were scheduled to play Munster, who played the exact opposite style of rugby in Thomond Park in December 1979. We decided that we were going to confound the stereotype that we were "fancy Dans" by playing rugby that day the Munster way. It has become the conventional wisdom that only two men and a dog watched those interprovincial matches back then but they were hanging out of the rafters in Thomond Park that day.

'We hammered them. 4–3!'

THE LIVE MIKE

Even after his retirement from rugby, Campbell still found his name linked with Tony Ward's. He was invited on Mike Murphy's radio show at one stage. Before the broadcast he was asked if there were any subjects he did not wish to discuss. He said 'Tony Ward' because he thought it had been flogged to death. The first question Mike asked him was: 'I see here, Ollie, that the area that you have said you do not want to be questioned about is Tony Ward. Why is that?'

A TONI AWARD

For the next thirty-nine years after the Australian tour in 1979 both men would be inextricably linked in the public consciousness. Inevitably in the lead up to Ireland's tour to Australia in 2018 the story was recycled in many media outlets. When Ireland won the series both men breathed a sigh of relief thinking they could finally put the story to bed. Campbell sent Ward a text which simply stated: 'It's over.'

The next day he was out on a social engagement when a young lady asked him to pose for a selfie.

As he smiled for the camera the lady said, 'This is for my Dad. He is a massive fan of Tony Ward.'

'Sorry.'

'My Dad is a huge fan of Tony Ward.'

'I see. And what is your name?'

'Toni.'

CAMPBELL'S KINGDOM

In 1985 Campbell was on a business trip in Kerry. He found himself at a loose end one evening and heard that the Kerry team, then considered the greatest Gaelic football team of all time, were training nearby, so he went to watch them. He slipped into the grounds as inconspicuously as possible and sat at the back of the stands. He did not speak to a single soul and was convinced that nobody had noticed him. He was blown away by the training session and could not believe that amateur players would train for so long with such savage intensity and especially that they would run and run and then run even harder.

Some time later Ollie and the Kerry lads were guests of honour at a charity fundraiser. The Kerry players called Campbell over and asked him if he remembered the training session. 'Of course I do,' replied Campbell, 'I've never seen a team train so hard.'

He was a bit taken aback when one of the Kerry players said to him: 'What happened was that Mick O'Dwyer noticed you watching us. He stopped the session and called us together and said, "Do ye see who is up there in the stands? Let's put on a show for him." We wanted to kill you because he gave us the hardest and longest session we ever had. We were stiff and sore for days afterwards!'

DELAYED REACTION

Injury forced Campbell to retire at twenty-nine. He joked recently: 'My psychiatrist said I'm just beginning to deal with it.'

DEMOLITION JOB

Ollie is best summed by Shakespeare's description of Antonio in *The Merchant of Venice*: 'A kinder gentleman treads not the earth.' However, he retains a keen sense of mischief. A few years ago he collected Michael Lynagh at the airport when he was visiting Dublin to attend a dinner. The legendary Australian out-half had his young son with him. When they drove past the new Aviva stadium Ollie told the boy, 'Your dad scored a famous try in the old stadium here in the last minute of the 1991 World Cup quarter-final and the Irish people were so disappointed they knocked down the stadium.'

The young boy blurted out, 'Dad how could you do that to the Irish people?'

29

RUGBY SPIRITS IN THE SKY

Bod Meets God

Rivalry is at the heart of sport. Manchester United's rivalry with Liverpool is among the most high-profile of the species. Former United star Gary Neville retains a deep antipathy for Liverpool, as was evident when he was interviewed on Sky Sports after Thiago was transferred to the Merseysiders from Bayern Munich.

Martin Tyler commented, 'His dad won the World Cup with Brazil, Thiago was born in Italy but represents Spain because he grew up there, and he speaks and understands English perfectly.'

Gary Neville replied, 'That will be no use to him where he's going.'

Munster and Leinster constitute the greatest rivalry in Irish rugby. During an interpro match there was a lightning strike and both Brian O'Driscoll and Paul O'Connell were sadly killed. They both ascended into heaven and, given their status in the rugby hierarchy, they bypassed St Peter at the Pearly Gates and were brought in the VIP entrance, where they were greeted by no less than God himself. 'Greetings. Heaven is enriched by having both of you here. Come on, I'll show your accommodation. I hope you'll both be comfortable.'

God took Brian by the hand and led him off on a short walk through beautiful fields of flowers until they came across a pretty thatched cottage by a stream, with a beautiful garden, lovely flower beds and tall trees swaying in the gentle breeze. The thatched roof formed the shape of the tricolour, the birds in the trees were whistling 'Ireland's Call', and the gnomes by the garden path were images of great Leinster rugby heroes: Ollie Campbell, James Ryan, Phil Orr and Karl Mullen.

O'Driscoll was left uncharacteristically speechless. Eventually he muttered, 'I don't know what to say.'

THE MUNSTER WAY

God then took O'Connell up the path. As they were strolling away, Bod looked around him and, further up the road, he saw a gigantic mansion. On the manicured lawns, there were huge 20ft golden statues of Munster legends Moss Keane, Keith Wood, Peter Clohessy, Ronan O'Gara and John Hayes, overlooking a beautiful, magnificent garden. Massed choirs of birds were singing 'Stand Up and Fight' in harmony that Simon and Garfunkel would have marvelled at.

A little flustered, Drico ran after God and his old rival, tapped God on the shoulder and said, 'Excuse me God, I don't wish to sound ungrateful or anything, but I was wondering why Paul's house is so much more stylish than mine.'

God smiled beatifically at him and said, 'There, there, Brian, don't worry, it's not Paul's house. It's mine!'

30

BIG MAC

Willie John's Education

We talked as the fog and mist met in the middle like secret lovers on a midnight tryst.

I once heard a journalist saying about him, 'If he was any sharper he'd cut himself.' Another said, 'He would pull a bull through a slippery yard', which I assumed meant that he was very tough.

The great American sports writer Red Smith said, 'I went to a fight and an ice hockey match broke out.'

One of the most famous tours in rugby history was that of the Lions to South Africa in 1974. On the pitch the tour saw some very physical exchanges. One of the props, Gloucester's Mike Burton, was well able to look after himself in these situations. The following year he became the first English international to be sent off in a Test match, following a clash with Australian winger Doug Osbourne. In the canon of rugby literature Burton's autobiography, *Never Stay Down*, stands out. He devotes a chapter on the best punches he encountered in his career!

When Joe Kinnear was manager of Wimbledon he famously said, 'Psychology won't work on us – we have too many psychos in the side.' The idea of 'get your retaliation in first' came from the great Welsh coach Carwyn James during the Lions tour to the All Blacks in 1971.

Willie John McBride's philosophy was that the Lions would 'take no prisoners' and 'get our retaliation in first' as he recalled for me:

'South African rugby was always physical and we had always been dominated, played second fiddle, in years gone by and they just couldn't believe that we could stand up to this. Of course we were physical but we were definitely not dirty. In fact, we went out of our way not to be dirty because we knew we were the better players and the better team when we played rugby. You can't be a good team and a dirty team at the same time.'

McBride was responsible for a tactic that has now become part of rugby folklore: the infamous '99' call used by the captain as an emergency measure when things looked like getting out of hand. On his signal, all fifteen Lions would 'take on' their nearest opponent, not only to show the South Africans that they were not going to back down but also to reduce the risks of a sending-off as the referee was highly unlikely to dismiss an entire team. The call was used twice in the bruising third Test but was only used as a last resort.

But 1974 was memorable for Willie John for another reason. He was joined in the Irish second row for the first time by Moss Keane in the cauldron of Parc des Princes in 1974. Moss was stamped on and was feeling very miserable. Consolation came in the form of his colleague Stewart McKinney: 'Cheer up, Moss, it could have been a lot worse. You would have suffered brain damage if you'd been kicked in the arse.'

CHIPPING IN

On Moss's first cap in Paris, Willie John McBride sensed that his huge frame needed extra nourishment and took him out for a bag of chips the night before the game. They were coming back to the team hotel via a rough area and one of the locals decided to do the unthinkable and steal the chips from Moss. The Keane edge surfaced immediately and Moss floored him with a right hook. His friends, however, all ganged up on the two Irish players and a brawl broke out. Before long there was a trail of bodies on the ground – all of them French. Within minutes four gendarmes arrived. Moss explained the situation: 'They started it. They stole my chips.' One of the officers responded, 'Messieurs, we didn't come to arrest you. We came to save the mob.'

DO NOT DISTURB

Willie John was playing for Ireland at a time when the joke was that it was harder to get off the Irish team than get on it. In contrast England were changing the team regularly. One time he found himself playing against debutant Bill Beaumont. When they first found themselves standing beside each other in the line-out, Wille John said, 'You're new aren't you?'

Beaumont replied, 'Don't worry. I won't be disturbing you.'

SPEED MERCHANT?

Early in his career with Ireland Willie John played with a winger Cecil Pedlow, who was supposed to be very fast. This was a time when forward supremacy was the key, so when Willie John was asked if that was true, he replied, 'I've no idea if he was. We never gave him the ball.'

It was the time when the wingers threw in the ball. Years later Cecil told Willie John, 'I used to throw the ball to you in the line-out.'

McBride told him, 'You might have thrown the ball in but I don't recall you ever throwing it to me!'

NEW POSITIONS

Willie John played in a time when forward play was fast and furious. He has no time for the way forward players are (in his eyes) pampered today, particularly at scrum time, when the referee slows things down and says, 'Touch, pause and engage.' When Willie John conveyed his disgust to Cecil Pedlow, he replied, 'That's what my wife says to me now in the bedroom.'

31

SLEEPING BEAUTY

Willie Duggan Has Sweet Dreams

When he was sixteen, Sam Warburton's father gave him a replica Lions jersey. He wore it constantly for three years and then suddenly stopped. When his father asked him why, Sam told him that the next time he would wear a Lions jersey was when he was selected to play for the Lions. The next time the Welsh international wore a Lions jersey was when he captained the Lions to a series win on their tour of Australia in 2013. Sometimes you have to dream big dreams.

One player who took this idea perhaps too literally was Willie Duggan. Ireland's tour to Australia in 1979 provided perhaps the funniest moment in Willie's rugby career. The night before the First Test the squad had a team meeting. The coach, Noel 'Noisy' Murphy, always got very worked up when he spoke at these meetings. The problem was that he generally said the same thing each time. He always started with: 'This is the most important match you will ever play for Ireland.' The night before the first Test, sure enough, Murphy's first words were: 'This is the most important match you will ever play.' The team were just after eating dinner and the room was very warm because there were so many of them. Murphy was talking away for about five minutes and just as he said, 'Jesus Christ ye're wearing the Irish jersey and do you realise this is the most important f**king game you will ever play?', there was a massive snore. It was, of course, Willie Duggan. Murphy said, 'F**k it. I'm not doing this.' Then he stormed out.

UNORTHODOX

It's been said that rugby is a game for thugs played by gentlemen. But rarely was that said of Willie Duggan.

Willie's Lions captain in 1977, Phil Bennett, loved Duggan's willingness to take on physical confrontation in the most intimidating of environments. Hence his joking description of Willie, 'A fuse deliberately seeking a match.'

Serge Blanco was the god of French rugby. The Biarritz fullback embodied the French desire to play rugby with sublime skill and effortless élan. He also smoked like a movie star. Willie Duggan also enjoyed the pleasures of cigarettes. His preparations for big games could be unique.

Scottish referees, like their goalkeepers, sometimes get a bad press. A Scottish referee, who will remain nameless, was making his international debut, in Twickenham in an England–Ireland Five Nations Fixture in the 1970s. Willie Duggan was having a fag in the Irish dressing room. The time had come to run on the pitch but Duggan had nowhere to put out his cigarette. He knew that if he ran out in the tunnel with the fag in his mouth the cameras would zoom in on him straight away. When the referee came in to tell the teams it was time to leave, the Irish number 8 went over to him and said, 'Would you hold that for a second please?' The obliging referee said yes but Duggan promptly ran out on the pitch – leaving the ref with no option but to put out the fag. He went out to face the glare of the cameras and the first sight the television audience had of him was holding a cigarette! Asked about the incident afterwards the referee said, 'I've had a wonderful day – but this wasn't it!'

The referee did have the last word, though, at the post-match dinner when Duggan asked him if he minded his smoking. He said, 'I don't mind your smoking, if you don't mind my being sick all over you.'

POLITENESS PERSONIFIED

Duggan sometimes got into trouble with referees. He was always phlegmatic about it: 'I don't consider I was sent off. The referee invited me to leave the pitch and I accepted the invitation.'

32

DOYLER'S DISCIPLE

Mick Doyle Changes the Face of RTÉ

An elderly farmer in a remote part of Kerry finally decided to buy a television. The shopkeeper assured him that he would install the antenna and TV the next day. The next evening the farmer turned on his new TV and found only the rugby pundits on RTÉ on every channel. The next morning he turned the TV on and found only the RTÉ rugby pundits no matter what channel he put on. The next day the same again, so he called the shop to complain. The owner said it was impossible for every channel to only have the rugby pundits talking but agreed to send the repairman to check the TV. When the TV repairman turned on the set, he was stunned to find the farmer was right. After looking on the set for a while he went outside to check the antenna. In a few minutes he returned and told the farmer he had found the problem. The antenna had been installed on top of the windmill and grounded to the manure spreader.

The repairman sagely remarked, 'Rugby pundits are like nappies. They need to be changed often and for the same reason.'

DOYLER

During Harold Macmillan's time as Prime Minister of the UK he received a grave message about a diplomatic disaster during a Parliamentary recess. BBC radio reported the event as follows: 'These dismal tidings were delivered to the PM on the golf course where he was playing a round with Lady Dorothy.' The words read fine in print but when spoken the sentence took on a very different connotation!

Jimmy Hill asserted that Romania's success in the 1998 World Cup group matches could be attributed partly to their players having dyed their hair blond. According to Jimmy it made it easier for them to see their passing options.

In 1996 Anna Kournikova sent men's pulses racing at the French open. Although for two weeks most of the media comments were about her, not surprisingly she didn't make it to the final. The final pairing was Steffi Graf and Arantxa Sanchez-Vicario. Former English tennis player Chris Bailey was commentating on the match for the BBC and at the end the producer asked him to give a snappy soundbite to sum up the tournament. He said, 'A great Vicario win – all the talk may be of the young glamour babes coming through, but just look at the podium, there is life in the old dogs yet.'

Pat Spillane's media career was shaped most by a former Irish rugby coach and fellow Kerry man: 'The biggest influence on my style as a pundit was the late Mick Doyle. Mick was a great friend of mine. Doyler and Mandy were at my wedding and it was probably Doyler more than anyone else who encouraged me to become a sports pundit. Mick used to come to Kerry on holidays and bought a house there and we became good friends. Unconsciously I suppose I imitated Doyle's style on the telly as I have a lot of Doyler's traits in me.

'I was at the game in March 2004 when Ireland beat Scotland to win the Triple Crown. What I remember most forcefully from the game was listening to *Ireland's Call* before the match. It would not psych up a person to go into battle.

'The night before the game Mick Doyle was asked what it was he most disliked about rugby today. He replied: "I'm not sure whether it's Brian O'Driscoll's hair or *Ireland's Call*."'

SURE THING

Spillane shared Doyler's certitude: 'I had no doubts before Kerry played Galway a few years ago that the Westerners in the Super 8s were going nowhere. They beat us. I'm always like that. I may often be wrong but I never have any doubts!

'Getting predictions wrong does not faze me unduly. I always get my predictions wrong and a few times a week I will meet people who will say something like, "Spillane, you're only a chancer. You know nothing about football. You were wrong again last Sunday."

'On such occasions I always quote the lines of the Declan Nerney song: "If I knew then what I knew now, I'd be a wiser man."

'The great thing is that RTÉ pay me to come and tell the nation what I think will happen. Then when I make a dog's dinner of it and get it badly wrong, *The Sunday World* pay me the following Sunday to explain why I got it so wrong!

'I suppose what I took most from Mick Doyle was a desire to marry analysis with entertainment. There are, though, a number of pitfalls facing a television pundit. The golden rule is to be careful what you say – not something I am noted for!'

33

BUNDEE AS SHERLOCK HOLMES

Aki Saves the Day

Bundee Aki arrived in Galway as a twenty-four-year-old that had spurned a chance of representing the All Blacks. He was an instant fan favourite, tearing into defences and bringing Connacht to the cusp of the Champions Cup. By the end of his second season, he had not only been the inspiration for Connacht to win the Guinness PRO12 title but was also named the league's best player. He really bought into Connacht's team ethos.

This was most tellingly revealed when Robbie Henshaw had his laptop stolen. There was a tracking advice on the computer so Aki rounded up Jack Carty (I should declare at this point that as I am from the same parish as the great Connacht fly-half – our cat is called Jack in homage to the great one) and half the team went in search of the thief. A short time later they showed up at Henshaw's door and handed him back the laptop. Details of their exchange with the thief are as strictly guarded as the third secret of Fatima.

MURDER MOST FOUL

In 2001 Harlequins travelled to play Munster in the Heineken Cup. As it was a crunch match and Munster were very difficult to beat at home, the Quins players went to bed early. Two of Quins' English internationals, Will Greenwood, aka Rodney Trotter according to some English fans, and Tony 'Dippers' Diprose, were rooming together. Very early in the morning they were rudely woken up by a loud banging on the door. They assumed it was someone straggling in from a nightclub who didn't know where they were and didn't respond. But the banging continued. Then a booming voice said, 'This is the police, open up.'

The two internationals replied in unison, 'Yeh, yeh, sure, p*** off, will you.'

'Open up immediately, there has been a murder,' said the booming voice.

'Very funny, now p*** off.' They were convinced it was a wind-up. As the banging persisted, and because of the tone in the man's voice, Dippers eventually got up and opened the door, where he was confronted by two massive policemen. 'About time too,' said one. 'There has been a murder, we would like to question you.'

The rugby stars were immediately freaked out – worrying that one of their teammates might have been killed. The talkative policeman walked into the room and immediately recognise Greenwood, the centre with a phenomenal try strike rate who had twice toured with the Lions: 'Oh, hello Will, howya doing?' The fact that he was in the middle of a murder hunt was forgotten.

For his part Greenwood was bursting to know the details of the crime and have his anxieties about his teammates placated but the policeman continued: 'Nice to welcome you to Munster,

I'm sure there'll be a warm reception for you at Thomond Park this afternoon. Anyway, the weather is due to be blustery, may be a hint of rain, wasn't it a great result for the Irish, beating you recently?'

The two English players were subjected to the policeman's views on every aspect of the game for almost half an hour, but no reference to the murder. The two players were anxious to get the details and then get back to sleep and eventually managed to steer the policeman to the murder. He replied: 'Oh yes, that murder, it obviously wasn't you two, we know that, but lovely to chat. Oh and by the way, Munster will win today.'

He was right.

34

DALY CHORES

Ireland Win the 1948 Grand Slam

The former BBC commentator Cliff Morgan, himself one of the all-time great fly-halves, said to me once, 'Jack Kyle was the very best, the loveliest of players and the loveliest of men.'

That says it all.

Cliff often talked about his first international for Wales against Ireland. He had heard so much about his legendary opponent, Jack Kyle, and was all set to take him down a peg or two. As the match progressed, Kyle was not featuring prominently and Morgan relaxed, believing that the Irish man did not live up to his reputation. Suddenly Kyle made a break and scored a stunning try. That was an eloquent testimony to Kyle's genius. He only needed one opportunity and he stamped his class all over a match.

Jack Kyle OBE was the undisputed star when Ireland won our first ever Grand Slam in 1948, as well as three international Championships in four years in 1948, '49 and '51. Those years are known universally throughout the rugby world as 'the Kyle era'. His arsenal of gifts was amazing: tactically astute, razor-sharp in decision-making and with great pace off the mark that made him a very difficult target to nail down. At five foot nine and twelve stone six, he was a lightweight who packed a heavyweight tackle. He made his official Ireland debut against France in 1947 and went on to win 46 caps between 1947 and 1958, which may not seem a lot by today's standards but they spanned eleven seasons in the days when there were only four regular internationals a year.

It is no accident that his time in the green shirt coincided with one of the greatest ever eras in Irish rugby. He first played for Ulster as an eighteen-year-old and made his Ireland debut against France in 1947 and eleven years later he made his final appearance in a 12–6 victory over Scotland at Lansdowne Road. He also captained Ireland on six occasions and in the course of his 46 caps he scored 24 points from 7 tries and a drop goal. In addition he toured with the Lions in Australia and New Zealand in 1950, starring in sixteen of their twenty-three games including all six Tests, and scoring 6 tries.

Yet for all his achievements and all the plaudits heaped upon him, he was the personification of modesty: 'Tony O'Reilly famously said, "The older I get, the better I used to have played." I am in the same category!'

Jack enjoyed the great characters of Irish rugby:

'A great character in the team was Barney Mullan. The night before the game in Paris we had a team meeting as per usual. Barney came up with the idea that if we were under pressure during the game and got a line-out he would call a short one and throw it out over the forwards' heads and lift the siege. True to plan we got a line-out on our own twenty-five. The French players were huge. They looked like mountains to us, so we needed to out-think them. Mullan threw it long and Noel Henderson grabbed it, passed it to me, I fed it to Des McKee and he returned the compliment for me to score under the posts. The glory was mine but it was Barney's tactical awareness that earned us that try.

'Travelling to Paris for us at the time was like going to the edge of the world. We were as green as grass. After our win we were invited to a reception at the Irish embassy. Of course champagne was the order of the day, which was a very novel experience for most of us. We were knocking it back as if it was stout! To me the incident that best illustrated our innocence was when the Dolphin pair Jim McCarthy and Bertie O'Hanlon asked for red lemonade!'

Jack Kyle's clearest memory of the Grand Slam winning side was of Jack Daly.

'At the time we always faced playing the Welsh on their own patch with trepidation. In 1948, though, when we played them in Swansea, Jack sat in the dressing room punching his fist into his hand, saying: "I'm mad to get at them. I'm mad to get at them. I'm mad to get at them." His enthusiasm rubbed off on the rest of us.

'Jack was an extraordinary character. Before the war he only played with the thirds for London Irish. As he departed for combat he said, "When I come back I'll be picked for Ireland." He was stationed in Italy during the war and had to carry heavy wireless equipment on his back. As a result his upper body strength was incredible. Before internationals he did double somersaults to confirm his fitness. Having scored the winning try to give us the Grand Slam in 1948 he was nearly killed by spectators at the final whistle. His jersey was stripped off his back and people were wearing pieces of it on their lapels for weeks afterwards. Jack was whisked off from the train station in Dublin the next day by a girl in a sports car whom he had never met but who was sporting a piece of his jersey on her blouse. He stayed with her for a week and lost his job when he went back to London!'

MEDICAL SERVICE

Jack Kyle is one of the greats, not of Irish rugby but international rugby. However, his father knew how to put him in his place: 'When my late father read that I had been selected to head off on a six-month tour with the Lions, his words across the breakfast table were: "Does that young fellow ever intend to qualify in medicine?"'

Did the players receive any reward for their unique achievement in winning the Grand Slam in 1948?

'The only thing we got was a photo of the winning team and the team crest!'

TACTICAL INNOVATION

Jack witnessed some strange sights at team meetings:

'I remember my former teammate Andy Mulligan telling the story of an Irish team talk given by my late brother-in-law Noel Henderson, when he was captain of Ireland: "Right, lads, let's decide how we're going to play this game. What do you think, Jack?"

I responded, "A few wee punts at the line might be dandy, and maybe young Mulligan here can try a few darts of his own."

'Noel then sought Tony O'Reilly's opinion. O'Reilly replied, "The programme here says a midget's marking me. Just give me the ball and let me have a run at him."

'Then it was Cecil Pedlow's turn. Cec's answer was, "I think a subtle mix of runnin', jinkin' an' kickin' should just work out fine."

'Picking up the ball to go out, Noel summed up: "Right, lads, that's decided – Jack's puntin', Andy's dartin', Tony's runnin', and Cecil's doin' all three."'

LOSING MY RELIGION

The only story ever told against Jack Kyle is that he could be a little bit absent-minded at times, like when he turned up at an Ireland training session with only one boot. For his part, Kyle greatly enjoyed some of the characters on the Irish team. He had a particular appreciation for the quick wit of former Irish rugby international Andy Mulligan, who once went up for a job from Dublin to Belfast and his prospective boss asked him: what religion are you, Mulligan?

Quick as a flash Andy responded, 'What religion did you have in mind, sir?'

JOY AND SADNESS

After his retirement from surgery Jack lived in a 'wee village' on the County Down coastline. He was a gentleman in both senses of the term and someone who placed a high value on friendship. One of his friends had always wanted to visit Paris. Jack brought him there for his ninetieth birthday. His friend was suitably impressed by the wonders of one of the great cities in the world. At one stage they were sitting by the Seine sipping coffee when a large number of beautiful women passed by. Jack's friend turned to him and shook his head sadly: 'Ah Jack, if only I was seventy again!'

THE BARE ESSENTIALS

The past is a different country and listening to Jack was like travelling in a time warp: 'We were really innocent. I suppose this was particularly shown when we went to Paris in 1948. We had our banquet in the Hotel Laetitia. It was a bit of an eye-opener! There were six different glasses, a different wine for every course, all vintage. I will never forget the wine waiter coming along to pour for some of the Irish lads and they telling him, *"Non, non merci, avez-vous un jus d'orange, s'il vous plaît?"* After that, we headed to the Folies Bergère, or in the immortal words of Bill McKay, the Folies Bareskins!'

GRAND CENTRAL

Kyle had some peculiar experiences playing rugby in Ireland. Shortly after the Grand Slam triumph in 1949 Jack drove down to Cork. On the way he came to a level crossing at a railway station which was halfway across the road. He sat in the car for ten minutes, then got out and found the station master and asked, 'Do you know the gate is halfway across the road?'

'I do,' replied the station master. 'We are half expecting the train from Cork.'

DOCTOR, DOCTOR

Jack told me a few stories about his time as a doctor. One of his colleagues, known for his extraordinary treatment of arthritis, had a waiting room full of people when a little old lady, bent over almost in half, shuffled in slowly, leaning on her cane. When her turn came, she went into the doctor's office. Within five minutes she came back out walking completely erect. A woman in the waiting room who had seen all this rushed up to the little old lady and said, 'It's a miracle! You walked in bent in half, and now you're walking erect. What did the doctor do?'

'Gave me a longer cane,' the woman replied.

EYE-CATCHING

A seaman met a pirate and noticed that he had a peg leg, a hook and an eye patch. 'So how did you end up with a peg leg?' the seaman asked.

'I was swept overboard and a shark bit my leg off,' the pirate replied.

'What about your hook?' asked the seaman.

'Well, we were boarding an enemy ship and one of the enemy cut my hand off,' the pirate said.

'So how did you get the eye patch?' the seaman finally asked.

'I got something in my eye,' replied the pirate. When the sailor looked confused, the pirate continued: 'It was my first day with the hook.'

GLORY DAYS

One of the giants of Irish rugby in the golden era of Jackie Kyle was his brother-in-law, Noel Henderson. In the course of a radio commentary of an Irish international, Henderson was being slated by the commentator. Noel's father was so outraged at the stream of insults that he threw the radio out of the window!

35

ENGLISH LESSONS

Mick English Tours with the Lions

In normal circumstances former Irish rugby international Hannah Tyrrell had more pressing plans for the second week in April 2021. But Covid-19 came along and turned things upside down and inside out. As a result Tyrrell found herself starring for Ireland against Wales in a rescheduled Six Nations Championship instead of celebrating a weekend she had pencilled in her diary long before the emergence of a global pandemic: 'I was supposed to get married (on Friday) but unfortunately Covid put an end to that and we pushed it out a little bit. But I'm out here doing what I love with my teammates. What else could I ask for?'

Ireland defeated their hosts 45–0: 'We waited a long time to play this game – it has been a long six months for us working hard. It was nice to reap the rewards and get a few points on the board. We effectively got the nerves out in the first few minutes. We were raring to go.'

In 1959 Mick 'the Kick' English and Noel Brophy were selected to tour with the Lions to Australia and New Zealand.

Sadly they were both injured and had to return home together by boat. The journey home took weeks and, on the way home, they became best friends. Forty years to the day that they came home, Mick's son married Niall's daughter. It was only after the happy couple returned from their honeymoon and looked at the dates on an old photo that they appreciated the serendipity of their wedding date. It is a closely guarded secret but there is romance in Irish rugby.

THE SUPREMES

Nothing quite unites the island of Ireland like the Irish rugby team, and since Ireland's first ever international against England at Kennington Oval in London on 15 February 1875, when rugby was a twenty-a-side game, Irish rugby has produced many exceptional players and even more amazing characters.

If laughter be the food of rugby, play on. On the World Cup and Grand Slam index, Ireland does not feature very prominently. Yet no student of the game would disagree that Ireland has given international rugby a disproportionate number of the great characters of the game. In this category are people like Jack MacCauley. He was said to be the first married man to be capped in international rugby in 1887 – according to rugby folklore he got wed just to get leave of absence to play for Ireland!

Even club players have entered international rugby's informal hall of fame with their celebrated wit. A case in point is Sam Hutton of Malone, not least because of his famous chat-up line: 'Excuse me, darling, haven't you met me somewhere before?' They may not know how to win many titles but they certainly know how to have a laugh.

Mick English (nicknamed 'Mick the Kick' because of his proficiency with the boot) won 16 caps for Ireland from 1958 to 1962. He was in the right place in the wrong time because he would have won many more caps had not the first part of his career coincided with that of Jack Kyle and the latter part with that of Mike Gibson.

He is famous throughout the rugby world for his quote when discussing an incident during an international against England that led to a try for his opposite number, Phil Horrocks-Taylor. 'Horrocks went one way, Taylor the other and I was left holding the bloody hyphen.'

GET AN EARFUL OF THIS

When I met Mick English, he told me the story of a rugby player who was hurt very badly during a scrum and had both of his ears ripped off. Since he was permanently disfigured, he decided to give up playing rugby for good.

His club and insurance company ensured that a large sum of money was paid out to him.

One day, he decided to invest his money in a small but growing sportswear business. He bought the company outright but after signing on the dotted line realised that he knew nothing about business. He decided to employ someone to run the shop. The next day he set up three interviews.

The first guy was great. He knew everything he needed to and was very enthusiastic. At the end of the interview, the former rugby player asked him, 'Do you notice anything different about me?'

And the man replied, 'Why, yes, I couldn't help noticing you have no ears.'

The rugby player got angry and threw him out.

The second interview was with a woman, and she was even better than the first guy. He asked her the same question, 'Do you notice anything different about me?'

She replied: 'Well, you have no ears.'

He got upset again and showed her the door.

The third and last interview was with the best of the three. He was a very young man fresh out of college. He was smart and handsome and seemed to know all about the sportswear business. The rugby player was anxious, but went ahead and asked him the same question: 'Do you notice anything different about me?'

To his surprise the young man answered, 'Yes, you wear contact lenses.'

The former rugby player was shocked, and said, 'What an incredibly observant young man you are. How in the world did you know that?'

The young man fell off his chair laughing hysterically and replied, 'Well, it's pretty hard to wear glasses with no flipping ears!'

36

WE ARE THE CHAMPIONS

Ulster Are European Champions

The out-half requires a cool head because they are known as 'the general' in rugby jargon as they are the link between the backs and the forwards. It can be the glamour position and conversely if things go wrong it is the place not to be! Ireland's former out-half David Humphreys has seen both sides of the coin. On the way he amassed a number of records, becoming Ireland's record point scorer and Ireland's most prolific drop-goal scorer.

The highlight of his career came in January 1999 when he captained Ulster to victory in the European Cup:

'We didn't have a very good team but we got on a roll. There were just a few hundred people at our first match but our success struck a chord initially across the province and then throughout the whole of Ireland. Driving down to Dublin for the final in Lansdowne Road all the flags of support for us really inspired us.

'All of Ireland got behind us as we were bidding to become the first Irish side to win the competition. I suppose it was all the sweeter for me as I was captain. Mark McCall was captain for the opening match but he got injured and the captaincy fell onto my shoulders by default. The whole day was an incredible experience.'

A number of prominent Ulster Unionist politicians were at Lansdowne Road for the occasion. One found himself in the proximity of a staunch Republican who was very much on the opposite end of the spectrum in terms of attitude to Northern Ireland. The Unionist turned to this staunch Nationalist and said, 'How does it feel to belong to a 32 county Ulster?'

AN IMPORTANT CLARIFICATION

One of the Munster players is believed to be responsible for the story that surfaced at the end of Humphreys's wife Jayne's third pregnancy when David rang the operator.

Operator: '999. What's the nature of your emergency?'

Humphreys: 'My wife is pregnant and her contractions are only two minutes apart.'

'Is this her first child?'

'No, you idiot. This is her husband.'

TIME TO SAY GOODBYE

Humphreys has a lot of happy memories from his time in rugby:

'Probably my favourite rugby story goes back to 2003 just before the World Cup. The international players were away with the Irish squad and Johnny Bell was made captain of Ulster for a Celtic League match. Just before the game Johnny gathered all the players around him, brought them into a huddle and said: "Right lads, there's just two things I want from you in this game." He paused dramatically. You could have heard a pin drop as the lads were hanging on to his every word. You could almost cut the tension with a knife as he said: "Honesty, commitment and work-rate." The lads almost fell on the floor laughing at his gaffe. Ulster lost badly and Johnny's career as a captain came to an abrupt and undistinguished end!'

37

TRUMPED

Franno Becomes a Twitter Star

Some people are comfortable bending the rules. A case in point is Donald Trump. Indeed, Rick Reilly's book about Trump's relationship with golf is called *Commander in Cheat: How Golf Explains Trump*.

The Donald loves golf and while he was president he appeared to spend as much time as he could at the courses he owns as he did in the Oval Office. How he conducted himself at one place related directly to his behaviour in the other.

On the basis of testimony from playing partners, caddies and golf club executives, Reilly outlines how Trump lies about the number of club championships he has won, 'stiffs' his golf-course contractors, lies about his handicap and worst of all — he lies about his lies. Reilly suggests that Trump does golf sort of the way he did the presidency, which was to operate as though the rules are for other people.

One of the phrases most associated with Donald's presidency was 'fake news'. Former Irish international and now pundit Neil Francis understands his frustration. Franno does not have

a Facebook, Instagram or Twitter account. Like other prominent personalities such as Rob Kearney and Pat Spillane, he
does have a Twitter impersonator who does a good job of, in
Franno's own words, 'ripping the piss' out of this star who is
summed up as: 'Huge triceps. Indescribably wealthy. The first
global superstar.'

Franno's fictional self lives in luxury in south county Dublin,
where he is waited upon by his butler Von Smallhausen. He
only drinks vintage Champagne or the very best Bordeaux and
anyone who lives outside south county Dublin is described
as some form of subhuman. He has had lunch with Vladimir
Putin, who worships at his altar. The caviar was Sevruga rather
than some cheap alternative.

A target for much of Franno's comments in this parody
account is Munster and Munster rugby such as: 'I've been
asked to explain remarks where I called Markey Street in San
Francisco a "cesspit". To clarify, compared to where I live, most
places are cesspits. Especially Clonmel.'

His election manifesto during the 2020 General Election
included the proposal to have Limerick annexed from Ireland.

In this alternate reality, shaking his belly like a bowlful
of jelly, Franno's claims: 'I am hearing reports Joey Carbery
broke his arm milking a heifer at Munster training today.
Terrible blow.'

Humility does not feature prominently in these posts: 'I'm
reasonably indifferent having been offered an honorary knight-
hood. I guess I should have lots of people to thank but the truth
of the matter is that I did it all on my own . . . When I played my
last game in Lansdowne Road they made plans to immediately
demolish the stadium.'

In fairness to Franno he does not need a fake account to bring
colour to the rugby landscape. Witness his observation: 'In the

movie *Trainspotting*, the crew always seemed to retire to one of their kind who was both a heroin user and a dealer. His nickname was "Mother Superior" because he had the longest habit. If you say winning is a habit, then Leinster, certainly over the last dozen years, have got into it.'

FENDER BENDER

Francis played in the inaugural Rugby World Cup in 1987. His tour was more memorable for events off the pitch than for those on it. His highlights included puking on a dog because he was forced to eat the hotel food, the entire squad sneaking out in the middle of the night to get some KFC because of that hotel food, and an early morning pool session with an Irish fan.

However, the most memorable moment came when the team saw the Webb Ellis trophy. While the Irish squad were waiting for the rest of the teams to arrive, he went over to the table and lifted the trophy off its plinth, knocking the lid off it in the process. Star forward Philip Matthews went over to put the lid back on just as the All Blacks walked in. An awkward silence fell on the room. Franno claims that the Irish team felt like a boy who was caught playing with his older brother's Fender Stratocaster.

38

SHAKIN ALL OVER

Archie O'Leary Succeeds in Rugby and Racing

One of Ireland's leading writers, Joe O'Connor, once posed the question: is football better than sex? Joe's witty argument could readily be transposed to the world of rugby. At first glance this might be considered a highly contentious statement as the two activities are so remarkably different. One involves the complete engagement of the senses, wild abandonment, heart-stopping elation and above all orgasmic bliss.

The other is sex.

Few know the sheer toe-curling ecstasy of winning and the adrenalin rush of having the small hairs standing on the back of the neck at Cheltenham better than Florida Pearl's owner and former Irish rugby international Archie O'Leary. Spectating is no sport for the unfit. At best it leaves you shattered; at worst it could kill you. When Florida Pearl won his first race in Cheltenham in 1997, Archie did not enjoy it. He normally did not get overexcited before a race once he saw the horse was settled down but that day he was so nervous his glasses were shaking. Ted Walsh said after the race that having a winner at

Cheltenham is like losing your virginity to Kim Basinger – it's all downhill afterwards. Mind you, when Archie heard that, he had to ask his wife who Kim Basinger was!

DUAL STAR

Archie was a thrice-capped Irish second-row forward. He toured Argentina and Chile with Ireland in 1952. Archie claimed that rugby was more fun then, although it was pretty tough on the pitch. In fact one of his clearest memories of his Ireland career is going down on a ball, getting kicked and breaking two ribs, and having to play on because Mick Lane had already gone off. On the Monday afterwards, he had an X-ray done which cost £1 11s 6d so he sent the bill to the IRFU. In return he got a snotty reply which said this was an amateur game and that there was no way in hell they were going to pay for it.

SILENCE IS NOT GOLDEN

Professionally, Archie was an insurance mogul – employing over a hundred people in his insurance business. Apart from his headquarters in South Mall in Cork, he also had offices in Mallow, Galway and Dublin. He was proud of his achievements: 'I started off on my own in 1961 with one fella and a girl. As if that wasn't scary enough the fella wouldn't even talk to me!'

REVEALING

His father was a doctor in Cork. He was the first to scale the flagpole at UCC, then Queen's College, to haul down the flag that was there, and put up the tricolour. He was wearing an Irish kilt at the time!

LOST IN TRANSLATION

Cork was a huge part of Archie's life. He once told me a story of a French priest who came to work in Dublin. On his first day he heard confessions. His last penitent was a troubled man. At the end of his confession the man asked the priest, 'Are you from Cork?'

'No I'm from Paris.'

'I thought you were from Cork. I don't understand anyone from Cork.'

JACK'S BACK

One of the people Archie most admired was Jack Doyle. Jack was a jockey, a trainer of an Irish Grand National and a finder of new talent, notably Mill House, who won the Gold Cup in 1963, and Bruni, who won the English St Leger in 1975. Doyle also earned one cap for the Irish rugby team against Wales in Belfast in the mid-1930s.

Doyle had the distinction of first introducing Robert Sangster to John Magnier in the early 1970s and therefore indirectly responsible for a revolution in the international bloodstock arena. That meeting spawned 'the syndicate' with Vincent O'Brien that ultimately led to the establishment of the Coolmore Stud.

The Sangster–O'Brien–Magnier triumvirate benefited enormously from a decision taken by Charlie Haughey when he was Minister for Finance, when he decreed that all income generated by stallions should be exempt from tax. This led to a steady stream of top thoroughbreds crossing the Atlantic from America to Ireland. When it was subsequently suggested that Magnier might have been the real brains behind the tax decision, Magnier replied with typical self-deprecation: 'Sure I was only milking cows at that stage.'

Jack Doyle died in October 1998. A few months before he died a function was held in his honour. One of the guest speakers was Tony O'Hehir, who told a story about his father, the legendary Micheál O'Hehir. One day he called with the racing correspondent Louis Gunning to collect Jack from his house in Shankill. They were waiting a long time for Jack. Like all of us Jack had his ups and downs and periods when money was tight. So eventually the two boys were sent a message that whatever door Jack was coming out, it would not be the front door!

AN UNFORTUNATE ERROR

Another story Archie recalled to me was of Jack's experiences as a jockey at a race meeting in Navan when there was a terrible pile up at the third last fence. Horses and jockeys were sprawled everywhere. Despite two broken ribs Jack managed to remount and with agonising pain and great applause from the crowd he was the only one to finish the course. The trainer greeted him with a kick in the bum and said, 'You big dope. You remounted the wrong horse!'

Archie was sceptical of what Brendan Behan memorably described in a typical phrase as the 'horse-arse Anglo-Irish' from Kildare and Meath. Archie believed that the Cork-born jockey Mick Fitzgerald was a truer representative of Irish sport. He is as famous for his euphoric soundbite as he is for his victory on Rough Quest in the Martell Grand National in 1996. 'Sex will be an anti-climax after that' was his description of the experience. He described the National as the best twelve minutes of his life. His fiancée Jane Brackenbury responded by saying, 'He's never lasted twelve minutes in his life!'

SPEECH MAKERS

For top jockeys the corporate part of their livelihood is developing. Each day of a big meeting like the Cheltenham festival, leading jockeys act as corporate speakers for guests by providing pre-race analysis. This aspect of a top, professional jockey's life will increase significantly in the years to come. For that reason an agent's most important job during the festival is to synchronise their jockeys' timetables so that they show up to the sponsors when they are expected but are back with their horses whenever they need to be.

Inevitably in this high pressure environment there can be the odd faux pas.

A case in point was what happened to Mick Fitzgerald. Mick was due to address some clients before racing in Windsor in the corporate box. Through no fault of his own he arrived a bit late and had to go directly to racing. He had rides in the first two races and had a first and a second. As he was free until the last race, he rushed up to the sponsor's box and apologised most profusely for having missed the pre-race analysis. For forty minutes he launched into a masterly incisive and entertaining analysis of the day's racing. As he finished he went around to everybody and again apologised profusely for missing the pre-race analysis.

Later an agent asked the sponsor what he thought of Mick Fitzgerald. The sponsor said he had never turned up. Mick had been given the wrong directions and through no fault of his own had gone to the wrong box!

PARADISE LOST

For many rugby players of the past racing is the best fun they can have with their clothes on but sometimes they can lose your shirt. Most punters are dismissive of the story of a rich bookie, a poor bookie and the tooth fairy who are in a room with a £100 note on the table when the lights go out. When the light comes back on the money is gone. So who took it? It's got to be the rich bookie because the other two are figments of the imagination.

Rugby people too love stories about punters like the late Barney Curley making fools of the bookies. He had a stud farm in Wicklow populated with moderate horses and began to place them in weak races where he knew he could make a killing. His most famous coup was with Yellow Sam at Bellewstown (in the 2m5f Mount Hanover Amateur Riders' Handicap Hurdle) in 1975. The horse had odds at 20/1. Barney had men laying odds on the horse at shops all over the place. It was a simple plan really. Punters could only place bets via off-course bookies, phoning through to the course to offset the bookies' potential liabilities. The system prevented fancied horses going off with big odds. By the time the horse ran the odds should have been 1/2. The beauty of the situation from Barney's point of view was that there was only one phone line into the ground and this huge, calorifically-challenged guy got hold of it claiming his mother was sick and he wouldn't let go of it until the race was over. So nobody knew what was going on outside!

THE PIANO MAN
A crucial difference between the English and Irish at Cheltenham is the way they react to victory. The English tend to temper their reaction with some of their hallowed reserve and aloofness. The Irish let their emotions run wild and there are no inhibitions. Who will ever forget the exuberance of Dawn Run's famous victory?

For years Danno Heaslip was the heart of the Galwegians rugby team, from the scrum-half position. Danno and his brother Mick provided Ireland with another Cheltenham win when their horse For Auction won the Champion Hurdle at 40/1 in 1982 under the stewardship of Colin Magnier. Part of racing folklore is their special bet for the champagne money, netting £2,000 in the process. On arrival back to their hotel Danno is said to have instructed the manager to open one hundred bottles of champagne. His second instruction was to the manager to get a piano.

'But we don't have a piano in this area,' the manager replied.

'Then buy one,' said Danno.

BOOK HIM DANNO

Probably the only Irishman with mixed feelings about the victory was Danno Heaslip's friend, former government minister Des O'Malley. He had been all geared up to attend the festival, but then a general election intervened and he found himself back in office at the start of March, and at the last minute had to cancel his trip to Cheltenham. He instructed Danno to put £25 each way on the horse for him. Danno went to Cheltenham on the Sunday but before leaving posted a letter to O'Malley's home in Limerick, saying that so many people had asked to him to back the horse that he could not possibly get it all on, particularly as he was backing the horse himself. The only problem was that O'Malley had left for Dublin before the post arrived on the Monday morning and didn't get the letter until after the race – having calculated that he had just won £1,250 on his investment!

39

THE KEANE EDGE

Kerry Win the Munster Final

The last time I spoke with Moss Keane, I asked him how he would like to be remembered. He answered indirectly as was his wont. He reminded me of the inscription on Spike Milligan's tombstone: 'I told you I was ill.' However, Moss suggested an alternative: 'I told you I was old.'

The entire Irish nation went to mourning in 2010 with news of the death of Moss Keane. Few sports personalities were more loved.

SENSITIVE SOUL

Moss's wife Ann put his date of birth and death in Roman numerals. While Moss, leaning over the banisters of heaven, would be happy to have people know his age, he would have been even happier if people did not know.

Since his capture on 8 February 1983, Shergar has been at a stud in the Middle East, galloping around the Scottish Highlands, peacefully grazing in a Channel Island's meadow, part of the mafia mob, part of a Kentucky killing and even giving riding lessons to runaway British aristocrat Lord Lucan. Likewise, if even a fraction of the stories about Moss were true he would have needed a brewery of his own to supply him in Guinness, broken down more doors than most people have eaten hot dinners and generally been responsible for extraordinary levels of mirth and mayhem.

Moss had originally made an impact as a Gaelic footballer. However, he was not known for being 'fleet of foot'. According to folklore, after a less than resoundingly successful career as a Gaelic footballer, his conversion to rugby came when he over-heard a friend saying in a pub that, 'A farmer could make a tidy living on the space of ground it takes Moss to turn.'

Keane's sporting career began when his father told him when he started to kick a ball around with the friends in the corner of a field, using goalposts they had cut for themselves, 'No cursing, kicking, scraping or biting. Get the ball in hand and then kick it. It's catch and kick. That's what it is. It's not soccer you're playing. Hit hard with the shoulder but hit fair. And let there be no pulling and dragging at jerseys or jumping up on fellas like in that oul' rugby. And no crying.'

Moss once threw out a pass to Billy Morgan (the Cork foot-baller) in such a way that Morgan got hammered by a tackler. Morgan and Moss were great friends, but Morgan made it clear what he thought of the quality of the pass: 'Mossy, that oval-shaped yoke is a ball and you are supposed to pass it and not shovel it out like cow sh*te from some Kerry dunghill.'

Stories about Moss are more common than showers in April – though many are not printable in our politically correct times. Some are even true! Moss had a nice line in self-depreciating humour: 'After I left university I found I had no talent for anything so I joined the civil service! I won 52 caps – a lot of them just because they couldn't find anybody else.'

BUTTERFINGERS

Moss enjoyed a good relationship with legendary Roscommon footballer Dermot Earley. The two had become friends after attending a charity auction for GOAL in 1979. Dermot donated the jersey he had worn in the League final, which raised £100. He was not sure if he should feel complimented with the price or insulted when the buyer Terry Rodgers told him, 'My father was from Roscommon but thanks be to God he got out early.'

Moss brought the house down when he told how Ireland had lost narrowly to Wales in Cardiff Arms Park earlier in the year despite a breathtaking performance by Tony Ward.

In his own distinctive style Moss held up a plastic bag and recalled how he had gone into the Welsh dressing room after the game to swap jerseys with Allan Martin the Welsh forward. On his way out, big Moss remembered that Martin had not been a good man to buy a round of drinks on the Lions tour, so he went back inside and 'borrowed' Martin's tracksuit while he was in the shower, to compensate for all the drinks Keane had bought him on the Lions tour.

Moss also said you have to pick your fights. To illustrate, he recalled how he was once selected to play for the Welsh Barbarians against a touring South Africa team. The game turned violent, with numerous bouts of fisticuffs. At one stage twenty-nine of the players on the field were fighting ferociously. Moss was the sole non-combatant. Asked later why he was so uncharacteristically Gandhian, Moss replied, 'I might die for Ireland but I'm f***ed if I'm going to die for Wales.'

HEY MR POSTMAN

Moss also spoke about driving from Dublin for a match in Tralee with Dick Spring. The two boys always shortened the journey by doing the crossword from *The Irish Times*. Moss proudly held the record for getting the crossword done before they got to Kildare. On this day, though, Spring was on fire and answering every question. Spring was driving that day and Moss noticed that he was not pushing his foot on the pedal as hard as they approached Kildare, with a new record in sight. Moss called out a clue: 'Postman loses mail.'

Spring scratched his head and observed, 'That should be easy to do.' He repeated the clue a number of times. Finally he asked, 'How many letters?'

Moss gleefully replied, 'Every f**king one of them!'

THE SWEETEST FEELING

Folklore about Moss grows with every day and distinguishing fact from fiction is not easy. Moss was playing for the Wolfhounds, and in the side was Charlie Kent, the big blond English centre. Charlie was a diabetic, and at half-time this rather puffed-up ambulance man arrived in the players' huddle and tapped Moss on the shoulder. The man asked Moss if he was the man who wanted a sugar lump; Moss said, 'Arra Jaysus, who do you think I am, Shergar?'

DO THE MATHS

Internationally Moss too was a much-loved figure as Welsh legend Ray Gravell told me, 'Willie Duggan was an awesome player and a great man to knock back a pint! I would probably say the same thing about Moss Keane. These guys were legends on the pitch and legends in the bar! Sometimes too much drink is not enough! It only took one drink to get them drunk. The problem was they could never remember was it the twenty-fourth or the twenty-fifth!'

HIGHFLYERS

Like Willie Duggan, Moss had a fear of flying and generally the only way they got on a plane was with the benefit of a lot of Dutch courage. As he drove to the airport for the Lions tour in 1977 Moss was so nervous about the flight that he crashed his car. The story is told that he rang his mother just before he took off and said, 'The car is in the airport. It is wrecked. See you in four months.'

Moss was once asked, 'Are you afraid of flying, Mossie?'

He replied, 'Afraid of flying? No. Afraid of crashing? Yes.'

Moss habitually had to sit in the back seat whenever he took the plane. Asked by Ciaran Fitzgerald why he always took the back seat he replied, 'I've never seen a plane back into a mountain yet.'

MATCH OF THE DAY

When Moss went on his first tour to New Zealand with the Lions, he was the only player in the first seven weeks who the BBC had not interviewed because they did not think his strong Kerry brogue would work well with a British audience. Eventually the Lions players said they would refuse to do any more interviews for the BBC until Nigel Starmer-Smith interviewed Moss. Nigel reluctantly agreed to this demand and asked on live television, 'Well Moss, you've been here now for two months and you've played in your First Lions Test, met the Maoris – what's been the best moment of the trip for you?'

In his thickest Kerry accent Moss replied, 'When I heard that Kerry beat Cork in the Munster final.'

NO BULL

In 1983 Will Duggan rang up Moss to wind him up by telling him he was selected for the Lions tour to New Zealand at a time when Moss was at the end of his career and was not a contender for selection. The Doog was surprised when Moss replied, 'My cow died.'

Duggan responded, 'I'm sorry to hear that but the good news is that you've been picked for the Lions again.'

Moss: 'My cow died.'

Willie: 'That's tough but playing for the Lions will compensate.'

Moss: 'My cow died.'

Duggan: 'Why are you constantly telling me that you cow died?'

Moss: 'So you will know that I don't need any bull.'

40

NO JOHN BULL

John Hayes Eats Out

I am not always sure about his music but one of my favourite pop stars is James Blunt. I love the way he pokes fun at himself all the time. I liked the way he called his book *How To Be A Complete and Utter Blunt: Diary of a Reluctant Social Media Sensation*. My favourite Blunt moment came when a critic tweeted: 'Can we all take a moment and remember just how terrible James Blunt was.'

Quick as a flash the singer tweeted back: 'No need. I have a new album coming soon.'

Irish rugby's equivalent of James Blunt is John Hayes, though it is difficult to imagine the Bull crooning *You're Beautiful*. Like Blunt, he is not a man to take himself too seriously. There is never any bull from the Bull.

His record is 217 Munster games, 105 Ireland caps and two Test appearances for the Lions. One snapshot illustrates his personality. His most famous try came in Munster's thrilling Heineken Cup semi-final win in Toulouse in 2000. The giant from Cappamore had made a carry and was still kneeling on the ground ahead of play when Dominic Crotty broke through two phases later. Then came a period of ten seconds when the Bull had not got up off the ground. He always claims that the ten-second gap fooled the opposition and he was in the right place at the right time to score a try.

FAST FOOD

Although he was a model professional and not a drinker, he did enjoy his food. The 1990s were good times in Shannon as they won four consecutive All-Ireland Leagues, and Hayes shone with the likes of Alan Quinlan, Mick Galwey and the late great Axel Foley. While many of the team enjoyed liberal liquid refreshment, the big thing for the Bull on a night out was the chipper afterwards. One night in Kilkenny there was a big queue in the chipper. All the way up along towards the counter, there was a shelf with bits of free food, such as leftover chips. The Bull shocked his Shannon friends because he did such a brilliant job of demolishing all the spare food that when he got to the counter he was unable to eat any more.

BIG SOFTIE

Although he is an imposing physical presence, the Bull has a soft side. I imagine that, when possible, he has a gentler touch than Gandhi stroking a pussycat.

This was shown when the GAA revoked Rule 42 and opened up Croke Park to Ireland's soccer and rugby games while the old Lansdowne Road stadium was being demolished and the Aviva was being built. Nobody will ever forget the extraordinarily unique atmosphere that day Ireland played England in that never to be forgotten rugby match in 2007. The emotion that day was unreal, as was evident in the sight of big John Hayes bawling his eyes out while the anthems were being played.

FIRST DATE?

Unlike some of his colleagues, Hayes is unwilling to cause embarrassment to former internationals. Hence his refusal to name the recently retired rugby international who went into Tesco's and bought a sandwich and a bag of crisps.

His keen eye was caught by the beautiful young woman who was serving him and asked: 'Would you like to get a drink?'

The player gulped and said: 'Thanks for asking but I have a girlfriend.'

The woman smiled and watched in amusement as the former star's face turned a purple shade of red when she replied: 'The drink is part of the meal deal, sir.'

TRUE LOVE WAYS

Alan Quinlan was so upset when he heard that the founder of sexual innuendo died that he rang John Hayes, who always has a word of consolation. Hayes replied, 'His wife has taken it really hard.'

41

MY HEART WILL GO ON

Donncha's Titanic *Performance*

The Bull has clearly a romantic sensibility as he married Irish rugby royalty Fiona Stead.

The build-up to their wedding did create a unique moment in the annals of Irish rugby as Eric Miller recalled for me:

'As the tour of South Africa in 2004 was coming to an end we organised John Hayes's stag party. We dressed John up in a gymslip. The sight of a twenty-stone man in a gymslip is one that I never want to see again! Colin Farrell was filming there at the time and he came to join us for the party. He was a very sound guy and certainly knew how to have a good time! We gathered around in a circle with John in the middle and everyone got to ask Colin a question. Everything was going to plan until Donncha O'Callaghan, as only Donncha can, asked, "What was it like to be the star of *Titanic*?" The whole place cracked up and we nearly fell off our seats laughing.'

ANIMAL FARM

It is not surprising that Donncha's adventures from that tour spawned another story. In this account Donncha stayed on afterwards to go on a safari holiday. While there, he came upon an elephant, in great pain, with a giant thorn in its foot. Donncha very carefully approached the elephant, and gingerly removed the thorn from its foot. The elephant began to walk away, then turned and stared at Donncha for a full minute, locking eyes with him. The elephant then continued on its way. 'I wonder, if I ever see that elephant again, will it remember me?' Donncha mused to himself.

The following Christmas Donncha was back in Munster at a circus. He noticed that one of the elephants kept looking at him, almost like it knew him. Donncha wondered, 'Could this be that elephant I helped so long ago?' He decided to get a closer look. With the elephant still giving him the stare down, Donncha moved in closer, getting right up in front of the elephant. They locked eyes. A knowing look seemed to cross the elephant's face. It reached down, picking up O'Callaghan carefully with its trunk and lifting him high in the air, then threw him crashing to the ground and stomped him near to death.

Turns out it was not that elephant.

DONNCHA'S DAYS

Stories about the Claw's Munster teammates are the stuff of legend, like Donncha O'Callaghan's experiences touring South Africa waiting to be served in a posh restaurant. The Irish lock was frustrated that he had to spend so long waiting for his dinner. When the meal finally arrived O'Callaghan said, 'You tell me you're the same fellow who took my order. Somehow, I expected a much older waiter.'

GUMP

Donncha O'Callaghan is the clown prince of Irish rugby. Yet he has a serious side and has a big heart, as is evident in his charity work for UNICEF and his mercy mission to Haiti after their earthquake in 2010.

His sensitive side was on display after Rob Henderson required fifteen stiches in his lip following a 'clash' in a Celtic League match in autumn 2004. Noticing Hendo's concern about his appearance, his ever-helpful teammate O'Callaghan called him 'Bubba' after the character in Forest Gump.

Donncha tells the story of the Irishman who approached an English foreman for work on a building site. The latter fancied himself as a great wit. 'What's your name, Paddy?' he enquired of the Irish chap.

'Michael Moran,' came the reply.

'Anything to do with the Mountains of Mourne?' the wit asked.

'No, but my mother was one of the Hills of Donegal.'

FORLORN IN THE USA

According to legend O'Callaghan went to Dallas after the 2011 World Cup for a well-deserved vacation. He checked into a downtown hotel, but when he got to his room he immediately called the front desk. Donncha said, 'This here bed can sleep the whole Munster team! I only wanted a regular-sized bed.'

The clerk responded, 'That is a regular size bed, sir. You have to remember that everything's big in Texas.'

O'Callaghan went to the hotel's bar and ordered a draught beer. When he was served, he said to the bartender, 'This is as big as Peter Clohessy. I only asked for a glass of beer.'

The bartender answered, 'That is a glass of beer, sir. You have to remember that everything's big in Texas!'

When the waiter in the hotel's dining room brought out the steak Donncha ordered for dinner, O'Callaghan exclaimed, 'That steak's as big as John Hayes's thigh and the baked potato is bigger than Reggie Corrigan's head. Where'd this come from?'

The waiter replied, 'It's all local, sir. You have to remember that everything's big in Texas!'

When the waiter asked O'Callaghan if he wanted to see the dessert menu, Donncha said he might be able to squeeze something in, but after consuming all that food and drink he needed to use the restroom first. The waiter directed him to go down the hall to the first door on the right.

By this time, O'Callaghan was quite inebriated and mistakenly went through the first door on the left. He walked across the tiled floor and fell into the swimming pool.

When the rugby legend came spluttering to the surface, he yelled out, 'For f**k's sake, please don't flush.'

THE NO CLOTHES SHOW

The phrase 'wardrobe malfunction' was coined when Janet Jackson exposed her breast during the 2004 half-time Super Bowl entertainment. One Donncha O'Callaghan appearance remains in the memory for all the wrong reasons. He lost his shorts in a ruck during Munster's 22–12 victory over the Cardiff Blues in a Heineken Cup match in 2006, revealing a pair of bright red briefs, and sought to play on. He took his place for a line-out before the referee insisted that he leave the pitch for replacement shorts.

42

FROM DOWN UNDER

Campo Joins Old Belvedere

Throughout the Covid lockdown in 2021 Old Belvedere hosted a very enjoyable series of webinars for their members, ably hosted by the former Leinster out-half Andy Dunne, with four special guests: John Robbie, Joe Schmidt, Sir Ian McGeechan and David Campese.

Inevitably, Campo's conversation touched on his most famous game in Ireland.

It's funny the things that go through players' minds during a big game. During the 1991 World Cup quarter-final Australia's great centre, Tim Horan, was in a panic. After Gordon Hamilton scored a sensational try to give Ireland the lead in the dying minutes, Tim thought it was all over for them and they would be on the plane home the following morning. He had put a lot of his clothes in the laundry that morning and his big fear was that the clothes would not be ready for the following day! Then Michael Lynagh intervened and took them out of jail with his try.

I WANT YOUR SEX

In the World Cup final itself that year Horan had an even more pressing distraction. In the build up to the final the Australian team had an amazing amount of support from well-wishers, not just the fans who cheered them on their way but many who sent messages to the team hotel. In the lead-up to the final from time to time the players went into the team room into the hotel to read the messages. The messages were incredible: some offered free accommodation at five-star hotels, free evenings at massage parlours, free beach holidays, but then came the classic. A woman from Adelaide had faxed in: 'To whoever scores the first try in the final, I will offer you fantastic free sex.' Then she added her phone number.

The first break in the match happened to come from Horan. He was racing down the right-hand side with only Will Carling between himself and the try line, with this incredible offer at stake. Was he about to get lucky twice in the one moment? He decided to chip through but the ball went into touch. From the ensuing line-out the Australians managed to pilfer possession, and the forwards drove over the line. The prop, Tony Daly, crashed over the line to score this crucial try and became an unexpected hero, scoring the only try of the match. Tony was a wonderful old-fashioned prop, who won 41 caps for Australia, but had no future as a male model and was no George Clooney.

As the whole of Australia watched the game on television the nation's telephone company had its quietest two hours ever. They only took a single call. A lady from Adelaide had rung in to say that she wanted her number changed immediately!

Daly was also famous for his impression of John Eales. When Eales became team captain he was famous for the lengths he went to in order to reach a consensus. Daly regularly entertained his colleagues on long bus trips by mimicking the way Eales called line-outs: '19, 67, 45, 22 . . . if that's okay with everyone I mean. Anyone got any thoughts? I'm very happy to change it. Everyone's got to be in agreement with the decision.'

A PALE IMITATION

Daly also called Eales 'City Ford' because he said 'Yes' more often – after a television advertisement that used it as its slogan.

Daly was also believed, though it was never proved, to be responsible for a classic wind-up of David Campese. While the team were staying in a hotel in London a woman approached Campo in the lobby and said: 'Are you John Eales?'

Campo replied, 'No, I'm not.'

'I'm glad. I wouldn't like to see him looking so bad.'

AGONY UNCLE

On tour to England David Campese took a taxi with a few of the other players after a drinking session one evening back to the team hotel. The taxi driver was a bit obese and was also 'hygienically-challenged', with a less than enticing aroma emanating from his body. In addition he recounted a tale of woe about his lack of success with the opposite sex. After the Aussie lads paid their fare the taxi driver said, 'How about a tip?'

Before anyone could even thinking of reaching to their pockets for a second time Campo interjected, 'Certainly. Start using a deodorant and you might have some chance with the Sheilas.'

LASSIE COME HOME

In 1992 Campo was on tour with Australia in Wales. John Eales was approached by his prop Ewen McKenzie and asked him if he had read the biography of the Scottish rugby captain, David

Sole. Ewen proceeded to show him a passage that immediately drained all the blood from the great man's face: 'There is probably nothing I can say about Campo that he hasn't already said himself! Or even as the Wallaby lock John Eales said: "David fell in love with himself ten years ago and has remained faithful ever since!"'

Eales wished the ground would open up and swallow him. He had jocosely mentioned that phrase in the course of a private conversation with Sole as one of the Wallabies' favourite lines. However, he never expected to read it in cold print, with Australia's most iconic figure sitting just a few yards away from him. After the initial fear subsided Eales decided to deal with the problem head on and go into the lion's den and broach his indiscretion directly with Campo. He knocked timidly at Campo's door and after some prevarication eventually mustered up the courage to meekly ask: 'Campo . . . have . . . have you . . . have you seen David Sole's new book?' Much to Eales's relief Campo replied with typical indifference: 'Naaaah, mate, I wouldn't read something like that if you paid me. Who cares?' Eales almost danced with joy and said: 'Good. You're not missing much. It's really terrible.'

It was a much-relieved Eales who went to bed that night. The following morning Eales confided his faux pas to prop Tony Daly. Daly told him that all his angst was futile: 'You needn't have bothered speaking to Campo about it in the first place. He couldn't be bothered even reading his own book yet, so there's absolutely no way he would even think about reading David Sole's!'

43

LOVE STORY

Jim McCarthy Is Enchanted

It was the stuff of Hollywood.

Shortly before he left for the Lions tour in 1950, Jim McCarthy went to the Cork Opera House and met a ballerina called Pat. It was love at first sight. When Jim went away he brought Pat's picture with him. When he woke up the first thing he did each morning was to take out Pat's picture and kiss it and say: 'I love you.' Shortly after he returned from the tour they were married.

Jim liked to give Pat flowers. She told him that he was becoming obsessed with flowers. Jim turned from her and asked, 'Where is this all stemming from my petal?'

IT SAYS IN THE PAPERS

Jim McCarthy was known as Jack Kyle's outrider because of the protection he gave one of Ireland's greatest stars. He has a unique distinction. He was best man at both of Tony O'Reilly's weddings, though he only played the one season with Tony at international level. When O'Reilly arrived on the scene he was the darling of the media and could do no wrong. After his first match against France the *Irish Independent* said that Jim had played poorly and had not protected Tony well enough, even though he was not playing in the centre. He was dropped for the next match after that report and never played another international. Twenty-five years later, when O'Reilly had become the owner of the paper, Tony put him on the board of the *Irish Independent* just to make up for their injustice to him all those years ago.

LADIES' MAN

As a gentleman to his fingertips Jim would also not reveal Tony O'Reilly's roommate when he played for Ireland the night before Ireland took to the field against England at Twickenham. O'Reilly was out having a good time and his bored roommate was sitting in the room alone when the phone rang. A young woman's voice came over the line: 'Can I speak to Tony please?'

'I'm sorry, he's not in right now. Can I take a message?'

'Do you know what time he'll be back?'

'I think he said he'd be home around ten.'

Silence. Awkward silence.

'Do you want to leave a massage for Tony? I'll be happy to pass it on to him as soon as he comes in.'

'Well . . . he said he would be in at this time and asked me to call him.'

'Well, he went out with Karen about an hour ago and said he would be back at ten.'

A shocked voice now: 'Who the fu . . . who is Karen?'

'The girl he went out with.'

'I know that! I mean . . . who the fu . . . who is she?'

'I don't know her last name. Look, do you want to leave a message for Tony?'

'Yes . . . please do. Tell him to call me when he gets in.'

'I sure will. Is this Mary-Kate?'

'Who the f**king hell is Mary-Kate?'

'Well, he's going out with Mary-Kate at ten. I thought you were her. Sorry. It was an honest mistake.'

'Tony's the one that made the mistake! Tell him that Liz called and that's she's very upset and that I would like him to call me as soon as he gets in.'

'Okay, I will . . . but Samantha isn't going to like this.'

The phone was slammed down with venom.

AND AS FOR FORTUNE AND AS FOR FAME

McCarthy believed that tours are rugby's tales of the unexpected. One episode which proves the veracity of that remark came in 1951 when Ireland toured South America. It was a total success off the field and a disaster on it. They were the first international team to be beaten by Argentina. When the Irish team got there, they were told they couldn't play any rugby because Eva Peron had just died. They sent the boys in green down to Santiago, Chile to teach the cadets how to play. After eight days the cadets beat the Irish.

The players didn't take the playing side very seriously. At one stage Paddy Lawler went missing for a few days and nobody had a clue where he was. When he returned a team meeting was hastily called. The team manager solemnly announced that he had been talking to Dublin, which was a big deal in 1952, and then looked around menacingly and said, 'I'm deciding whether or not to send some players home.' Paddy stood up straight away and replied, 'We've been talking among ourselves and we're deciding whether or not we should send you home.'

44

CLAWSOME

Peter Clohessy Makes His Mark

He is one of a kind.

It was Mae West who famously observed, 'A hard man is good to find.' In Irish rugby we found one in Peter Clohessy. He knew how to mix it. He believed that a good prop forward should be so mean that if he owned the Atlantic Ocean he would not give you a wave.

Clohessy earned the nickname 'Judge Dredd' in the dressing room because his word was law. It was evident from an early age that the Claw was going to be the strong, silent type. According to folklore, when he was four he went to the dentist, who then tried to strike up a conversation with the would-be rugby legend.

'How old are you?'

No response.

The dentist then asked, 'Don't you know how old you are?'

Immediately four fingers went up. 'Okay.' The dentist then asked, 'And do you know how old that is?'

Four little fingers went up once again. Continuing the effort to get a response, the dentist asked, 'Can you talk?'

The young Clohessy looked at him menacingly and asked, 'Can you count?'

DOWN TO EARTH

Clohessy is said to be the only man in Limerick who can leave his car unlocked.

As the Claw once told me, though, he could be the focus of strong criticism even in his home city:

'One Tuesday evening after a particularly galling loss to Shannon I was heading on to the field to go training for Young Munster and there was this old lady, I'd say she was eighty-five if she was a day, and she called me over to the wire. I knew I was in for an earful straight away. She shouted at me: "What the hell was wrong with you on Saturday, you were hoisted so high in the scrum, I was going to send you a parachute!"'

The home of Limerick rugby, Thomond Park, is famous for the 20-foot wall which envelops it but which is insufficient to prevent the ball from leaving the ground from time to time. When balls were lost the crowd were wont to shout: 'Never mind the ball, get on with the game.'

Yet Clohessy also had a sophisticated rugby intelligence. There was a lot more to his game than 'hump it, bump it, whack it'. This approach might be, for those of a certain disposition, a recipe for a good sex life but it will not win you 54 caps and a Lions selection.

Clohessy's keen brain was to the fore in one of the bonding exercises before the Lions tour in 1997. As is common practice with rugby teams, they were taken to a military base for exercises. At one point they were given an instruction in unarmed self-defence. After their instructor presented a number of different situations in which they might find themselves, he asked Clohessy, 'What steps would you take if someone were coming at you with a large, sharp knife?'

The Claw replied, 'Big ones.'

FAST EXIT

The Claw has happy memories of an English World Cup hero:

'I always got on well with Justin Leonard. When we played England there was always a bit of banter between us because we'd been playing against each other so long. With about 20 minutes to go of our trouncing in Twickenham in 2002, Justin took me by surprise when he said: "Peter, I believe you're away to a wedding straight after the game?" I am not sure how he knew that but I was indeed off to a friend's wedding in Cork immediately after the match. I replied: "The quicker I get out of this place the f**king better".'

45

TOUCH WOOD

Keith Wood Becomes a Lions Legend

Keith Wood boasts: 'I've a one hundred per cent record in Twickenham. I never won there!'

He is also very honest: 'I hated playing England. I hated the English players and if they took that personally they were meant to!'

Wood was a stickler for preparing properly. This sometimes brought problems in the run-up to his marriage. His wife-to-be was telling him about her dreams for their wedding. Keith, though, had his mind on one of Ireland's upcoming internationals and was not listening properly. His fiancée noticed this and decided to test him on how much he had taken in: 'So, what's my favourite flower?

Woodie thought deeply: 'Self-raising.'

UNCLE FESTER

The bald wonder first made his name with Garryowen but in 1996 he crossed the channel and joined Harlequins. The following year he became the club's captain and he remained with the club until his retirement, except for the 1999–2000 season when he returned to play with Munster, leading them to the narrowest of defeats in the European Cup final. He first captained Ireland against Australia in November 1996 and immediately established himself as an inspirational leader. His motivational qualities were very evident in one of the most tangible legacies of the 1997 Lions Tour when England's John 'Bentos' Bentley made as big a name for himself off the pitch as he did on it with his critically acclaimed video account of the trip *Living with Lions*, which set the bar for all subsequent fly-on-the-wall sporting documentaries.

Woodie's passionate outbursts before games was one of the most striking features of the video. It was as if his tactics were to try and equalise before the other side scored. However, Woodie's one blemish was also to emerge on the trip. Bentley had the misfortune to be rooming with him. As a result of his shoulder problems, Keith could only sleep in one position. He propped two pillows under both shoulders and as soon as he began to sleep he started snoring loudly. After seven sleepless nights Bentley could take no more and sought medical advice. On the eighth night as soon as Woodie started sleeping Bentley kissed him on the cheek. For the next three nights Woodie lay awake in case Bentley would make further advances on him.

SLEEPING WITHOUT BEAUTY

Tom Smith the Scottish prop and star of the 1997 Lions tour was known as 'the silent assassin' because he was so quiet. However, one night on that tour he was sleepwalking and his roommate Mark 'Ronnie' Regan woke up to find Smith coming towards him with his hands out as he was ready to choke him. Henceforth Smith was rechristened as 'the Boston Strangler'.

Jeremy Davidson was dubbed 'Dangerous' on the Lions tour in 1997 because he seemed to injure player after player. Matt Dawson recalls touring with Davidson on that tour. The two of them were joined by Neil Back and went to a bar in a remote part of Pretoria. They stood drinking so long that the barman asked them to lock the door when they left.

HAIR-RAISING

Keith Wood wreaked havoc on that tour – mostly on Matt Dawson's hair. Finding himself rooming with Wood, Dawson decided the baldest man on the tour was the best man to give him a haircut. Woodie though was more interested in recalling a story about a man from Cork with a one-eyed dog who walked into a lamppost that he was not really paying attention and left Dawson with what the scrum-half described as 'a reverse Mohican' – having cut a swathe out of the middle of his hair. Dawson realised something was seriously wrong when the unthinkable happened: Wood went completely quiet. Woodie had shaved off all his hair.

BROTHERS IN ARMS

In 1997 before the Lions went on tour to World Champions South Africa, a Cape Town reporter carried the headline: 'These are not Lions but pussycats.' The Lions had the last laugh as they won the series.

Key to the success of the tour was the unity of purpose shared by all in the party, players and management, a unity that was missing four years later. The players did some unusual things to keep spirits up.

New nicknames were lavishly doled out. Lawrence Dallaglio was nicknamed 'Lawrence Bowleggio', because you could drive a bus through his legs. Jeremy Davidson's nickname was transformed into 'Buzz Lightyear' because of his jaw, especially as it looked like he was always chewing marbles. Will Greenwood was nicknamed 'Shaggy' because he looked like the character in Scooby-Doo. Keith Wood became 'the Irish Sperm Whale' or 'Uncle Fester', because he looks like Fester in *The Addams Family*.

The Lions kept tabs to ensure that miscreants were punished appropriately for their misdemeanours such as poor dress sense. Austin Healey, 'the Gimp' for his transgressions on tour, was stripped to his underpants and an apple was stuck in his mouth and tied to his head with electrical tape, in a re-creation of the scene from *Pulp Fiction*.

When a friend rang from England Will Greenwood took the call and said: 'Austin can't come to the phone. He's a bit tied up at the moment.'

While he was bound Healey asked if he could go to the toilet. 'Only if you recite the alphabet,' replied Lawrence Dallaglio.

'Okay,' said Austin. 'ABCDEFGHIJKLMNOQRSTUVWXYZ.'

'Where's the P?' asked Dallaglio.

'Halfway down my leg,' said Healey.

GREEN FINGERS

English winger Dan Luger tells the story about the man who loved his garden in the days when Keith Wood was an amateur. One day his world almost ended when he woke up to see that his pride and joy was scarred by a proliferation of molehills. He was distraught. He soon wiped his tears, got out the yellow pages and saw an ad which read: 'For the best mole catcher in town, call Keith Wood – simply the best.'

Woodie's days as a rugby pro were still ahead of him and he was on the job instantly. He promised the man he would solve the problem. He stood on watch all night hoping to catch the mole but with no luck. The next night he repeated the vigil but again with no sign of the mole. By now the garden owner was irate and said to Wood, 'When you catch this damned mole, make him die the worst death you can imagine – really nasty.'

The next morning Wood was jubilant. 'I caught him, just as I promised.'

'That's wonderful news. How did you kill him?'

'Horribly,' replied Woodie, 'I buried him alive.'

LUCKY STREAK

Another story in that category told about Woodie goes back to the 2001 Lions tour. Graham Henry was surprised to see Wood hanging up a horseshoe on the wall. Henry said with a nervous laugh, 'Surely you don't believe that a horseshoe will bring you good luck, do you, Keith?'

Wood chuckled. 'I believe no such thing, coach. Not at all. I am scarcely likely to believe in such foolish nonsense. However, I am told that a horseshoe will bring you good luck whether you believe in it or not!'

MURRAY THE MARVELLOUS

New Zealand's Murray Mexted was one of the great number 8s. For nine years he was the All Blacks number 8. However, as a broadcaster he is not quite so peerless. Like George Best he has an interesting personal life. He married Miss Universe. The conventional wisdom is: those who can, do – those who cannot, talk about it. Mexted is the exception to the rule. After his retirement from the game, he became one of the best-known rugby commentators Down Under, though more for his idiosyncratic use of language than for his insights into the game. He described a helicopter drying a ground in New Zealand as: 'It's just like a giant blow job.' His analysis of a ball kicked on a wet ground was: 'My father used to call it a testicles kick because you actually ended with your balls up.' His most famous comment about an Irish player concerned Keith Wood tackling like a man possessed: 'You don't like to see hookers going down on players like that.'

SO LONG

When Brian O'Driscoll was appointed captain of Ireland for the first time he met his predecessor, Keith Wood. The hooker wished Bod the best of luck and ushered him aside: 'Just a little advice, as tradition goes from one outgoing Ireland captain to the next, take these.'

He handed him three envelopes.

'If you fail to lead Ireland to victory,' he said, 'open an envelope, and inside you will find some invaluable advice as to how to proceed.'

Immediately after Drico's first defeat he remembered Wood's envelopes and opened the first one. 'Blame the referee,' it said.

He walked confidently into the press conference and said, 'Well, there wasn't much between the teams really. In a match like that, small mistakes can change the complexion of the game completely and in that respect I felt that the ref made some decisions that went against us, which had a big bearing on the final outcome.'

The journalists nodded wisely. Fester's advice was working well.

Another defeat quickly followed. Bad news, Drico would have to use the second of the three envelopes.

'Blame the place-kicker,' it said. Off the aspiring Captain Fantastic went to face the media.

'Well. I thought it was nip and tuck, we had them under pressure, but unfortunately Rog didn't have the best of days with the old shooting boots and so the chances slipped away.'

Again the journalists seemed satisfied with his response. Thank God for these get-out-of-jail-free envelopes, Drico reflected.

His third defeat. Bod was heartbroken and gutted not to have won. There was only one consolation, help was at hand. He walked into the dressing room, looking forward to some first-class advice from the third and last white envelope. He rummaged in his bag, pulled it out and tore it open. The advice was simple, 'Start writing out three new envelopes.'

46

THE GEORGE BEST OF RUGBY

Geordan Murphy Stars for Leicester

In the build-up to the 2003 World Cup, rugby pundits throughout the world predicted that Geordan Murphy was destined to become one of the stars of the tournament and one of the giants of world rugby. Tragically, injury intervened and Geordan missed out on the world stage his rich talents deserved, having emerged as the star of the previous Six Nations. It was a catastrophic setback to Ireland's chances for glory. With Murphy in the side Brian O'Driscoll would have got extra space because opposition defences would have to work out which one of Ireland's two big threats would make the break. Geordan developed the capacity to cut through to score while playing in the rugby equivalent of a sardine tin.

A FAUX PAS

Geordan cringes at one of his earliest memories from his time in Leicester:

'I had a real Homer Simpson moment standing beside this guy at the club one day and I didn't recognise him from Adam and I asked him if he got a chance to play much rugby at the club. I knew immediately from the way he looked at me that I had said something incredibly stupid. It was the Scottish international Craig Joiner. To complete my shame, when he turned around I saw on the back of his jersey was the word Joiner!

'Mind you, when I started playing for Ireland I found myself regularly the victim of mistaken identity. Even in the Irish squad people mixed up my name with those of Girvan (Dempsey) and Gordon (D'Arcy). So now and again I found the odd member of the Irish squad addressing me as "Girv. . . . Gord . . . Geordan." The best one, though, came after Ireland famously spoilt the World Champions England homecoming party at Twickenham in 2004 after Girvan Dempsey scored that great try. As I was injured, I didn't play in the game, so I was doing some corporate work and after the game I was in my jeans and T-shirt and a man congratulated me on scoring in the corner!

'With Leicester there were also great characters and practical jokers. We had a decent spread of them throughout the squad but it comes as no surprise that Austin Healey is the tops in this respect. He is always willing to get a laugh and that is great to have someone like him in the squad because he keeps morale up. Of course he can rub people up the wrong way and often has done so! He does the craziest things. To give a typical example of an Austin activity, when he was away with the English squad he was bored and decided to liven things up by having a game with the English forward Lewis Moody. They sat about ten feet away from each other with their legs apart and the idea was to throw an orange at each other's groin. The problem for Austin was that he was not very good but Lewis was the world champion!

'When I asked Austin why so many people took an instant dislike to him he just shrugged his shoulders and said: "It just saves time."'

OZ-WORLD

In 'Oz-world', the world according to Healey, pranks sometimes boomerang back against him. After he came into the England side in 1997 he put a pair of tracksuit bottoms down the back of his shorts and walked around calling Clive Woodward 'Rhino Bum' in front of everyone in the English squad. Woodward said nothing. Then Healey scored his first try against Wales in their next game and a few days later the WAGs of all the lads in the squad received a pair of G-string knickers through the post with 'I love Austin' printed on them and a note which read: 'Just wanted to thank you all for your support at the weekend. As you are aware I scored my first try for England. I think you'll admit it was one of the best tries seen at Twickenham. I know how much you girls admire my play, so I thought I'd send you a pair of these knickers each. Lots of love, Austin.' Healey actually knew nothing about it until he was summoned to appear before his furious squad mates. Then he got a phone message from Clive Woodward, who was laughing hysterically, saying: 'Don't ever take the mickey out of me again.'

DANCING KING

Austin Healey is the rugby player who is most proud of his body, which is why he often paraded around his hotel room naked when he was on tour. When he appeared on *Strictly Come Dancing* he named his biceps 'Con' and 'Crete'.

GROIN STRAIN

Geordan has many happy memories from his rugby career:

'One of the funniest came before playing a European Cup final with Leicester. In the warm-up before the game I was throwing the ball around. I tried to do a clever dummy pass and ended up a firing the ball into one of my teammates' groin. It made me laugh. It made him cry!'

DEMPSEY'S DEN

It was supposed to be Mission Impossible but Girvan Dempsey guaranteed himself a place in Irish rugby immortality when he scored the try that beat England 19–13 in 2004. Against all the odds Ireland ended England's twenty-two-match winning streak at 'Fortress Twickenham', stretching back to the 1999 World Cup, when they were beaten by New Zealand. It was England's first championship home defeat under Sir Clive Woodward, whose coaching regime began in November 1997. To add the icing to the cake, the English were parading the Webb Ellis trophy at Twickers for the first time since their World Cup victory in Australia.

The defeat immediately spawned a rash of jokes. One notice appeared:

For Sale:
  One chariot (low-swinging, sweet type), in urgent need of repair (wheels have come off again). One careless owner, details from Clive. Tel: Twickenham 19–13.

Another came in the form of a death notice:

In Memoriam Slam, G: passed away, March 6th, 2004, sorely missed by Clive and the boys.

47

ORGASMIC

Mick Galwey Shows No Fear

In Kerry you are considered to have an inferiority complex if you only consider yourself as good as anybody else, so it comes as little surprise to discover that Kerry men like Mick Doyle who played for Ireland did not lack in confidence.

Doyle was not a man to lavish praise on the Irish team with wanton abandon, so when he described an Irish victory as an 'eighty-minute orgasm' one had to sit up and take notice. The performance which prompted this vintage 'Doylerism' was Ireland's 17–3 victory over England in 1993. In the green jersey it was Mick 'Gaillimh' Galwey's finest hour as he put the result beyond doubt with a try in the corner.

THE LYONS DEN

In a previous life Galwey played senior football for Kerry. The high point of his career with the Kingdom came when he came on as a sub in the All-Ireland semi-final against Kerry in 1986. It was a bruising encounter as he found himself marking one of the hardest men in the history of the game, Meath's Mick Lyons.

One Kerry fan was less than impressed by Galwey's defection to rugby: 'He was a great footballer until rugby destroyed him.'

History casts a long shadow in the area in Kerry where Mick Galwey grew up. Memories of the civil war lasted a very long time. This was most tellingly revealed in a conversation between a de Valera and a Michael Collins fan in the 1960s.

The Dev fan said: 'De Valera was as straight as Christ and as spiritually strong.'

The Collins fan replied: 'Wasn't it a great pity the hoor wasn't crucified as young.'

The encounter with Lyons was the second biggest fright of Galwey's life. According to legend, the biggest came one night in his courting days when he took a shortcut through a grave-yard and he heard a tapping sound. As he walked the tapping got louder and his fright grew into terror. Suddenly, he came across a man crouched down, chiselling at a gravestone.

'Oh thank goodness,' Gaillimh said with great relief. 'You frightened me. I didn't know what that noise was. What are you doing?'

The other man turned his face into the moonlight as he said to the rugby star, 'They spelt my name wrong.'

PUTTING THE BOOT IN

Mick Quinn tells a story about Galwey and Will Carling. The famous English captain was not loved universally by his team-mates. When Ireland played England it was a typically robust match. After a heated ruck, where boots were flying with more frequency than planes at an airport, everyone picked themselves off the muddy pitch to reveal the man at the bottom of the pile of bodies. It was Carling. He had a huge gash under his eye. The referee, slightly shocked that the English captain should be the victim of such thuggery, asked: 'Right, own up, who did this?'

Immediately Galwey piped up, 'Take your pick ref, it could have been any one of twenty-nine of us.'

THE APPRENTICE

Mick is one of rugby's great diplomats. He is loath to criticise anybody. Like many Kerry people you have to read between the lines to figure out what he is saying. When asked his opinion about Brian Ashton's tenure as Irish coach, he kicks for touch. Galwey denies that towards the ignominious end of Ashton's reign, one of the Irish squad said to him: 'Tell me, how long have you been with us, not counting tomorrow?' It was rumoured that a prominent Irish official said to Ashton: 'Today I'm going to mix business and pleasure. You're fired!'

OLD RIVALRIES

In 2004 a new chapter in Gaillimh's life began when he was appointed coach of Shannon, having enjoyed such great success with the club as a player. It was a difficult appointment, particularly given the fierce competition between Shannon and local Limerick rivals Young Munster and Garryowen. In 2003, immediately after England won the World Cup, BBC 5 Live were getting the responses of ecstatic English fans at the match when they stumbled across a sad-looking Shannon supporter. He was asked if he was happy with the result.

Fan: 'Not at all, I'm Irish, I'm from Limerick.'

Reporter: 'But would you not support England when Ireland are no longer in the competition?'

Fan: 'No way.'

Reporter: 'Why not?'

Fan: 'Eight hundred years of oppression.'

Reporter: 'Is there ever any time you would support England?'

Fan: 'If they were playing Young Munster or Garryowen.'

COMPLEX SURGERY

Another favourite Gaillimh story is about the four surgeons who are taking a coffee break. The first one said, 'Accountants are the best to operate on because when you open them up everything inside them is numbered.' The second surgeon said, 'Librarians are the best: everything inside them is in alphabetical order.' The third surgeon said, 'Electricians. Everything inside them is colour-coded.' The fourth one said, 'I prefer English rugby players. They're heartless, spineless, gutless and their heads and arses are interchangeable.'

48

THE WIZARD OF OZ

Rob Henderson Plays for the Lions

My first meeting with Rob Henderson was memorable. On the eve of a Munster–Leinster Celtic League match Rob invited me up to his hotel room. When I knocked at the door he ushered me in. I was more than a little taken aback to discover that all he was 'wearing' was a bath towel! Despite many hours of expensive therapy I have never been able to erase that very disturbing image from the dark corners of my subconscious.

SO THIS IS CHRISTMAS

During his playing days with London-Irish, Henderson came under the stewardship of Clive Woodward. Apart from getting to know him as a coach, they got to know each other socially:

'I've spent some time with him. I've even had Christmas dinner with him. I invited myself! We had a delightful Christmas. He's a lovely fella and he's very smart. He was as good at business as he was at organising the England team. The guy is focused to the nth degree. I expected that he would do a great job coaching the Lions. I told that to everyone I could think of who knew him before the tour in the hope he might pick me! He got the results he did with England because he got the best out of people. He did that by giving everything he had himself to it. He doesn't do anything unless he does it wholeheartedly.

'I played golf with him one day. I'd only started playing two or three months beforehand but I'd got all the gear from a sponsor. We came to the first tee and I hit one down the middle, which was a miracle. I was really keyed up but by the time I got to the eighth hole I had lost all the balls in my bag and about fourteen of Clive's. He loves his golf and when I hit another ball into the woods he just looked at me sadly and said: "I think we better go in now."

'I gave him the green jersey I wore when I won my first cap for Ireland. I presented it in a grand manner as befits Clive – in a Tesco bag! He wasn't there when I dropped it into his home so he wrote to me and said when I eventually grew up he would return it to me!'

THE TOURIST

The late Cliff Morgan described touring with the Lions as 'breaking bread with the rest of the world'. The high point of Henderson's career was the Lions tour of Australia in 2001. To make the trip in the first place was fantastic but to play in all of the three Tests was wonderful. Hendo's awesome power was the perfect foil for Brian O'Driscoll's sublime skills, and they provided the coach, Graham Henry, with the perfect midfield combination of strength and flair. Henderson's teammates were not so appreciative of his off-the-field activities. Rooming with Henderson was the ultimate nightmare according to Austin Healey because he smokes like a chimney and he snores liked a blocked up chimney and because sarcastic is his middle name and he could turn any sentence into a jail term.

RALA

Rob loves the big personalities in Irish rugby:

'A real character is Patrick O'Reilly. He played hooker for Terenure and for years was the kit-man for the Irish team. Everybody knows him as "Rala". He got the nickname because when he was in Irish class at school he was brought up to the blackboard and told to write his name. After he wrote Rala he couldn't remember the Irish version of the rest of his surname so all the kids called him Rala and the name stuck for the rest of his life. If you ever needed advice, shoelaces or you were ever in a scrape or you needed help he was the "go-to man" as they would say in the NFL. If he couldn't do it he would find someone who could. The only problem was that he delegated his work to everybody else. He might have fifteen bags but he'd have sixteen people who wanted to help him carry them! He's a guy who I will never forget.

'He tells a great story of playing against Garryowen when his opposite number was the former Irish hooker, and later manager, Pa Whelan. It was a windy day with a howling gale. A call came in from the second row but Rala couldn't hear it. One of the second rows stepped forward and said to Rala: "Low and hard at number 2." Rala shrugged his shoulders and stepped back. He then threw the ball very hard at Pa Whelan! Rala spent the next forty-five minutes both apologising and running away from Whelan.'

ANGIE

Rob's most loyal fan was his wife, Angie, who offers a revealing insight into the legendary status of one player in the Irish set-up:

'Peter Clohessy left more than just a hole in Irish rugby when he retired in 2002 – he left his seat at the back of the bus vacant too! I was amused to find, like a school bus, the team coach had the naughty, big boys who always sat on the back seat. The "usual suspects" included Claw, Woodie, Axel Foley and Rob. In 2003 after joining the team on their coach to travel the short journey across town for a celebratory dinner, I found a spare seat, that just happened to be next to the man I married. The conversation unfolded as follows:

'Me: "Oh that's nice, darling, you saved me a seat . . ."

'Rob: "That's Claw's seat . . ."

'"But Rob, Claw's not here, he didn't play, he's retired."

'"Yeah . . . but it's still his seat."'

49

DONAL'S GEMS

Donal Lenihan Calls It As It Is

Donal Lenihan was a big admirer of Moss Keane: 'My first full cap against Australia in 1981 was really a natural progression from all that went before. Trevor Ringland also made his debut that day. There's always a special friendship between players who won their first caps on the same day. I usually roomed with Moss Keane. He was coming to the end of his career at that stage. Our room was like an alternative medical centre with pollen, garlic tablets and a half-dozen eggs. The mornings of internationals I woke up to see Moss eating three raw eggs. It's not the sort of sight that you want to wake up to!'

BIG QUESTIONS

Put-downs were a particular speciality of Donal Lenihan. During the 1989 Lions tour of Australia, Lenihan's ready wit was to the fore on a number of occasions. At one stage Bridgend's Mike Griffiths asked, 'Can I ask a stupid question?'

'Better than anyone I know,' answered Lenihan.

Another time the touring party were driving through Sydney when they passed a couple coming out of a church after being married. Then in all earnestness Jeremy Guscott asked: 'Why do people throw rice at weddings?' Lenihan replied immediately: 'Because rocks hurt.'

He then turned defence into attack, 'Why do you think they are getting married, Jeremy?'

'I suppose, Donal, it's because they love each other.'

'I wanted a reason, and you gave me an excuse.'

Jeremy replied, 'Don't be so cynical. Marriage is a great institution.'

Donal nodded his head in agreement, 'Marriage is a great institution all right. It's holy deadlock.'

Scott Hastings grew impatient when his brother Gavin seemed to prefer playing tennis or going windsurfing with Ieuan Evans rather than with him. Lenihan commented: 'Ieuan's like the brother Gavin never had.'

'What about me?' asked Scott.

'You're the brother he did have,' responded Lenihan.

PHANTOM OF THE OPERA

Rob Andrew was the only one to put one over on Lenihan on the tour. On a night off he invited Donal to *La Traviata*. Thinking they were going to a nice Italian restaurant Lenihan agreed. What he failed to realise was that they'd been given complimentary tickets to the opera!

FATHER AND SON

After defeating Australian Capital Territories on the 1989 Lions tour, Donal Lenihan brought the touring party to the Friends of Ireland bar where they were greeted by a priest. Following much liquid refreshment, it was time for the team to return to their hotel. The priest bade them farewell. Slightly under the influence, Andy Robinson told the cleric he was wearing his collar back to front.

'I'm a father, Andrew,' said the priest.

'I've got kids myself,' replied Robinson.

'No, I'm the father to hundreds of people in this area,' explained the priest.

'Really. In that case, it's not your collar you should be wearing back to front, it's your bloody trousers!'

UNFAIR

Lenihan was left musing on the historical unfairness of Ireland's relationship with Australia. We gave them thousands of our emigrants which helped to make their county great. What did they give us in return? *Neighbours* and *Home and Away*.

SAILING INTO THE SUNSET

Injuries forced Lenihan to depart from the international stage slightly ahead of schedule, having captained Ireland seventeen times: 'I knew it was time to retire when the bits and pieces started falling off my body.'

He cut his teeth as Ireland team manager but resigned to concentrate on his job the Lions. The former England rugby coach Jack Rowell was once asked what it was like to be a top rugby coach. He replied, 'You have fifteen players in a team. Seven hate your guts and the other eight are making up their minds.' Lenihan was to find out what he meant. His stewardship of the Lions in 2001 was made more difficult by damning claims made about the preparation and training methods of the squad in articles during the tour by two Lions players, Matt Dawson and Austin Healey. That controversy and the fact that the Lions lost the series did take away some of the shine of what should have been the crowning glory of Lenihan's career. It was a case of what might have been. A friend of Donal's put the scale of the disappointment well: 'It was like thinking you have gone to bed with Liz Hurley only to wake up to the terrible realisation that you slept with Red Hurley.'

50

THE FLYING FINN

Moss Finn Wins the Triple Crown

In 1982 after Ireland won the Triple Crown, the Ireland team travelled to France hoping to win the Grand Slam. The team bus entered the stadium and was surrounded by French supporters who were going crazy, thumping the side of the bus and shouting abuse at the team. The Irish team was very tense and everyone was silent. Donal Lenihan was sitting beside Moss Finn. The French fans were screaming: *'L'Irelande est fini. L'Irelande est fini.'*

Moss Finn stood up and said, 'Christ, lads. Isn't it great to be recognised.'

PARK LIFE

Finn was a great character. The morning of his international debut the Irish team were staying in the Shelbourne Hotel and Moss was telling the players how good he was feeling. It was his first trip to Dublin and he went on to say that he had been out for a lovely walk in front of the hotel to see the ducks in the Phoenix Park. He had really been to St Stephen's Green but he genuinely thought that was the Phoenix Park.

WORDSMITH

Finn's teammate Michael Kiernan is a master of the put-down. Witness the following: 'Fergus Slattery was superb on the pitch during matches; he led every training session: sprints, push-ups, you name it – and he was a great man to party. He was last out of every reception but first to training next morning.

'Donal Lenihan was much the same as Slatts, bar the matches and the training.'

THE NUMBERS GAME

One of Finn's favourite stories goes back to Munster's All Blacks win. Tom Kiernan was an accountant by profession and had a great head for figures – most of the time at least! After the All Blacks were beaten by Munster in 1978 Tom, as their coach, was asked by a local journalist if it was a one-off. In all earnestness Kiernan is reputed to have replied: 'You could play the All Blacks seven times and they would beat you nine times out of ten.'

51

LABOUR OF LOVE

Dick Spring's Successes and Failures

The lush tapestry of the GAA has been greatly enhanced by its cross-fertilisation with Irish rugby. One of Kerry's most famous sons, Dick Spring, was a noted Gaelic footballer. In fact, before he played rugby for Ireland, he played football for Kerry.

As a boy his hero was Mick O'Connell, probably the greatest Gaelic footballer of them all. Spring claims that in Kerry they have taken and applied the words of the Olympic motto 'higher, faster, stronger' for their sporting heroes. As has been said of the Jesuits, 'They are tops in everything, including modesty.' But modesty is not something Kerry people have had much opportunity to experience.

Spring still follows even club football in Kerry, like the progress of Laune Rangers. Someone said in the 1990s that they are the best side in Kerry since Tonto was their manager. This reminds Spring of the Galway wit who described an old Corinthians team as being the best since St Paul wrote to them!

In 1979 Spring was capped three times for Ireland at rugby. He is probably best remembered, though unfairly, as he was a much better player than he was given credit for, for an incident in the Wales match, when Ireland gifted the home side with 15 points to lose on a scoreline of 24–21. After twenty-two minutes Ireland led 6–0 courtesy of two lengthy penalties from Tony Ward. In the twenty-fifth minute the picture changed dramatically. The Welsh fly-half lofted the kick towards the Irish posts but Spring was under it and there seemed to be no danger. Somehow the ball slipped through his hands and bounced over the Irish line for Allan Martin to rush on and score a try which Steve Fenwick converted.

While his political career flourished in the 1980s and 1990s, Spring has never been allowed to forget that incident and has been the butt of jokes about 'a safe pair of hands'. Throughout the enormously popular series on RTÉ Radio One *Scrap Saturday*, Spring was consistently referred to by Dermot Morgan, who went on to find fame as Father Ted, as 'Butterfingers'. As a result Spring always claims that the highlight of his career was his first cap against France. That's the game he shows to his kids. He claims he cannot remember what happened in the Wales game!

MAJOR CREDIT

John Major was quite impressed when he heard Spring played for Ireland. Major played rugby himself when he was very young but did not prosper at the game because at that time he was too small, even though he is a tall man now. Major's great passion is cricket and his moods fluctuated a lot depending on the fate of the English team. Spring was always wary about having sensitive negotiations about the peace process in Northern Ireland with Major when England were playing. He found the best time to negotiate with Major was when England were doing very well at cricket. The only problem was that did not happen very often!

THEATRICAL PAUSE

One trick Spring used when he gave a speech to a rugby audience in Wales to get their attention was to start by speaking for the first three minutes in Irish. By the time he started speaking in English they were ready to hang on to his every word!

SPRINGTIDE

Dick Spring was invited to be the guest speaker in Llanelli by Ray Gravell. In order to impress the then Tánaiste, Ray pulled out all the stops. He flew Spring over on a private jet and collected him in Cardiff in a friend's posh Jaguar. The problem was that Ray forgot to ask his friend what all the switches were for. The rain was sheeting down and Ray thought he was switching on the wipers but in fact he opened the roof and could not get it back down; as a result Spring was soaked in his elegant dress suit as he arrived to the prestigious event.

52

McGANN THE MAN

Barry McGann's Weighty Matters

Barry McGann was one of the great Irish rugby fly-halves and a great soccer player. He was also a little 'calorifically challenged'. Around the time he was first capped for Ireland he moved from Cork to Dublin and was persuaded to play for Shelbourne. They had some tremendous players at the time like Ben Hannigan and Eric Barber. Barry always got a great slagging whenever he went back to play in Cork. One time they were playing Cork Celtic. As he ran onto the pitch he heard a voice saying on the terraces: 'Who's that fella?'

'That's McGann the rugby player.'

'Oh, wouldn't you know it by his stomach!'

An even more damning indictment of McGann's bulk was subsequently provided by Tony O'Reilly's quip: 'Twice around Barry McGann and you qualify as a bona fide traveller!'

WEIGHTY MATTERS
Barry always had a bit of a problem with the battle of the bulge. Ray Gravell recalled his experiences of Barry for me: 'With Ollie

Campbell, another superb kicking out-half I came across for Ireland was Barry McGann. Barry was the fastest out-half I've ever seen over five yards. The problem is that he was completely f**ked after five yards!'

TWINKLE TOES

However, the classic comment about Barry was: 'Given his waistline, the only thing that Barry McGann could ever dodge was a salad!'

SLOW SPEED

Jack Kyle had three speeds: fast, very fast and very, very fast. One of Barry's great expressions was: 'He had two speeds – slow and very slow.'

WARM-UP

Asked about his outstanding memory from his Irish days Barry McGann pauses only briefly:

'It was towards the final days of my international career. I was a sub for Mick Quinn at the time. Syd Millar was the coach then. I had the reputation of being a very laid-back player but I was serious when I needed to be. Because of work I was late for a training session, although genuinely I got there as quickly as I could. The training session at Anglesea Road was in full swing when I arrived. I went over and apologised to Syd for being late and asked him what he wanted me to do. I had a strong feeling he didn't believe I had made much of an effort to be there but he told me to warm up. Instinctively I rubbed my hands together and blew on them and said: "Okay coach I'm ready." Moss Keane was in stitches but I'll never forget the bemused look on Syd's face. I think that incident probably cost me 10 caps!'

FLY-ING LOW

McGann is a very genial man and because of that features in a number of stories. He is known for his speed of thought. At the Lansdowne club dinner, the president droned on with his long-winded speech. The players were saying to each other, 'I wish there was a way to shut him up.'

'Leave it to me,' said McGann, who scribbled a note on a paper napkin and passed it up to the president, who read it, quickly finished his speech, and sat down.

'Brilliant!' said his teammates. 'What did you put in that note?'

Barry replied: 'Your fly is undone.'

MR PRESIDENT

The president of the club was retiring after many years of loyal service. At the dinner given in his honour by the club, McGann rose to make his speech.

'It is said,' he began, 'that when a child is born, its guardian angel gives it a kiss. If the kiss is on the hands, the child will become a musician or an artist. If the kiss is on the head, it will become a great thinker or scientist. If on the lips, it will grow up to be a singer or an actor. Now I don't know where our Bob here was kissed, but he's certainly been a damn good president.'

53

A PASSAGE TO ROMANIA

Leinster Tour Romania

Rugby tours can be a good test of the player-coach relationship. When a rift emerges because they are eating, sleeping (in a sense) and drinking together it can be like a volcano waiting to explode. When the Australian team were on tour, their coach, Rod Macqueen, couldn't believe how popular he was with the players when they got to the golf course. Everyone wanted to play a round with him. The players never carried much spending money and knew that when they played with Rod he would feel obliged to pay the green fees. Hence his nickname: the ATM machine – Automatic Teller Macqueen.

IT'S NOT THE WINNING THAT COUNTS
On the 1989 Lions tour to Australia, the players were invited on a rare day off to the Royal Perth Yacht Club. It was just after Australia had lost in the final to the US in the America's Cup yacht races. Not all the tour party were present but among the group were three Welsh backs. The president of the yacht club was showing them around the club and took them onto the

Kookaburra 2 – the boat that the hopes of the nation had rested on in the race – only to be thwarted when the American boat *Stars and Stripes* had won the head-to-head race. The captain of *Kookaburra 2* was then introduced to the players. One of the Welsh threesome innocently asked: 'Do a bit of racing then, do you?'

'Yeh, mate. In fact we've just been in the America's Cup where we sailed against the Americans.'

The second Welsh back: 'How did you get on, then?'

'We came second.'

The third Welshman interjected: 'Second. That's bloody good, isn't it!'

That same year the Lions toured to Australia. After a night on the town David Sole was at the bar when he spotted someone he recognised from back home in Scotland. He rushed up and greeted his 'friend' effusively: 'What brings you over to Oz?'

'I live here,' was the reply in a tone that, had David been less inebriated, would have told him that the man had absolutely no idea who the rugby player was and in accent that would have told him he had not an ounce of Scottish blood in him.

'Didn't you used to have a beard at one time?' asked Sole.

'No.'

'You used to be taller. You must have shrunk but it's great to see you all the same, Sam.'

'My name isn't Sam, it's Cliff.'

'Good God. You've changed your name as well.'

WHATEVER THE WEATHER

Gavin Hastings recalls watching the news on the television during the 1987 World Cup in New Zealand and the newscaster was reading out the weather temperatures for towns throughout New Zealand:

Auckland 20 Wellington 18

Christchurch 14 Invercargill 10

Palmerstown North 16 Wangaum 12

One of the Scottish props walked by, saw the TV and said: 'Crikey, these scores are pretty close!'

MUNSTER MOVE

Tony Ward retains vivid memories of touring Romania in 1982 with Munster:

'You hear about how in communist regimes you're all equal? Well these people were all equally poor. There were queues of people literally starving, queueing for food and handouts. After the Lions tour to South Africa in 1980, I didn't go back with Ireland in '81 because my social conscience had been really pricked.

'You always came back from tours with your bags bulging with souvenirs and different things, but I hardly came back with anything in my bag from Romania. I gave away all my gear and that to the players we were playing against because they just didn't have it over there, it was just so tough on them at the time.

'That was the height of Romanian rugby, and because Romanian rugby was very much based on the French model, they were very talented players too. They used the ball well, it wasn't just power and fitness by any means. Mircea Paraschiv, the scrum-half and captain, I got to know him quite well. And one of the second rows, Gheorghe Dumitru, and Enciu Stroika (flanker), there were a few of them who were big names at the time.

'I do remember, everywhere you went there were people around in the background, and we were warned about that beforehand. We didn't really go out and about. We were definitely very aware that there were people in the background and that they were government agents or whatever. We were all complaining because the only thing you could get to eat was a bit of pork on a plate, nothing with it, and an apple. That was your dinner,' Ward says.

Posters in Iasi advertised the visit of *'The only team to beat the All Blacks'*, but Munster struggled to an 18–12 win on a scorching hot day. As only he could, Moss Keane told reporters he had not experienced such heat since the last time he was in Kerry!

Tony Ward retains one keepsake from that tour:

'I'm not great for keeping my souvenirs. I don't believe in having jerseys in your drawers and I've given almost everything away over the years. But one thing I have kept, I have it in my hand here at the moment . . . I have this wooden spoon, which is appropriate in one way, that an ordinary guy had made out there. It has these markings on it, little designs, *"Romania v Munster, 19 September"*, then he has myself, Mossie and Colm Tucker highlighted on the spoon part. On the back here is the 1982 tour, all the Bucharest team, Constanta team, then down the bottom, *"Rugby world – Parc des Princes, Ravenhill, Murray-field, Lansdowne Road"* . . . It's just beautiful. I've kept it to this day, and it's probably worthless, but it means an awful lot to me because of the person who gave it to me, the fanaticism of those Romanian people about rugby. It typified the game out there at the time.'

TUCKING HELL

Colm Tucker was one of the stars of Munster's win over the All Blacks. Colm caused some amusement for his teammates, notably when Ireland played France at the Parc des Princes in 1980. In the match programme his surname was spelt with an 'F' instead of a 'T'.

Munster toured Romania in 1982. The food was absolutely dire throughout the tour. The Munster players had been warned in advance that it would be like that and were told to bring a few bars of chocolate. Noel McGlynn was a butcher and he had the wherewithal then to bring plenty of fantastic meat, vacuum-packed, to sustain him throughout the tour and to store it and keep it fresh. He only shared his 'treasure chest' with Colm Tucker and Ginger McLoughlin! The three wise men dined royally on the tour while the rest of the squad watched enviously on their paltry rations.

LEINSTER TOUR

Despite all the poverty in the country Leinster's tour to Romania had generated some comic moments. In 1980, the year Jimmy Carter had arranged a boycott of the Moscow Olympics because of Russia's invasion of Afghanistan, Leinster, under Mick Doyle and Mick 'the Cud' Cuddy, toured Romania. The Cud was a master of the art of the misnomer. One of his many classic comments was: 'There were so many people they were coming out of the woodworm!'

JIM'S HIGH JINX

One of the players on the tour was Jim Glennon. As a player Jim always gave 150 per cent. Although he is not an arrogant person he does make one proud boast: 'Nobody used his arse better in the line-out than Jim Glennon did!' Glennon was never a great line-out winner but was very hard to get a line-out ball from. He formed a very effective second-row partnership with George Wallace for Leinster. They were christened *'Urbi et Orbi'* by Mick Doyle.

LATE NIGHTS

A vivid memory for Glennon is of going to see Romania play Russia with Phil Orr and George Wallace. The Russians were staying in the same hotel as Leinster but on a different floor. That night the three amigos met up with the Russian captain and invited him and his colleagues up to their room for a jar. They had stared disaster in the face earlier when they discovered that there was only one bottle of whiskey in the hotel. Worse still, that bottle was in the Cud's room and not intended for public consumption. The Cud was annoyed (to put it mildly) when he discovered it 'missing'.

The next morning the manager of the Russian team came into the lobby and asked to speak to 'the leader of the Irish delegation' and invited Leinster to tour in Russia. It was a pretty strange spectacle because the Russians had KGB types following them everywhere watching their every move. Glennon thought this invitation might provide the key to a rapprochement with the Cud, so he headed in before the Russian delegation to explain the situation. The Cud was not impressed. He said, 'Look Glennon, would you ever bleep off and tell them Russians to bleep off and while you're at tell them to bleep off out of Afghanistan as well!'

HERE ORR THERE

The tour provided Phil Orr with one of his happiest rugby memories:

'We were soon fed up with the food on offer. On a bus journey the two big jokers in the side, Paul McNaughton and Freddie McLennan, walked up the bus with a list taking the lunch orders. We were told they could choose between T-bone steak or grilled chicken, and we had to indicate whether we wanted chips, baked or sautéed potatoes, and select from a choice of vegetables as it all had to be ordered in advance. All the players got very excited, and great care was taken over the menu. We arrived at an impressive looking restaurant for a big meal. There was a buzz of expectancy – which turned into a stunned silence when the food arrived. Each dish was the same: a big bowl of clear, greasy soup and in it was a huge fish head complete with eyes. Nothing was eaten. McNaughton and McLennan had to be led out – they were laughing so much they couldn't walk.'

THE MAYOR OF VENICE

Leinster were confident of better treatment when they made a tour to Venice. It was a pretty bizarre event. They travelled to the match by boat. They were on one side and their opponents were on the other. The boat brought both teams back together and the meal did not start until a quarter past midnight. The mayor of Venice invited the officials and a few of the players for a reception in Venice's most prestigious building. The Leinster delegation were all dressed up in their official blazers. As they went into this very impressive building they noticed there was a sheet covering a table. They were all a bit taken aback when the Mayor, who was a communist, strolled out in the most casual of clothes, a grandad shirt and jeans. Then the sheet was taken off the table and they saw that their reception was in fact a few bottles of minerals. The officials were less than impressed but the players thought it was absolutely hilarious.

SOCIABLE

Jim Glennon was involved in Mick Doyle's first and last representative games as coach: in 1979 when Leinster played Cheshire and in 1987 when Ireland played Australia respectively. He lays claim to an unusual distinction – he once saw Doyle speechless. Having suffered a heart attack during the '87 World Cup, Doyler rejoined the Irish team after a ten-day stay in hospital. They were staying in a motel type place. A few of the lads, known on the tour as the 'amigos', were out late one night and sneaking furtively in. There were uncarpeted stairs outside Doyler's room and he was woken up by the activity. He recognised one of the voices. The next day the culprit was given a right ticking off in front of the whole squad. As Doyler delivered his attack, the player in question stood and listened but when the coach had finished the bad boy said: 'Jaysus, Doyler, there's none so pure as a converted hoor.' Doyler was left too stunned to speak.

54

ALARM-ING

Tom Clifford Lays Down the Law

No one had a greater passion for rugby in Limerick than Tom Clifford. He was first capped for Ireland against France in 1949. His name lives on through 'Tom Clifford Park', a ground which had been variously described as 'The Killing Fields', 'The Garden of Get Somebody' and 'Jurassic Park'.

BIG TOM

Tom was first capped for Ireland against France in 1949 and won the last of his 14 caps against France in 1952, a match that also saw the end of the international careers of Karl Mullen, Des O'Brien and Bill McKay. Clifford was a key part of the '49 Triple Crown victory and toured with the Lions to New Zealand in 1950. He was one of nine Irish players to make the tour with Karl Mullen, George Norton, Michael Lane, Noel Henderson, Jack Kyle, Jimmy Nelson, Billy McKay and Jim McCarthy.

According to legend Tom's rugby affiliation was evident at an early age. When he was in primary school he got a new teacher who came from a different part of Limerick and as a result she was a fanatical Shannon fan. On her first day she asked Tom what team he supported. Tom replied, 'Young Munster.'

'And why do you support Young Munster?'

'Because my mum and dad support them.'

'And I suppose if your parents were Shannon fans you would be a Shannon supporter.'

'No, Miss If my parents were Shannon fans I would be an idiot.'

A WEE DROP

Tom Clifford was famous for his singing. One of his favourites was, 'When I was a wee tot, they put me on a wee pot, to see if I could wee or not.'

A GOOD PROP-OSITION

For Jim McCarthy Clifford was not only one of the great props but perhaps the greatest character in Irish rugby:

'When I look back it's the matches with Munster that stand out for me. Bill Shankly's famous saying that "football is not a matter of life or death but more important" applies to rugby in Munster, especially in Limerick. For me the person that encapsulated that feeling was the late, great Tom Clifford. He was the character among characters. I'll never forget his funeral. The church was teeming with rugby folk. The priest giving the homily had been a lifelong friend of Tom's and told us how he had invited the legend of Irish rugby to his ordination Mass. After the ceremony he asked Tom what he thought of it. Tom replied: "You spoke too long. The next time if you go on for longer than ten minutes I'll set off an alarm clock in the church." The next Sunday the priest saw Tom arriving in at the church and noticed he had a bulge in his overcoat. When Tom caught out his eye, he pulled out an alarm clock!

'I was on the Lions' tour with Tom in 1950. Tom was a larger-than-life figure, especially when he sang his party piece, "O'Reilly's Daughter". His only rival in the character stakes was probably Cliff Davies, a Welsh coalminer. Cliff was greeted by the New Zealand Prime Minister, S.G. Holland, who said: "Glad to meet you, Cliff." Cliff retorted: "Glad to meet you, Sid."'

A NEW JOB

Having successfully negotiated the Lions tour, Clifford was immediately involved in an accident when he returned to Ireland. He took a taxi in Dublin and, anxious to ask the taxi driver if he knew what time the next train was to Limerick, he leaned forward and tapped the driver on the shoulder. The driver screamed, lost control of the cab, nearly hit a bus, drove up over a footpath and stopped just inches from a large plate-glass window. For a few moments everything was silent in the taxi. The startled Clifford apologised to the driver, saying he didn't realise a mere tap on the shoulder would frighten him so much.

'No, no,' the driver replied. 'It's all my fault. Today is my first day driving a taxi. For the last twenty-five years I've been driving a hearse.'

THE KILLING FIELDS

Clifford's motto was: 'Kick anything that moves above the grass and if doesn't move kick it anyway.'

Hence the joke told by visiting teams from Dublin:
Why does the Shannon run through Limerick?
Would you walk through Limerick?

55

LITTLE AND LARGE

Ciaran Fitzgerald Plays in an All-Ireland Final

Ciaran Fitzgerald, who captained Ireland to the Triple Crown in both 1982 and 1985, played for Galway in the All-Ireland minor hurling final against Cork in 1970. His problem was that when he played in that All-Ireland he was marked by Martin Doherty, who subsequently made it big with the Cork senior team. Big was the word for Martin. Fitzgerald would have needed a stepladder to have competed with him in the air.

At times, though, claims about the GAA's connection with rugby have been exaggerated. Former Irish out-half Mick Quinn's father was not a sporting man but he was very proud that his son played for Ireland. He seldom drank but when he did he really knew how to enjoy himself. Once he was having a few drinks with John Joe Whyte of *The Irish Times*. He told John Joe that Mick had acquired his ability from him and that he himself played for Monaghan in the 1928 All-Ireland Gaelic football final – not even knowing at that stage if Monaghan had played in the final that year. The next day this story appeared verbatim in *The Times*. John Joe had not realised he was being wound up and did not bother to check out the facts.

WORDY

The young players on Fitzgerald's Ireland team looked up to Moss Keane as if he was God. New players from the north found his thick Kerry accent particularly difficult to decipher. The senior players devised a little ritual for those new players. When Trevor Ringland was brought onto the team for the first time, Fitzgerald put him beside Moss for dinner and Trevor was in awe of him. They primed Moss to speak for two minutes in fast-forward mode. He was talking pure gibberish. Then he turned to Trevor and asked him what he thought of that. Trevor answered lamely, 'I think you're right,' not having a clue what Moss had said. Then Moss launched off again, only faster. The panic on Trevor's face was a sight to behold. He was going green. All the senior players were killing themselves trying to keep a straight face until Trevor found out he was being wound up.

THE TOWER OF BABEL

Language problems can be a serious problem in exhibition games. In the 1970s an all-star cast was assembled to play a club team. The celebrity team included Gareth Edwards, Gerald Davies and the Scot Ian Barnes. Barnes was a second-row forward from the Borders who spoke with a thick Scottish accent. His scrummaging partner was Moss Keane, who spoke with a thick Irish accent. Both were sorting out tactics before the match but were incapable of communicating through words. By using gestures and amid vigorous nodding of the head they seemed to have worked something out. The scrum was a total disaster. The touring side were losing by 20 points at half-time.

Barnes went to Edwards and said, 'Hey Gareth, I cannae understand what he's saying. I'm pushing on the wrong side of the scrum. Would you think you could get him to swap sides with me?' A minute later Keane went up to Edwards and said, 'That bloody Scot can't speak fu**ing English. I'm pushing on the wrong side.' Edwards brokered a compromise and the tourists were a transformed side in the second half and won the match.

CROWNING GLORY

In 1982 before the Triple Crown decider against Scotland, Bill Beaumont rang Keane to wish him well. "Moss. If you win they will build a statue of you in Cork."

"Billy, you bolli*. I'm a Kerryman."

Moss himself was confused. After the game was over, he approached Ciaran Fitzgerald and said, 'I'm taking the Cup to Currow next weekend. No more about it – my mind is made up.'

'But Moss, there is no trophy. The Triple Crown is a mythical trophy.'

'Is there a medal?' Moss asked.

'No, Moss.'

'You mean to say we went to all that f**king trouble and they won't even give us a f**king medal.'

BESTSELLER

Moss had his autobiography ghostwritten by Billy Keane. Shortly after he ran into Peter Clohessy. The Claw politely remarked: 'I see you got Billy Keane to write a book for you, Moss.'

Moss replied: 'Really? Who read it to you?'

56

POPPY-COCK

Nick Popplewell's Lions Tour

Nick Popplewell's status was reflected in the fact that he was an automatic Irish selection for the Lions tour in 1993. Mick Galwey was the only other Irish player to be selected on the original squad so to keep up the Irish spirit he brought out twelve bottles of poteen on the Lions tour.

At one point Nick was rucking beside Brian Moore. Poppy got a blow to the head and said to Moore, 'I can see two balls and cannot continue.'

Moore replied, 'Get back on the pitch and kick both.'

It would not be Popplewell's last encounter with Moore, who was notorious for trying to out-psyche opponents before key internationals. Indeed some of his colleagues on the English team remarked that when he played against France in Paris he was more focused on putting his opponent off than playing his own game. There was one famous occasion when he was hoisted with his own petard in Ireland's 13–12 win over England in Twickenham in 1994. The Irish players decided to start a fight with the English team early in the match to throw the English guys off their stride. In the dressing room beforehand the question arose as to who should start the fight. Poppy's eyes turned to Peter Clohessy. When the match started the Claw was looking around for a suitable person to fight with. He first considered Jason Leonard but he thought Leonard might be a bit of a handful to deal with so his eyes fell on Brian Moore when there was scrum in front of the English posts. Moore is perhaps not the most handsome man in the world. One of his teammates said of him, in an alcohol-induced moment, that his front teeth are in the back of his mouth and the back teeth are in the front and that he was born so ugly that his mother thought his face was on fire and she decided to put it out – with a shovel!

The Claw said to him, 'Listen pal, what are you doing to do for a face when Sadam wants his ars*hole back?' Moore immediately started a bust-up and because he struck the first blow Ireland got a penalty and three easy points.

LEGAL EAGLE

The 1993 Lions tour left Popplewell with many happy moments. It is important to have light moments on a tour whether it is with club, country or the Lions. Nicknames are one way of keeping up the levity. Another effort to break the monotony in a rugby tour is 'a court session' where players are judged by their peers and given an appropriate punishment for their transgressions. They generally involve taking in more than a modicum of alcohol.

People are fined for different reasons and the more fines they get, the more alcohol they enjoy. Players are charged for incidents in training or in matches, like somebody who dropped the ball a few times in training might be charged with being a 'butterfingers'. The fine might be to drink a bottle of beer without using their hands.

On the 1993 tour Former English prop Paul Rendall was known as Judge from his days dispensing justice in a players' court on a tour of Australia when he famously sentenced the team manager Geoff Cooke to eat a daffodil sandwich. Jason Leonard once asked: 'Judge, why don't you have a nickname?' Rendall took him aside and said: 'No one minds you making a complete tool of yourself every now and again, but for God's sake don't let the backs hear you say things like that. You're a forward and stupid comments are for backs only.'

Rendall sentenced Scott Hastings to listen to two hours of Richard Clayderman tapes on his personal stereo after being found guilty of having his hair cut in a style that was 'an affront to what little hair Graham Dawe had left'.

At one stage on that tour Nick Popplewell was the judge, Stuart Barnes was the defending barrister and Brian Moore was the prosecutor. Things got unexpectedly serious one night before the first test when Moore suddenly started talking about tactics. He said, 'I've got an idea to improve our chances on this tour.'

Barnes immediately said, 'Great. When are you leaving?'

On that tour Popplewell got to experience Barnes's unique sense of humour. In 1990 Bath beat old rivals Gloucester 6–3 in a closely fought match to reach the Pilkington Cup final. After the game the Bath players and their significant others retreated to the Rec for a celebration. Barnes was chatting with one of the supporters and offered to buy him a drink. 'What would you like?'

The fan thought he was in heaven to have a drink bought by the Bath captain. When the fan asked the rugby star what he was drinking Barnes said, 'I'd like something tall, cold and full of gin.'

'Then come and meet my wife,' answered the fan.

57

NEIL DOWN

Simon Geoghegan Lights up the Irish Attack

Simon Geoghegan did not have the good fortune to play with a good Irish team. However, in full flight he lit up the stage like a flash of forked lightning, flashing brilliantly, thrilling and, from the opposition's point of view, frightening. He scored 11 tries in his 37 caps for Ireland.

David Campese once remarked: 'The only thing you're ever likely to get at the end of an English backline is chilblains.' Geoghegan would have empathised with this scenario.

It was no coincidence that Ireland's best performances in the early nineties coincided with the best of the flying winger, notably Ireland's 17–3 victory over England in 1993. The tragedy was that it was too late for him to claim a place on the Lions' tour. When injury struck it was his partner on the wing, Richard Wallace, and not the golden boy of Irish rugby that got the call to go south as a replacement on the Lions.

Still basking in the glory of their win over the All Blacks, the English expected to extract retribution in 1994 in Twickenham but a splendid try from Geoghegan helped Ireland to secure another shock win – this time on a score of 13–12.

Eric Elwood's boot contributed the rest of the points in Ireland's win but the game is best remembered for Simon Geoghegan, following a good move featuring Richard Wallace and Philip Danaher, blazing past Tony Underwood and Jon Callard to score a wonderful try. It was England's first defeat in their own backyard in six years of championship rugby and Will Carling's first defeat as captain in a home Five Nations game.

During these years the Underwood brothers played on the wings for England. Whenever either scored a try, the Director of the BBC coverage of the English game always cut to the stands, where invariably their mother was dancing a jig with elation. After scything past Jon Callard and Tony Underwood to score that try, Simon is said to have turned to Underwood and remarked: 'I hope your mother saw that!'

EARLY BATH

Geoghegan's club side Bath at the time were the team of all the talents. At the time they even tried to sign David Campese but even their resources could not stretch to Campo's salary demands. The joke was that Campese was either going to play in France for the Cannes Openers or in China for the Peking Toms.

Geoghegan enjoyed the folklore about the giants of Bath rugby at the time. After their summer break Simon was talking to the English fly-half Stuart Barnes about his trip to Switzerland. In particular he asked Barnes if he had enjoyed the beautiful scenery.

'Not really,' Barnes replied, 'I couldn't see much because of all the mountains in the way.'

Another concerned Jeremy Guscott. The centre was walking in Bath one day when an old man stopped him and held out a paper and pen. Jeremy gave him his best smile and assumed it was an autograph seeker. His ego took a bit of a blow when the old man said, 'Can you address this postcard for me? My arthritis is acting up and I can't even hold a pen.'

'Certainly, sir,' said Guscott. He wrote out the address and also agreed to write a short message and sign the card for the man. Finally he asked, 'Now, is there anything else I can do for you?'

The old man said, 'Yes, at the end could you just add, "PS: Please excuse the sloppy hand-writing?"'

FACE-OFF

The most distinctive face on the Bath team was Gareth Chilcott. He was a very effective prop forward but no Tom Cruise. His wife was complaining about her husband spending so much time in the club bar, so one night he took her along with him. 'What'll you have?' he asked.

'Oh, I don't know. The same as you I suppose,' she replied. So, Chilcott ordered a couple of Jack Daniels and threw his down in one shot.

His wife watched him, then took a sip from her glass and immediately spit it out. 'Yuck, that's terrible!' she spluttered. 'I don't know how you can drink this stuff.'

'Well, there you go,' cried Chilcott. 'And you think I'm out enjoying myself every night.'

LOSS BY MISADVENTURE

Tragically injury brought Simon Geoghegan's career to a premature end, and Irish and world rugby were deprived of one of its most thrilling wingers. Geoghegan's performance has not always been enhanced by his Irish teammates. He was rooming with Neil Francis the night before the Fiji game in November 1995, Murray Kidd's first outing as team coach. Francis got thirsty during the night and disposed of a glass of water in the bathroom. The next morning when Geoghegan went to retrieve his contact lenses he discovered that Francis had unwittingly drunk them and the glass of water.

58

VERBAL LYNCH MOB

Seán Lynch Stars for the Lions

In 1971 Colin Meads prematurely dismissed the Lions forwards as 'Too many sweat bands, not enough sweat.' Seán Lynch was one of the men who made Meads eat his words. Capped 17 times for his country, Lynch is not a player to take himself too seriously. Lynchie was on the Irish tour to Argentina in 1970.

Lynch was one of the surprise stars of the Lions tour to New Zealand in 1971. He was to play a more central role than anybody could have foreseen at the start of the tour. The week before the first Test in Dunedin the Lions had lost their two first-choice props, Ray McLoughlin and Sandy Carmichael, with long-term injuries in the infamous 'battle of Christchurch'. The match confirmed an old adage: 'New Zealand rugby is a colourful game – you get all black and blue.'

GONE FISHING

Mick Quinn has a number of stories about Lynch. Typical of this kind is the one where Lynch goes on a fishing holiday with

Willie Duggan. They rented a boat and fished in a lake every day. After six days they still had caught nothing but on the seventh day they caught thirty fish. Seán said to Willie, 'Mark this spot so that we can come back here again tomorrow.'

The next day, when they were driving to rent the boat, Lynch asked Duggan, 'Did you mark that spot?'

Willie replied, 'Yeah, I put a big X on the bottom of the boat.'

Seán said, 'You stupid fool! What if we don't get that same boat today!'

MIGHTY MOUSE

Lynchie's prop partner with the Lions was the squat Scot, Ian McLauchlan, 'Mighty Mouse'. One of his opponents scornfully dismissed him in the words: 'You'll be Mickey Mouse by the time I've finished with you.' Yet it was the Lions who had the last laugh winning 9–3. The crowd's silence after the game bore eloquent testimony to the scale of the shock.

On the non-playing side Lynch's greatest memory of the Lions' tour is of visiting a vineyard. He had red wine, white wine, blue wine and everything that was going. Smiling like a nun with concussion, he claimed that rugby was the curse of the drinking class!

THE BLACK MARKET

Lynch's club St Mary's toured Russia in 1977. It was a strange environment at the time because they had two Russian police going everywhere with them who were keeping tabs on everything they did. It was the pre-glasnost and perestroika era and everybody in Russia was mad for Western goods, especially jeans. They had all their team blazers and jumpers and O'Neills (a native Irish clothing company) playing gear so they were able to sell off their jeans for about £100 in today's money. But their masterstroke was to convince the Russians that O'Neills was the Irish for Adidas! That tour cost the players virtually nothing as a result of their black-market activities.

59

THE LIFE OF O'REILLY

Tony O'Reilly Speaks

There are two types of people in the world: those who make things happen and those that things happen to. Tony O'Reilly was probably in both camps.

Rugby players sometimes suffer from 'Orson Welles syndrome'. Like the famous star of the screen, their crowning moment of glory came at the very start of their careers. Nothing that followed could match it. In the annals of Irish rugby a special place is reserved for Tony O'Reilly.

O'Reilly is very much the Roy of the Rovers of Irish rugby. Having first being capped against France as an eighteen-year-old in 1955, he really made his mark with the Lions.

In the opening Test the Lions won 23–22 in Johannesburg. It was the biggest attendance ever seen at a rugby game. The Springboks led 11–3 and to compound their misfortune the Lions lost their flanker Reg Higgins to a broken leg. At the time no replacements were allowed, so they had to play with fourteen men in front of over 100,000 partisan South Africans. Then 3 tries from Cliff Morgan, Cecil Pedlow and Tony O'Reilly gave the Lions a 23–11 lead. The Afrikaners replied with a vengeance. In the final minute Chris Koch crashed over for a try to cut the deficit to just one point. As van der Schyff faced a relatively easy kick to give the South Africans victory, the Irish members on the team turned to religion. The Limerick second row Tom Reid said, 'Jesus, if he kicks this I'm turning Protestant.'

To the horror of the home fans, van der Schyff pushed his kick left of the post.

O'Reilly's quick wit was evident. Asked as to what he had been doing looking the other way, he replied: 'I was in direct communion with the Vatican.' Van der Schyff missed and the tourists won 23–22.

FROM SIGHT TO INSIGHT
The late Tom Reid saw rugby as a 'little refreshment of my spirit' and was a great diplomat. On the tour O'Reilly and Reid were in a group of Lions tourists who were asked during an official reception what religion they were. An awkward silence descended on the party until Reid piped up, 'Well, sir, I think nothing of it. I come from Limerick in southern Ireland and I have my own political problems.'

Reid suffered from bad eyesight and went to live in Canada after that tour. In 1959 he memorably linked up with O'Reilly again. After the tour in New Zealand, the Lions stopped off to play a Test in Canada. O'Reilly was standing in line before the match when he heard a loud Limerick accent booming out over the ground, 'Hello Reilly, I know you're there. I can't see you but I can hear you all right!'

ROUGH PLAY
As a schoolboy O'Reilly also excelled at soccer, playing for Home Farm, but he turned his back on the game on foot of

an assault. During a match he made a bone-crunching tackle on an opponent. The boy's mother rushed onto the pitch and attacked O'Reilly with her umbrella. The future Lions sensation remarked: 'Rugby is fair enough – you only have your opponent to deal with. Soccer you can keep, if it involves having to deal with your opponent and his mother.'

BUSINESS SCHOOL

Belvedere College provided a nursery for both O'Reilly's rugby and entrepreneurial skills. When he was seven he was the only boy in his class to make holy communion. To mark the occasion a priest gave him an orange – an enormous luxury during the war years. Like most of his friends, O'Reilly had never seen an orange. O'Reilly subsequently claimed: 'After I ate the centre I sold the peel for one penny per piece, thereby showing a propensity for commercial deception which has not left me since.'

ISLANDS IN THE STREAM

Sir Anthony was once urged by the great Irish flank forward Ronnie Kavanagh to harden himself with a gruelling physical regime in the mountains. O'Reilly was typically unimpressed: 'Kav, it's not guerrilla warfare, it's rugby we are playing. We're not going to be asked to ford a stream at Lansdowne Road.'

TACTICAL AWARENESS

In 1963 following Ireland's 24–5 defeat at the hands of the French, O'Reilly was dropped for the only time in his career. Although the news came as a shock, O'Reilly had arguably never consistently reproduced his Lions' form in the green jersey. It seemed after 28 caps his international career was over. Seven years later in an ill-judged move, the Irish selectors persuaded him to come out of retirement to play against England at Twickenham in place of the injured Billy Brown for his 29th cap. To put it at its kindest, O'Reilly, now firmly established as a commercial giant because of his work with the Heinz Corporation, was anything but a lean, mean machine at that time. His shape prompted Willie John McBride to remark: 'Well, Tony, in my view your best attacking move tomorrow might be to shake your jowls at them.'

PAST IT

Ireland lost 9–3 and O'Reilly gave an undistinguished performance. In the final moments he dived boldly into the heart of the English pack. As he regained consciousness, he heard an Irish voice shouting: 'And while you're at it, why don't ya kick his fu**in' chauffeur too!'

NOT A BEAN

The Heinz slogan is: 'Beans Means Heinz'. After the match a WAG was heard to say: 'I never realised Heinz means has-beens!'

60

NUMBER TWO TO THE NUMBER TWO

Eddie O'Sullivan Assists Warren Gatland

Warren Gatland began his coaching career with Connacht. As a player he was in the right place at the wrong time. He established himself as the number two All Blacks hooker. The only problem was that Sean Fitzpatrick was the number one at the time!

Asked for her opinion about rugby, Elizabeth Taylor replied, 'It seems a neat game, but do they really bite ears off?'

South Africa's Johan le Roux bit Sean Fitzpatrick on the ear, tearing flesh in the 1994 series in New Zealand, and was sent home in disgrace and banned for nineteen months from international rugby. Afterwards the New Zealand media joked, 'Fitzy's fine but le Roux's in hospital with blood poisoning.'

When Fitzpatrick was fired up everybody knew the All Blacks were in a mean mood. In 1995 they defeated Japan 145–17 in a pool game in the World Cup, in a 21-try extravaganza. The mistake the Japanese made was scoring a try. If they had not the cheek to score a try the All Blacks would have let them off with a 50-points defeat. During half-time the Japanese captain was asked to say a few encouraging words to his team. All he could say by way of tactical insight was: 'We're going to retreat carefully!'

According to legend, when Fitzpatrick was asked what Japan needed to do to become a power in world rugby, he replied: 'The manager needs a new Chinese assistant: "Winonesoon."'

Mind you, Fitzpatrick has been the subject of the odd cutting remark himself notably when a journalist claimed that, after exhaustive research, he could reject the malicious rumour that when Fitzpatrick was a child they had to tie a lamb chop around his neck so that his dog would play with them. The journalist was so emphatic because he had proved conclusively Sean never had a dog.

FAST EDDIE

After the controversial dismissal in 2002 of Warren Gatland as Ireland's rugby coach, Eddie O'Sullivan succeeded him in one of the most high-pressure jobs in Irish sport. As a player Eddie lined out on the wing with Garryowen and he was pretty quick, so Neil Francis called him, 'Fast Eddie'. Eddie trained as a PE teacher in Limerick and played a lot of indoor soccer there. As he was a very incisive player he got the nickname 'the Dagger'. Since his alleged role in the dismissal of Warren Gatland, people have used that against him in a different context!

When O'Sullivan went to Garryowen he did a lot of weight training, which was very unusual in the 1970s, though now its par for the course in rugby. His teammates didn't think he was doing weights for rugby reasons, so they called him, 'the Beach Boy'.

Nicknames are an integral part of rugby culture. Rob Andrew's nickname was 'Squeaky' because he never did anything wrong. Given that his waistline was less than trim, Stuart Barnes was known as 'the Barrel'. Some are not very flattering. Jason Robinson, one of the stars of England's 2003 triumph, is often called 'Bible Basher' because he is a 'born again' Christian and because of his hatred of bad language. Mind you, others call him 'McDonald's' because of his love of junk food. English coach Andy Robinson was known as 'the Growler' because he always seemed to be in bad form and was constantly telling people off.

Austin Healey is known as 'the Leicester Lip' because of his constant stream of often annoying chat. Healey was also known as 'Melon Head' when he was young because of his big fore-head. Scott Gibbs, a key player for Wales and the Lions, was nicknamed 'Car Crash' because he did not tackle people, he obliterated them.

CRANKY

Eddie O'Sullivan may have been a little surprised when Keith Wood said after his retirement: 'I think I'll take a step away from the game for a while. I don't have the temperament to be a coach. I've known that for a while. Eddie may be a cranky man but he is not quite as cranky as I am.'

Eddie O'Sullivan believed in attention to detail. His philos-ophy was that of Abraham Lincoln – if he had a hundred hours to cut down a tree, he would spend ninety-nine hours sharpening the axe. In 2002 O'Sullivan led the Ireland rugby team to Siberia to play a match in an area renowned for its freezing temperatures. As the players are a very pampered lot, they can normally get everything they need. On this trip, incredibly, they found there was one thing they could not get – ice-cubes!

WATER, WATER EVERYWHERE

The Irish swimming fraternity has long been waiting for an Olympic-size swimming pool. In 2002 the IRFU began the first phase of its new pitch at Lansdowne Road. Ireland played autumn internationals against both Australia and Argentina during downpours. The pitch was covered in water in many places and barely playable. One swimming fan watching the Argentina match from the stands remarked, 'Congratulations to the IRFU in giving us our first ever 100-metre swimming pool.'

WISHFUL THINKING

In the run-up to the 2007 World Cup some fans were having difficulty accepting the verdict of the experts who predicted that Ireland would do well in the World Cup. To redress the balance they told a story about Eddie O'Sullivan.

In the middle of the night Eddie was woken up by a call from his local garda station in Galway. 'I'm afraid the trophy room has been broken into, sir.'

Horrified, O'Sullivan asked, 'Did the thieves get the cups?'

'No, sir,' replied the policewoman, 'they didn't go into the kitchen.'

MAKE A WISH

One day that year Eddie was walking along a beach when he came across a bottle. When he unscrewed the top, a genie appeared and said, 'I'm so grateful to get out of that bottle that I will grant you one wish.' O'Sullivan thought for a moment and said, 'I have always dreamed that there could be a motorway from outside my front door all the way to Lansdowne Road.' The genie thought for a moment and then said, 'I'm sorry, I can't do that. Just think of all the bureaucracy and red tape involved and all the local authorities who would have to be involved in putting that together. I'm sorry, but could you ask for an easier wish?'

Eddie said, 'Well there is one other thing. I'd like to coach Ireland to win the World Cup.'

The genie thought about it for a few minutes and then said, 'So do you want two lanes or four on that motorway?'

61

KNOCK YOUR SOCKS OFF

Ian McKinley Becomes a Pundit

Ian McKinley has literally changed the face of international rugby.

He played rugby at school for St. Columba's College in South Dublin. The day after his final exam for the Leaving Cert, he started training with Leinster aged eighteen:

'Coming from a non-rugby school to a full professional environment was certainly a massive challenge. My first memories would be meeting Dan Tobin (strength and conditioning coach) and him trying to get me up to speed with all the important lifts, e.g. squat, clean, deadlift. On the field it was very much about integrating with other Academy members, like Felix Jones and Dave Kearney. We played a lot of fitness games and in particular I remember a gruelling boxing circuit of fifteen rounds with Michael Cheika. I trained a lot with the first team as the season went on and I played my first game against the Dragons the week before the 2009 Heineken Cup final. I remember Felix Jones being so professional in all aspects. He was, though, quite light in weight and Dan, our fitness coach, would make him eat a lot to gain weight. One time he made him eat so much that Felix had to throw up.'

Then came the moment that would redefine McKinley's career:

'It was an AIL top of the table league game (UCD v Lansdowne) in Belfield. About two minutes into the game, I was at the bottom of a ruck, wrestling for possession. I went for one big rip and found myself on my back. In that moment a teammate accidentally stood on my face and his stud went straight into my left eyeball and it burst.

'There actually was no pain. My vision went straightaway, so I knew it was serious. The medical staff of UCD rushed in the field and they knew it was serious as my eye was out of place.

'I suppose I didn't realise how critical it was until I was in the A&E in the Royal [Victoria] Eye and Ear. There, after seeing me, they left me for a while in the room to try and get a senior surgeon to perform emergency surgery. That was actually quite a lonely time as I didn't really know what was happening.'

Thoughts about never playing again initially were not part of his subconscious:

'It never entered my mind. I just knew if my recovery was good I could get back on the field as soon as possible.'

In 2011 he was forced to announce his retirement. Then when things were looking bleak the rugby authorities threw him a lifeboat:

'I found out that IRB were looking at introducing eye protection for players worldwide. We got in contact with them and we found out that this was true. They were going to test the product on trial basis. The goggles became available in January 2014 and I managed to get a pair. From there I managed to play my first game back, three years after I initially retired, in Serie C with a team called Leonorso Rugby Udine in March 2014.

'Because it was a trial, every nation had a choice whether to participate in it or not. Ireland, England and France chose not to take part. As I climbed up the ladder with the quality of teams, I wasn't allowed to play in these countries. After many months of battling and campaigning, we managed to change this decision and now everyone who wears these goggles can play freely.'

There had to be a period of adjustment for him:

'It certainly took a while! To learn a new language, culture and to meet new people is challenging. I remember my wife went into the supermarket to ask for stock cubes. She looked up the direct translation in the dictionary and asked an assistant, "Where is the livestock?". The assistant as you can imagine laughed and laughed. So things like that happened all the time.'

IT'S ONLY NATURAL

Ian went on to play international rugby for Italy. His friends at home often 'amused' him by telling him that the Italian head coach took Italy out for training and told everyone to assume their normal position. So they all went to stand behind the goalposts and wait for the conversion.

GIVING IT SOCKS

In recent years Ian has returned to Ireland and has found new fame as a pundit on Virgin Media. It has been a welcome opportunity for him to reconnect with his family like his father Canon Horace McKinley Rector of Whitechurch parish in Dublin and his brother Philip who was ordained in 2021.

After his first appearance as a TV pundit Ian's family have altered his style in one area. They have encouraged him not to wear purple socks again. They are reserved only for bishops!

MATT-ER-OF-FACT

McKinley normally shares punditry duties with Matt Williams. When he coached Leinster because of their fondness for partying Matt told them that they were 'a drinking team with a rugby problem'.

With the retirement of Ian McGeechan, after the 2003 World Cup, Williams was appointed Scottish coach, after his term with Leinster. He should have known the magnitude of the task when BBC commentator Nick Mullins noted that his selection was akin to 'rearranging deck chairs on the Titanic'.

Managers play all kinds of mind games. As Scottish rugby coach, Williams had the number twenty-seven inscribed on the training gear of all his players to signify that they eat, drink and sleep the game twenty-four hours a day, seven days a week, 365 days a year. If you add up all those individual digits you get twenty-seven.

Scottish legend John Rutherford believes in the more traditional values that he himself illustrated as a player with his shrewd decision-making and great awareness of how to put a partner into space. Scotland's shocking slump during Williams's reign did little to convince Rutherford or other sceptics.

The dramatic decline in Scottish fortunes at the time was highlighted by a story doing the rounds that the international squad had their training delayed for two hours when one of their players discovered a suspicious white substance on the pitch. The police were called and then the drug squad investigated but could not confirm that the substance was safe. Training was allowed to continue, though, as there was absolutely no chance of any of the players getting near the try line.

Williams is one of the increasing number of coaches who have made the journey from 'down under' to Britain and Ireland, having begun his coaching career with New South Wales. Like many people in Scottish rugby, Rutherford has been unhappy with the growing influence of Aussies on Scottish rugby, not just at the coaching level but also amongst the playing community. The former Scottish international John Beattie joked that such was the Aussie influence on Scottish rugby during 'the Williams era' that Murrayfield would have to be rechristened 'Ramsay Street' after the celebrated street in Australia's most famous soap, *Neighbours*.

When Scotland axed Williams as coach to the national side they turned to two of Scotland's greatest ever internationals, John Jeffrey and John 'Rud' Rutherford, to take on key roles in the selection panel to determine his successor.

BORDERLINE

Rud came from the Scottish Borders club of Selkirk and grew up in a soccer background, with his father, Bill, a committee member of Selkirk AFC. He also starred at volleyball and basketball and first played rugby in school as a hooker.

He scored 3 tries in his first game for Selkirk rugby club and his rugby career took off. It is joked that the ethos of the club was probably typified by a story told about its chairman. He was sitting by his wife one evening as she lay on her deathbed: 'Jennie, I've got to go – it's an important practice session. If you should feel yourself slipping away while I'm gone, will you please blow out the candle.'

BAD NEIGHBOURS

It is not that Scottish rugby fans hate the English but . . .

One incident that sums Scottish fans' feelings for English rugby happened after Jonny Wilkinson played his first match in Murrayfield. The English squad walked past John Rutherford, who was talking to a sweet, elderly lady. Rud turned around to Wilkinson and said, 'Congratulations, Jonny.'

After exchanging greetings with Rutherford, the English out-half ran on to catch up with the squad. He was almost out of earshot when he heard Rud saying to the woman, 'That's Jonny Wilkinson, the English player.'

Her reply to this information was: 'I know. I hate him!'

62

PATTY'S PEARLS OF WISDOM

The Education of Colin Patterson

Tony Ward reflects on this time with great warmth:

'One of my happiest memories is of winning an Irish B cap against Scotland in Murrayfield. They had what would become a famous half-back combination playing John Rutherford and Roy Laidlaw. I immediately struck up an instant rapport with my half-back partner on and off the field. It was said that we went together like ham and eggs, and that Colin Patterson could find me in a darkened room. The scrum-half was heard to proclaim that I was not the first person he would want to meet in those circumstances!'

A HIGH-PROFILE PAIR

Patterson recalls this time with great affection:

'One of my clearest memories of winning my first cap is of a piece written about me in a local newspaper. The journalist in question had rung my mother a few times but had been unable to contact me. Yet when I opened the paper I saw a big piece full of quotes from me. I tackled the journalist about this afterwards. He said: "It's the sort of thing you would have said!" Throughout my career the amount of quotes attributed to me written by journalists who I had never even met defies belief. I didn't have that problem with *The Irish Times*. In their case the difficulty was that I never should have been picked for Ireland in the first place. I was described as Ireland's sixth choice.

'I later went on *The Late Show* with Tony when he has the golden boy of Irish rugby and landed him in big trouble. Wardy was involved in a serious relationship at the time and Gay Byrne asked him if he had a girlfriend. I quipped immediately: "One in every town." Tony had a lot of explaining to do to his young lady after that! He was also asked if he had thought about defecting to Rugby League. When Tony rejected the idea out of hand, Gay turned to me and said:

'"Tony is looking down on Rugby League, Colin, how about you?"

'"When you are only five feet five inches you can't afford to look down on anything," I replied.

'The personality difference between Tony and I were also evident on that visit. We were both asked what we would like to drink. I said two Irish coffees please, which was not what they normally provided and would take a bit of trouble on their part. Immediately Tony intervened and said:

'"Oh no. Don't go to any trouble for us."

'"Okay Tony, I'll drink yours as well," I answered and we both got our Irish coffees.

'I loved winding him up. Of course he gave me the ideal opportunity after the publication of his page-three style pose in his swimming trunks before the Scottish game in 1979. I pinned up the photo on the wall and kept gushing to him about his fantastic bum and how no woman could possibly resist him.'

Patterson was a rugby ecumenist singing the National Anthem with gusto before matches, even though he was not from Nationalist stock:

'Wardy taught me the first six or seven lines of the anthem and then I discovered that I could sing it to tune of "The Sash". I sang the first half of "The Soldier's Song" and the second half of "The Sash" just to give it a political balance!'

A SWITCH IN TIME

In 1979 Patterson got a new partner when Ward was dropped and replaced by Ollie Campbell on Ireland's tour to Australia:

'After the storm about Wardy being dropped off the team, the Australian press rubbished our chances of winning the first Test. One headline read: *Ireland to be Paddywhacked into Rugby Oblivion*. We beat them 27–12! If ever a victory was sweet, this was it. The place went berserk. I have a picture at home taken in the dressing room which shows Ollie and I together grinning from ear to ear. It was such a turn-up for the books. The only comparable story I can think of such a misjudgement came at the turn of this century. Two men, Mr Marks and Mr Smith, were talking. Mr Marks outlined his plans for a new shop and asked Mr Smith to be his partner. Mr Smith replied: "Nah. It'll never work." Mr Marks found a new partner – Mr Spencer. The result is history!'

WELSH WISDOM

Tony Ward toured with Colin on the 1980 Lions tour but it was a real education touring with the Welsh as Patterson told me: 'That was the era when you paid for your own telephone calls home. They had three great tricks devised never to pay for a telephone. Plan A was to charm the hotel receptionist into giving them the secret code they could use to make calls without having them charged to them. Plan B was to distract the receptionist and for one of them to sneak in behind the desk and steal all their telephone bills. Plan C was when a journalist asked for an interview, they traded it for a phone call.

'Best of all, though, was when we went into the Adidas factory. We were allowed to pick a bag of our choice and stuff it with gear. Most of us selected the most stylish bags and filled them with gear. All the Welsh guys, without exception, took the biggest bags in the shop and walked out with half of the gear in the factory!

'One night they did a classic wind-up on the English player Mike Slemen, who was the leading try scorer on the tour. All of them gathered into the one room and rang him up pretending to be from the BBC World Service, with a suitable posh accent. They fed him a lot of compliments and he started blowing his own trumpet and claimed that he probably was one of the best players on the tour. Eventually the Welsh lads could take no more and shouted: "Slemen you're a useless bolli*. The English man was mortified that he had been caught out so badly.'

63

PHONE IN

Terry Kennedy Tours in South Africa

Terry Kennedy's nickname is 'the Rat'. Everybody in rugby knows this but very few know its origins. On St Mary's tour to Russia in 1977, J.B. Sweeney, who was a great stalwart of the club, christened Kennedy 'Ratskinski' and it was then abbreviated. Hence 'the Rat'.

EBONY AND IVORY

Kennedy won the first of his 13 caps on the wing for Ireland against Wales in 1978.

He toured South Africa with Ireland in 1981. Before the tour John Robbie was called into his bosses' office (he worked for Guinness) and was told that he was not allowed to go. Robbie resigned, although he was married with a young child to support. He did retain his sense of humour through this difficult time.

'The great departure day arrived, and then we learned about the cloak-and-dagger methods that we were going to use to get to South Africa. I suppose it was necessary, and we were getting worried about running the gauntlet at Dublin airport, as we'd heard that a massive demonstration had been planned. I rang Terry Kennedy and in my best Peter Sellers Indian accent I told him that I was Kadar Asmal, the high-profile leader of the Irish anti-apartheid movement, and could I talk to him? Terry was very worried and when I asked him to confirm some secret arrangements for our departure, I could almost see the beads of sweat pouring from his brow. He was gibbering like an idiot and nearly collapsed in relief when I told him it was me.'

NAAS

On that tour the Irish team would get up close and personal with a giant of the game. Part of the fellowship of sport is that you would go to war with friends you would trust with your life. That's the theory and often the reality. But not always.

Naas Botha was one of the most prodigious goal-kickers of all time. Hence his nickname 'Dead-eye Dick' – a reputation enhanced by his performances against the Lions in 1980. However, he attracted a lot of controversy in South Africa because of his apparent reluctance to pass the ball.

Botha played a club match during a downpour. His team were on top all through the game and Botha was kicking everything. His right winger was going mad for a pass and eventually Botha gave him one but the winger dropped it and the opposition broke right up to the other end of the field. Botha screamed out, 'That's the last time I'm passing to you until you can drop it further than I can kick it.'

After he kicked his club side's 24 points to give them victory in the Cup final he was sitting beside another man on the plane. Botha was a bit surprised that his companion said nothing to him. After a half an hour of total silence he turned around and said, 'I don't think you realise who I am, I'm probably the most famous rugby player in South Africa.'

His companion quietly said: 'I don't think you realise who I am. I play for your team. I'm your first centre!'

After an injury to his arm Botha was telling a teammate that he had asked his doctor, 'And when my right arm is quite better, will I be able to pass the ball?'

The doctor replied, 'Most certainly – you should be able to pass with ease.'

His teammate replied: 'That's a miracle cure – you could never pass it before!'

A CHANGE OF HEART

Hugo MacNeill did manage to extract some fun out of the touring situation. Around this time there was a lot of money being offered under the table for players to play in exhibition games in South Africa. One of the ways Hugo sometimes wound up his colleagues in the Irish team was to ring them up, put on a South African accent and offer them £25,000 to play in such a match. It was always interesting to see who showed great interest.

In the 1980s, at the height of the apartheid era, there was a lot of money being offered under the table for players to play in exhibition games in South Africa. MacNeill has a great ability to do African and Australian accents and he often used them to great effect to tease his teammates on the Irish team. He rang one colleague who can't be named for legal reasons and pretended to be a chap called Fritz Voller from the South African Rugby Board. He said: 'I'm ringing you in connection with permission we got from the IRFU to allow you to play in a special match we've arranged between the Springboks and a world selection. The match will be played on October 14.'

The friend replied: 'I'm sorry. I'm totally committed to my responsibilities with Munster and Ireland and I'm unable to make the trip but thank you for the kind invitation.'

'But we would like you to captain our world selection.'

'I'm sorry I can't make it because of my commitments to Munster and Ireland.'

'But you could have a nice holiday and your wife could come with you and stay on for an extended holiday when you return to Ireland.'

'No. I can't because of my commitments to Munster and Ireland.'

'Okay I hear what you're saying. I don't want to put you under undue pressure. Thanks for listening. I suppose there's no point in saying that your match fee would be £30 thousand sterling.'

There was a pregnant pause.

'Sorry?'

'Oh, I was just mentioning your match fee would be £30 thousand sterling. It would be lodged into a Swiss bank account. But I wouldn't want to compromise your commitment to Munster and Ireland.'

'That's okay. Sorry, what date in October did you say again? Let me recheck my diary. Now that I think of it my poor wife, needs a little holiday!'

At which point Hugo rapidly reverted to his own accent and said: 'I've got you by the balls.'

64

Deano

Paul Dean Makes His Debut

Ireland's summer tour to South Africa in 1981 marked Paul Dean's initiation into the Irish set-up. It was to prove an education in every sense of the term.

'I am still learning what happened on that tour. There were three young lads in the squad: Michael Kiernan, John Hewitt and myself. We were going to bed very early at night, getting up early to go training and we couldn't understand why the older players were so tired in the mornings. We were on different clocks. They had a different agenda.

'The three of us were so naive and innocent. To give you an example, I roomed with one very senior player, who shall remain nameless, for four nights but I never saw him at night-time and I was so naive I thought he didn't want to room with me because he was afraid I'd be snoring!'

Dean's rugby past is a different country. Change is inevitable, except from a vending machine. Paul has noticed big changes in rugby since his playing days.

'There was an unwritten code about fair play back then also. I saw this over two years in internationals between England and Ireland. After we played England at home we had the post-match dinner, except for the first time women were allowed to attend. We were then on strict instructions from our girlfriends to get to the function in a "decent state", otherwise we'd be in trouble. Before the dinner a lot of drink had been consumed and one of my Irish teammates was "tired and emotional" and had to go to bed. When his girlfriend came down from her room there was an English player in the lift with her. He thought she fancied him so he grabbed her and groped her. She was terribly embarrassed. Her boyfriend didn't get to hear about it until the following day. The next year when Ireland played the return fixture, a line-out took place and the call was made to the Irish forward in question. He was marking the English player responsible. The English guy jumped and the Irish player "planted" him and put his opponent's nose to the other side of his face. The English player huddled up his forwards and told him the next time they got a line-out to throw the ball to him and he would plant his opponent in turn. The English players knew about the incident the previous year and told him he deserved it. That night the English player came to the Irish lad and apologised. The basic rule was what goes around comes around. Nowadays if you struck a player like that, especially with the media coverage and video evidence, you would be sued for GBH.'

For Dean the rugby friendships endure:

'A great character was the Scottish international John Jeffrey. He became a good friend of mine. The night before we played Scotland in 1985 we went to the cinema, as was the tradition back then. All I remember of the film was that it starred Eddie

Murphy and his catchphrase was: "Get the f**k out of there." As soon as the film was over the lights came on and when we stood up we saw that the Scottish team were sitting three rows behind us. We had a popcorn fight with them, which was great fun, and they started shouting at us: "Get the f**k out of here." Almost as soon as the match started the next day John Jeffrey tackled me very late. He knew exactly what he was doing. It was too early in the game for him to be penalised. As he pinned me down on the ground he whispered in my ear: "Get the f**k out of here." The nice thing was that we did get the f**k out of there – but with a victory.'

Closer to home Dean was particularly close with an international teammate:

'When I started with Ireland, I loved playing with Michael Kiernan because he was so fast. The problem was that, as he got older, he put on weight and started to lose his speed! My job was to make our talented backline look good. The problem was that I made Michael look much, much better than he actually was.'

Many rugby fans felt Michael Kiernan left the Irish team prematurely. For the first time Deano can exclusively reveal the real reason for Kiernan's premature retirement: 'He left because of illness. The truth is everyone was sick of him!'

65

A HOLY SHOW

The 1987 World Cup

Legendary Connacht second-row forward Mick Molloy saw some strange sights after he became Irish team doctor.

In the World Cup in 1987 the Irish team were coached by Mick Doyle. Doyler decided he was going to get into shape on the trip because he was two stone overweight. He started to train with the backs and when the lads saw this they stepped up a gear. At the end of the session Doyler was in bits. Later that night Donal Lenihan heard that he had been taken to hospital. As captain Donal went to see him that evening by taxi. He was in the front seat and Syd Millar and Mick Molloy were in the back. At one stage in the conversation Syd said Mick Doyle's wife, Lynne, had been on the phone and was very concerned about him and wanted to come Down Under to see him. Then he said his girlfriend, Mandy, was very worried about him and she too wanted to travel to see him. The Maori taxi-driver turned to Donal and said with real feeling, 'That stuff about holy Catholic Ireland is a load of crap!'

When Donal got back from the hospital Brian Spillane asked, 'Did he have a girl or a boy?'

Some years later, at a dinner, Donal told this story to a charming woman with an English accent whom he had never met before nor had any idea who she was, except that she was very well-versed in rugby matters. It turned out to be Doyler's ex-wife, Lynne!

MASS MISSER

Doyler had a wicked sense of humour. He was taking the Irish team for a Sunday morning training session. His prop forward, Jim McCoy, was not moving as swiftly as Doyler would have liked. Big Jim was an RUC officer and brought up in the Protestant tradition. Doyler shouted at him, 'Hurry up McCoy or you'll be late for Mass!'

LEAP OF FAITH

The definitive verdict on Moss Keane came from Mick Doyle: 'For the first half Moss would push in the line-outs and in the second, he'd jump in the scrums. That would always confuse the English.'

66

BETTER BAD DAYS

Ireland Win Wooden Spoon

In 1981 Ireland lost all four matches in the Five Nations, by a single score, after leading in all four at half-time. It was Ireland's best ever whitewash!

That summer a depleted Irish side toured South Africa. The tour saw one of the great wind-ups of Irish rugby. One Saturday, Freddie McLennan was 'duty boy' (the player in charge of informing players about travel arrangements and such for a particular day during a tour abroad. Each player takes it in turn). The squad had been given the day off and had to decide how to spend it. Freddie, himself a keen golfer, offered two choices. They could either go for a game of golf or take a trip around Johannesburg harbour. Eighteen players favoured the harbour trip on the basis that they could play golf at any time but would not always get the chance to do some sightseeing in Johannesburg. The next morning the players were ready at 8 a.m. for their trip around the harbour to be told that since the city was 5,000 feet above sea level it did not have a harbour and that the nearest seaside was a massive bus trip away.

ICE, ICE BABY

Johnny Moloney once saw the tables turned on McLennan: 'Mick Quinn would sometimes involve me as his partner-in-crime. He had this trick he played on every player gaining his first cap. A lot of players before their debut start to feel that they are a bit sluggish and not at their best. Quinny would pretend to be very sympathetic and tell them he had the solution. He would inform them in the strictest confidence that the top players always took a freezing cold bath to give them an edge in a big match. The only reason why this was not generally known was that it was a trade secret.

'The biggest casualty in all of this was Freddie McLennan. We put him in a cold bath and added buckets of ice. We told him he had to wait in there for twenty minutes otherwise it was no good. He was squealing like a pig. When his time was up, he couldn't move and had ice on his legs.'

Colin Patterson was a big fan of McLennan: 'Freddie is a great personality. Once, when we played England, Freddie and John Carleton were having a real jousting match. At one stage John sent Freddie crashing to the ground in a tackle. As he was going back to his position, Freddie shouted at him, "John, John. Is my hair all right?" If you watch the video of the game you'll see John cracking up with laughter and Freddie straightening his hair.'

67

MERCY KILLING

Peter Clohessy Takes Action

In conversation with this writer, Ronan O'Gara observed: 'I suppose the two greatest characters in my time were Mick Galwey and Peter Clohessy. They were old school and are a huge loss to the game, and the freshness they brought to the game and to the Irish squad was very uplifting. Probably my most abiding memory of my days in the Irish squad was when the players and management made a presentation to Peter to mark his 50th cap. Peter responded by singing the Frank Sinatra song: "I Did It My Way". What an appropriate song! He did things his way or no way. That's why I liked him and admired him so much.'

AH REF
The classic Clohessy story, which I stress is apocryphal, involves the referee who decides that he has to make a quick getaway after an Irish international against England in Lansdowne Road in which he sends off three Irish players and awards two controversial penalties. He drives too quickly, crashes coming

round a bend and is thrown through the windscreen onto the road. By coincidence, the car following him is driven by one of the players he sent off, Peter Clohessy, and he stops to see if he can help. He finds that the referee is in a bad way and makes a 999 call on his mobile.

'I think the referee's dead,' he shouts down the phone in panic. 'What can I do?'

'Calm down,' says the operator, used to dealing with emergencies. 'First of all, go and make sure the referee is dead.'

The operator hears a choking sound and the cracking of neck bone. Then the Claw returns to the mobile.

'Ok,' he says. 'I've made sure he's dead. Now what should I do?'

68

A RAY OF HOPE

Ray McLoughlin Upsets Gareth Edwards

Ray McLoughlin was one of the greatest prop forwards of all time.

Ireland were playing Wales in Lansdowne Road in 1974 when Ray and Willie John McBride combined to leave one of the Welsh forwards more than a little worse for wear. Gareth Edwards was furious and turned to the miscreants and said, 'I know it was one of you two f**kers who did that and you're going to pay for it before the game is finished.'

Willie John just peered down at him and softly asked, 'Gareth, are you speaking to us?'

Within seconds Edwards collapsed in a fit of laughter.

BROTHERS IN ARMS
Ray McLoughlin's brother Feidlim also played for Ireland. Feidlim modestly said, 'We have 41 caps between us.' What he neglected to point out was that he had only one and Ray held the remaining forty!

WIGS

Ray loved the camaraderie with former Irish internationals like Bill 'Wigs' Mulcahy. Wigs toured with the Lions in 1959. When they played Auckland, Albie Pryor was lining out for the home side and stamped on David Marques's head. To Mulcahy's astonishment Marques stood up and shook Pryor's hand. After the match Wigs asked Marques why he did that and was even more surprised to hear: 'You wouldn't understand, you're Irish. I shook his hand and called him a cad to make him feel small.'

Wigs was not impressed by either his sportsmanship or his interest in educating the colonies and witheringly dismissed him: 'With an attitude like that, no wonder you lost the British Empire.'

Wigs was also famous for his exchange with Ronnie Kavanagh. It was in a dressing room in Paris as Ireland prepared to face a tough French team, and captain Bill Mulcahy asked his team-mates if they had any final words of advice. Ronnie declared, 'I suggest we spend the next eighty minutes kicking the s**t out of them.'

Mulcahy replied, 'Bejaysus, men, we have a plan.'

MIGHTY MOUSE

Ray also enjoyed the company of his fellow prop-forwards on the international stage like Ian 'Mighty Mouse' McLauchlan.

Rugby tours have a number of striking similarities with a religious pilgrimage such as uniformity in dress codes, the chanting of familiar songs and a feeling of community and fellowship throughout. The analogy does not hold true for the Wasps tour to Malaysia in 1992 when some of the tourists bared their posteriors for the world to see. Not surprisingly in a Muslim country, this cheeky behaviour caused outrage and the offenders were severely fined and deported.

Rugby tours have a unique capacity to produce tales of the unexpected. On the 1974 Lions tour to South Africa, the visitors were playing Transvaal. Their tight-head prop was Johan Hendrik Potgieter Strauss, a beast of man and one of the toughest scrummagers in South Africa. Bobby Windsor wanted to psyche him out before the game so he went up to him and asked, 'Are you Johan Strauss?'

The Springbok replied, '*Ja*.'

Windsor sneered at him dismissively. 'Well, the Mouse will tune your piano for you this afternoon.'

69

NO MISTLETOE BUT LOTS OF WINE

Moss Has a Party

For the social aspect Lions captain in 1977, the late, great Phil Bennett, always enjoyed his trips with the Irish contingent. After one post-match dinner some of the Irish players were intent on stretching the evening a bit further and hit a local nightclub. After entering the premises, Moss Keane beckoned to Willie Duggan. 'What'll ye have, Willie?'

Duggan replied, 'Moss, I'll have a creamy pint of stout, from the middle of the barrel.'

After a brief exchange at the bar Moss returned and sad sadly, 'They've no beer here at all, Willie, only wine.'

'Oh,' replied Duggan, 'I'll have a pint of wine, so.'

Later that night Bennett said to Duggan, 'Moss Keane has legs on him like a drinks cabinet.'

Duggan replied, 'That's very appropriate considering the amount he drinks.'

COME DINE WITH ME
Moss linked up on the Irish team with another former distinguished footballer from Kerry, Dick Spring. After a match at

Twickenham Spring and Keane returned home and had a very late night session in St Mary's rugby club. They stayed in Moss's 'high class' flat in Rathmines. They woke up the next day at midday very much the worse for wear and went to 'Joe's Stakehouse' for some food. Moss ordered a mixed grill. Spring's tastes were more modest and he just asked for plaice and chips. When the food arrived Moss looked a bit queasy. He looked up and said, 'Springer, would you ever mind swapping?' Spring duly obliged. That day has entered folklore because it is said to be the only time in his life Moss turned his back on a big meal!

Another time Moss and Spring were together for a match in London. They were both starving on the Saturday night. The two of them crept into the kitchen of their hotel and sought out some food. Suddenly they were caught in the act by the porter. They expected to have the face eaten off them. After a dramatic pause he said, 'You know ye're lucky lads. There's now three Kerry men in the room.' The two thieves got the meal of their lives.

70

RAY OF SUNSHINE

Dr John O'Driscoll Shines in Crises

With Rodney O'Donnell, Colin Patterson, Ollie Campbell and Shannon's Colm Tucker, Dr John O'Driscoll was chosen on the Lions' tour to South Africa in 1980. Tucker was an interesting selection because he was unable to command a regular place on the Irish team. Tony Ward, Phil Orr and John Robbie subsequently joined the squad as replacements.

One of the occupational hazards John O'Driscoll faces because of his medical expertise is that he has to put up with a lot of medical jokes like:

Q: Who are the most decent people in the hospital?
A: The ultrasound people.

The Lions also had an Irish coach in the form of Noel Murphy (one on his instructions to the squad during a training session was: 'Spread out in a bunch.'). He was brilliant at motivating the Irish lads but not so good with the Welsh, who require a different type of motivation.

John O'Driscoll won 26 caps from 1978 to 1984 but he was prematurely cast off the Irish team that was whitewashed in 1984. He played in all four Tests on the 1980 Lions tour.

It was a horrific tour for two of O'Driscoll's Irish colleagues. Without O'Driscoll's presence, though, it would have been even worse. Tragedy struck against Griqualand West in the penultimate game of the tour when the Lions won 23–19 and Rodney O'Donnell sustained a serious injury tackling the massive Danie Gerber. Although he walked off the field, when he was examined in hospital it was discovered that he had dislocated his neck between the sixth and seventh vertebrae and that he had come within a fraction of an inch of being paralysed for life. Prompt intervention by O'Driscoll on the pitch prevented more severe repercussions. To compound the problems, when the ambulance finally arrived the driver got lost on the way back to the hospital, depriving the Irish player of the quickest possible care.

One person literally at the centre of the action that day was the great Welsh centre Ray Gravell.

There are moments of grace in every life when you cross paths with someone truly special – the late Ray Gravell was one of them for me. It is fair to say that they broke the mould after the birth of Raymond William Robert Gravell in Kidwelly in 1951. After Ray's passing in 2007, historian Hywel Teifi Edwards said: 'Loving Wales and revelling in its people were as natural to him as breathing. If you asked him where his *gwladgarwch* (patriotism) came from, he would look at you and tell you nobody asks why snow is white.'

He was part of the famous Wales team in the 1970s and played in all four Tests on the Lions tour to South Africa in 1980.

It was Ray who rechristened John O'Driscoll 'John O'Desperate'. He told me:

'Ireland supplied two great wing-forwards on that Lions tour in Colm Tucker and John O'Driscoll. Colm was such a committed player that it was a pleasure to play with him. I would die for John O'Driscoll. What a player and what a man. Mind you, John and Maurice Colclough were always trying to get me pi**ed. They were always pouring rum, without my knowledge, into my soup.

'I will never forget that we played a match a week before the first Test and they sprung this amazing kicker who could kick the ball eighty yards and was really crucifying us. Bill Beaumont said we must do something about him. The next time he kicked the ball I tackled him ferociously and broke his shoulder. John said to me: "Grav, what the f**k are you doing?"

'I replied: "I caught him a late one, early."

'It was such a shame that Rodney's career ended so prematurely on that tour. Rodney was actually lucky to still have the use of limbs after breaking his neck. If Dr John O'Driscoll hadn't been playing and shouted to the ambulance men when Rod went down not to move him, then he could have died or been paralysed. Moreover, John was only playing against the Junior Boks that day because Colm Tucker had sprained his ankle.'

A GOOD LITTLE ONE

With his small stature, scrum-half Colin Patterson was an obvious target for intimidation on the rugby pitch:

'I prided myself on my ability to take punishment. The tougher it got, the better I liked it. Whenever I got crushed by somebody, I got up immediately and said to him: "Good tackle soldier", which really annoyed them. At internationals there were a number of efforts to verbally intimidate me. I never let that sort of bullsh*t get to me. The best example of this was when we played Wales in 1980. Where Stuart Lane wasn't going to stuff the ball up my anatomy I can't say. I eventually turned around and said to him: "Stuart, you don't mean that." It was my last home game for Ireland so the BBC gave me the video of the match. When I watched it, I saw again Stuart bursting into laughter and saying: "You're a cheeky wee boll**ks." The more a player tried to intimidate me, the more I wound him up by waving at him in the line-out and so on. Apart from the fact that it helped me to win the psychological war, it's the only fun us small fellas get!'

In 1980 Patty was at the height of his powers when all was taken from him in an accidental clash:

'It all began with an innocuous incident. I was screaming in agony, the pain was so intense. My situation was not helped by the fact that the referee tried to play amateur doctor with me and started poking around with my leg. I was stretchered off but they are so fanatical about their rugby out there in South Africa that two fans rushed on. One took my discarded boot and the other my sock and he asked me if I would give him my shorts.'

The consequently wrecked medial ligaments from his injury caused Patterson to revise his career plans. Had he not got that injury, he had arranged to go out and play in Australia for a season. In fact he already had his ticket bought.

The Lions players had such huge admiration for John O'Driscoll because the official medical services were a long way from the professionalism they would expect today. On the 1980 Lions tour Ollie Campbell pulled a hamstring in the first week. To illustrate how amateur things were then, the team doctor, Jack Matthews (himself a former Welsh and Lions great), gave him a Zube (a sweet for when you have a sore throat) to suck on.

SIMPLY THE BLESSED

Despite his special talents Ray Gravell was always very insecure before big games. In fact on such occasions he sometimes told the selectors that he could not play because he had a blinding headache. It was all in his head.

He was pulled aside and told that he had just received a new wonder drug from America, which would cure him instantly. Gravell popped the orange pill into his mouth and immediately felt a surge of energy, power and strength that he had never experienced before.

It was only when he retired that Ray discovered the real truth – that the magic drug he swallowed was in fact . . .

. . . a Tic Tac.

THE COTTON DIET

The English prop, Fran Cotton's nickname was 'Noddy' because he liked his sleep. He had a serious health scare on that Lions tour to South Africa in 1980. He was erroneously diagnosed as having suffered a heart attack during the match against the Proteas. It transpired he had suffered an attack of pericarditis – inflammation of tissue around the heart. When Fran's English hooker, Peter Wheeler 'Wheelbrace', heard that the world's most famous heart transplant surgeon Christian Bernard had jokingly offered to perform his services on Fran, he said, 'They would never have found a heart big enough.'

When he was told by his doctors that he was out of shape because of too much red meat, fine wine and white bread, Fran replied, 'Fine. I'll give up white bread then.'

When he returned to England he went for a check-up. His concerned doctor told him to give up smoking, drinking, eating rich food and chasing women. 'Will that help me to live longer?' asked Fran.

'Hopefully,' said the doctor, 'but I'm not sure. You see no one has tried it yet.'

His Lions teammates sent him a get-well card. It read: 'Gone but not for Cotton.'

A few months later Cotton went back to his doctor. The doctor said: 'This is the diet you must follow. Three lettuce leaves, a slice of dry toast and a glass of orange juice twice a day.'

Fran replied: 'I see. Now is that before meals or after?'

BUM DEAL

Fran's captain on the tour to South Africa was Bill Beaumont. He was the one forward on the tour who, every time he went into a ruck the ball, came back on the Lions' side. Bill was not the most mobile forward but he still managed to get around: not the greatest line-out jumper yet he still managed to win the ball. He was not an awesome forward in the Wade Dooley sense though he had tremendous ability to use his own physique. He was always a great scrummager. He was nicknamed 'Sun Bum' on that tour because he had plenty of padding in those places which made him ideal for scrummaging. He was christened that by Peter Wheeler. Sunday was always their day off training and Wheelbrace arranged T-shirts for the squad which read: 'Sun Bum's Sunday Sessions Side.' Beaumont's backside was also jokingly known on the tour as 'the outboard motor.'

71

DOPEY

Tom Clifford's Captaincy

Tom Clifford was adept at psyching his team up for English games in particular. He once told the team about the three young children who go to heaven, but God says they are too young to die, and tells them to take a run off the cloud, and on the way back to Earth to shout out what they want to be. The first lad jumps and says he wants to be a successful teacher. Twenty tears later he is the youngest head teacher in the country. The second wants to be a successful lawyer and twenty years later he is the youngest judge ever appointed. The third young lad trips over his own feet jumping off the cloud and involuntarily shouts out: 'Clumsy bast**d'. Twenty years later he is playing scrum-half for England.

REVERSE PSYCHOLOGY

Tom was long before his time in his capacity to out-psyche his opponents. Before an international against England he went up to the two English props and said: 'I'm very sorry. I just heard the news. You don't deserve that – either of you.'

The two English players were puzzled. 'What do you mean?'

'I've just heard what everybody is calling the two of you.'

'Really. We haven't heard anything. So what are people calling us behind our backs?'

'Sim-bolic.'

'Symbolic? Why are they calling us that?'

Tom paused theatrically before replying: "Cos one of you is simple and the other is a bolli*.'

DEATH WISH

The Wallabies toured the British Isles in 1948. Things heated up when they played Munster. Munster had a very simple way of dealing with touring sides. That was as soon as possible to bring them down to their level and then it was an even match. Nick Shehadie, one of the stars of the Australian side, was confronted by Tom Clifford. Shehadie was a bit taken aback by the opening greeting: 'Come in here son. You may as well die here as in fu**in' Sydney.'

DOCTOR'S ORDERS

A club team from Limerick was on tour in New Zealand. The fly-half was a Tom Cruise lookalike and was a big hit with all the ladies at the many parties they attended. One night he struck up a relationship with a Nicole Kidman lookalike and she brought him home and took him to bed. They were in the throes of passion when the woman's husband walked in. 'What the hell do you think you're doing?' he screamed.

'I'm . . . er . . . I'm a doctor and I'm . . . taking your wife's temperature,' stammered the medic.

'Right!' said the husband. 'I hope for your sake that thing's got numbers on it when you take it out!'

HIGH COUNT

Tom Clifford had a sympathetic streak in him. One of his forwards suffered a severe blow in the region of his essential equipment. Tom approached the injured player who was squirming on the ground with his hands clutched between his legs, moaning, 'Please, don't rub 'em. Just count 'em!'

INSPIRATIONAL SPEECH

Another story goes back to when he burst into the changing room as the second half of the game was about to begin.

'All right!' he roared. 'All of you lazy, no-good, thick-headed b*stards – out on that field – now!' All the players jumped to their feet and rushed onto the field – except for the little scrum-half sitting in the corner. 'Well!' roared Clifford.

'Well,' said the scrum-half, 'there certainly were a lot of them, weren't there.'

72

THE GOSPEL ACCORDING TO LUKE

Paul O'Connell Rooms with Peter Clohessy

One of the stories that illustrates Peter Clohessy's passion for the game goes back to the first time he saw his son Luke play a game and Clohessy senior was voicing strong opinions from the sidelines about the referee. After one of the Claw's many vocal contributions, the coach called Luke over to the sideline and said to him, 'Do you understand what cooperation is? What team is?'

Luke nodded in the affirmative.

'Do you understand that what matters is whether we win together as a team?'

The little boy nodded yes.

'So,' the coach continued, 'when a penalty is awarded, you don't argue or curse or attack the ref. Do you understand all that?'

Again Luke nodded.

'Good,' said the coach, 'now go over there and explain it to your father.'

BADLY BURNT

Before the 2002 Heineken Cup semi-final the Claw faced a serious injury when he was badly burned in a domestic accident. This prompted his wife to remark: 'I always knew you'd go out in a blaze of glory but I didn't think you'd literally do it.' The small matter of multiple skin burns was not enough to deter Clohessy from playing in the game. In solidarity with the Claw, Munster fans wore T-shirts to the game saying: 'Bitten and burnt, but not beaten.'

A BALANCED DIET?

There is one memory that will forever hold a special place in Paul O'Connell's memory chest. Waking as a boy on Christmas morning was like this – the sleepy thrill before remembering its source. He loves the stories of the 'old school' before rugby went professional and the way players combined drinking and other 'extra-curricular' activities and playing. It was part of another time and place. The players from that era carry for O'Connell the aura of another life which is half secret and half open. He got a taste of it when he spent a week with Peter Clohessy.

'I used to travel up with the Claw for internationals because we were both Young Munster and both of us lived in Annacotty. Claw was such a legend at the time that he roomed alone but as it was my first cap he was asked to room with me for the week. It was a week I will never, ever forget!

'Later I roomed with Anthony Foley and we knocked off at 11 p.m. and went to sleep. We ate a proper breakfast of muesli and scrambled eggs and drank lots of water. We also took protein shakes after training. We did our weights but went for a nap during the day to ensure that we were getting the proper rest. After having a proper dinner we might do some video analysis but then we were in bed early.

'My week with the Claw was very different! He was old school. On the way up to Dublin we stopped off in a petrol station. I had a tuna sandwich with no butter and a pint of milk. The Claw had a sausage sandwich with plenty of butter and lashings of brown sauce and cups of tea with shovels of sugar.

'When we were in our hotel room he was smoking fags the whole day. We'd be getting room service up all day, every day, with various not particularly healthy dishes like mayonnaise sandwiches. I would go to sleep about 11 and he'd still be up watching the TV. I'd wake up about two to go the toilet. Claw wouldn't be one for bringing water into the room. The TV would still be on and I would knock it off. I'd wake back up at four and the TV would be back on! I'd knock it off again. Then I would wake up again at seven. The Claw would be sitting up in the bed, smoking a fag and watching the TV.

'On our afternoon off the Dublin lads would go home to their families but we didn't have that luxury because the journey was too far. We were staying in the Glenview Hotel and we drove up the Wicklow mountains and went to a café for a healthy diet of rhubarb tart, ice-cream and custard!

'He did everything differently and yet before the match he was the one with the tear in his eye and he would get more up for the game than anyone else. He was the best player on the pitch against Wales by a mile. His understanding of professionalism was very different but he had a bigger heart than everyone else and that's why everybody loved him and still loves him.'

73

IN SEARCH OF RUDOLPH

Moss and Willie Play for the Lions

Moss Keane and Willie Duggan were flying to New Zealand on the Lions tour in 1977. It was a 30-hour journey and Moss woke up Willie and said, 'Willie, we're over the North Pole.'

Duggan replied, 'Well, if we are, I can't see any f**king reindeers' [sic] and promptly went back to sleep.

FEELING SHEEPISH

Moss had pulled a hamstring on the plane over and was unable to train for days and days. Eventually the frustrated tour manager went to Bennett and said, 'If Moss Keane doesn't train tomorrow, I'm sending him home.'

Benny spoke to Moss and the Irish legend agreed to train the following day. Not surprisingly it was lashing rain and freezing for the training session and Moss showed up in his shorts, a T-shirt and sneakers. Just before he left the hotel he told the waiter, 'Can you please have some hot coffee and a rasher sandwich ready for me when I come back?'

When Moss returned the waiter handed him a mug of steaming coffee, and then apologised. 'You won't believe it – we are out of bacon.'

Moss looked aghast and stared at him in disbelief. 'Three million sheep in New Zealand – how can you be out of bacon?'

REGULAR HABITS

On that Lions tour in 1977 Moss roomed with Peter Wheeler on the first night. Wheeler was woken up prematurely by Moss turning on his bedside lamp, lighting a cigarette and opening a can of beer. Wheeler exclaimed indignantly, 'It's five o'clock in the morning and we're on a Lions tour to New Zealand.'

Moss answered, 'It's five o'clock in the evening back home in Ireland and I always have a pint at this time.'

74

DOCTOR'S SURGERY

Karl Mullen's Delivery

A rugby player goes to the doctor and says, 'It hurts when I touch my arm, my chest and my leg.' The doctor says, 'You've broken your finger.'

UNTO US A CHILD IS BORN
Doctors feature prominently in the story of Irish rugby. Ireland's first Grand Slam win was captained by Karl Mullen, who was an obstetrician. It is claimed that in his life he delivered enough babies to fill Lansdowne Road. One of the babies he delivered was Fiona Coghlan – the first woman to captain Ireland to a Grand Slam.

PREGNANT PAUSE
Long after his retirement as a player Karl Mullen was involved in one of the most famous incidents in Irish rugby. During a match, he was attending one of the great folk heroes of Irish rugby, Phil O'Callaghan, who was in the thick of the action.

After Philo put out his shoulder, Karl Mullen was to experience his tongue at first hand when he ran on the pitch to give him medical care. Dr Mullen said, 'I'll put it back but I warn you it will be painful.' He did and it was.

According to the story Philo was screaming his head off with the pain. The doctor turned to him and said, 'You should be ashamed of yourself. I was with a sixteen-year-old girl this morning in the Rotunda as she gave birth and there was not even a word of complaint from her.'

Philo replied, 'I wonder what she bloody well would have said if you tried putting the f**kin' thing back in.'

IT'S A SIN

Philo also shares another famous quip of former Irish international Trevor Brennan's remark to referee Alan Lewis: 'It's not a sin bin you need, it's a skip.'

75

MURPHY'S LAW

Johnny Murphy Makes His Mark

Former Irish fullback Johnny Murphy was a great captain of Leinster. He had a bus and hearse business and turned up for training one night in his hearse with a coffin inside. Some of the Leinster players found it to be disconcerting to be doing their press-ups beside a coffin and grumbled to Johnny. He just said, 'She's not going anywhere and doesn't mind waiting.'

ORATORY UNSURPASSED

Johnny's speeches were memorable not least because he was great at taking off posh accents. His opening sentence after a Connacht match was, 'Mr President of Leinster, Mr President of Connacht, players and the rest of you hangers on.' He made more politically incorrect remarks and was told by the 'blazers' to tone down his speeches.

The next week Leinster played Llanelli and beat the pants off them. Everyone was dying to know what Johnny would say. He began, 'Well lads I've got to be very careful what I say this week. It was a great honour for us to have the privilege of playing against such a famous side. My only regret is that BBC's *Rugby Special* wasn't here to see us beating the sh*t* out of ye. I know people will say ye were missing some of yer star players but don't forget we were missing one of our greatest stars – Hugo MacNeill. He couldn't get his f**king place – I have it.'

The whole place was in stitches and Ray Gravell in particular had to be picked off the floor he was laughing so hard.

DELIVERY SERVICE

Stewart McKinney tells a great story about Murphy. Johnny was collecting the flanker for a match. As usual he was late and McKinney was hassling him for his tardiness and telling him that he needed the time for a really good warm-up. Before they got to the ground Murphy pulled up the car sharply and McKinney assumed there was an emergency when his driver asked him to jump out. He duly did, only to find his bag thrown out after him and Murphy shouting out at him: 'Run the last f**king mile to the ground and you'll be nicely warmed up.'

HUGO'S CALL

Hugo MacNeill was capped 37 times for Ireland and, were it not for him, Johnny Murphy would have won more caps. Hugo scored eight international tries, a record for a fullback making him one of Ireland's greatest attacking fullbacks of all time.

He was the victim of a good put-down, though: 'I was down in Cork with Moss Finn, Donal Lenihan and Michael Kiernan, and we were having lunch with five or six rugby fans. In any other place in Ireland sports fans would have passed the time by picking their greatest ever Irish team. Not so in Cork. They picked the worst ever Irish team! I kept my head down as they discussed the merits of three of my predecessors for the position, expecting to have my name mentioned at any minute.

After they made their choice for fullback I remarked with relief, "I suppose I can relax now." Quick as a flash someone said, "Hang on boy we haven't picked the subs yet!"'

CALL ON HOLD

Ireland's form in the post-Mick Doyle era slumped dramatically, culminating in a humiliating 35–3 defeat at Twickenham in 1988. At least the match generated one of the most celebrated stories in recent Irish rugby folklore. MacNeill went AWOL during the game. Although Ireland went in with a 3–0 lead at half-time, they were slaughtered in the second half. When the second half started Hugo was not there and nobody knew where he was. The joke after the game was that he went in to make a phone call. By the time he came back on to the pitch they had run in for 2 tries!

76

SLAM-TASTIC

Paul O'Connell Helps Ireland Win the Grand Slam

Paul O'Connell has to get some of the credit for Ireland's Grand Slam win in 2018. Keith Earls was in the form of his life and put his resurgence down to a quiet word from his former Ireland and Munster teammate. Earls observed, 'After speaking to Paulie and having roomed with him for a couple of years, we used to be a bit nervous before games. He said if he had his chance over again he wouldn't worry as much and I took something from that.'

MUNSTER MAGIC

In his distinguished career with Munster, O'Connell played in many of Munster's 'miracle matches'. In 2018 he witnessed one in the stands as Munster beat Toulon 20-19 with a stunning Andrew Conway try with four minutes left in a drama-filled European quarter-final. This led to bedlam in the stands. There was only one word to describe it – Munsteresque.

Immediately after the game Munster fans started to make their plans for the semi-final in France against Dan Carter and

Racing 92. Paul O'Connell was no different. When he went home that evening he told his wife Emily that he would be making the journey. She calmly informed him that he could not travel because that day they had to go to a christening. Paul shook his head fiercely and less calmly told her that there was no way he was missing a match of that importance for 'just' a christening.

A pregnant pause ensued.

Then Emily gave him the type of withering look that only a wife can give her husband after he has committed a terrible crime in her eyes.

She replied in a calm voice – but with a conviction that was not open to challenge: 'You do realise that it is our child that is getting christened.'

77

THE TERRIBLE TWINS

Galwey and Clohessy

Mick Galwey loves the rivalry between Cork and Limerick rugby. Some have said that in Munster rugby Cork is the political wing, Limerick is the military!

YOUNG AT HEART

Gaillimh retains fond memories of his time with Ireland: 'Keith Wood was one player who could turn a game. He played hurling and Gaelic football in Clare and that didn't do him any harm. Woodie was the world's number one hooker but he was still one of the lads. He was one of the Limerick Under-14s as we called them with myself and Peter Clohessy. Of course Clohessy is one of the great characters of Irish sport. I remember once playing in France with Munster when Peter got a bad knock in the knee and had to be carried off. It was the strangest sight I ever saw in a match because they guys who brought on the stretcher for him were wearing Wellingtons! I said to the Claw, "Don't worry. The fire brigade are coming."'

BON APPÉTIT

Galwey once joked that the way Clohessy prepared for playing against England was by eating a bullock alive. Chaos ensued before one game when there was no animal available – so he had to take the only available option which was to eat a clown. When Gaillimh asked him what it was like the Claw coolly replied: 'He tasted a bit funny.'

SWEET MEMORIES

The Claw looks back on his career with affection:

'I think the nice thing is when I look back now at my career what I remember most is all the good times we had on and off the pitch. Although we trained hard, we had a lot of fun.

'My fondest memory is before we played Scotland one time. The night before the match Mick Galwey discovered his togs were missing. There was a minor panic because nobody else had any to spare. Eventually someone got him togs. Ireland were sponsored by Nike at the time. The problem was that Mick's togs didn't have the Nike name or swish so someone gave him a black marker and he wrote the name Nike on the togs. Later that night I crept into his room and changed the word "Nike" to "Mike' and wrote "Mike loves Joan".

'The next day we were changing in the dressing room before the match when I saw Mick putting on his togs. He didn't notice the change but noticed I was laughing at him. He asked, "Okay, what have you done to me?" when I told him he had a great laugh. It was just an hour before a big international but it was a great way of breaking the ice for us.'

78

HOT STUFF

Moss in Dubai

One of Moss Keane's most famous trips was to Dubai where he had a speaking engagement. According to legend he required so much Dutch courage before taking off that he had to be lifted off the plane. As he was carried off, people watching thought it was part of the ritual of a Muslim funeral. When he returned home he was asked about his most striking impression of life in a Muslim country. He replied, 'If you steal anything they cut off your hand. If you tell a lie they cut off your tongue. I didn't see one flasher in the whole place.'

He was also asked about the food and drink:

'The drink was fine but the food was mad hot. No wonder these people are called the Shiites.'

MODERATION

Yet a further classic story about Moss goes back to one of his tours with the Barbarians in Wales. At one stage his team went to the bar after a game of golf. Although everybody else was drinking beer, Moss, with commendable patriotism, was drinking Guinness and was knocking back two pints to everyone else's one. As dinnertime approached it was decided it was time to return to the team hotel. As people prepared to leave somebody shouted 'One for the road'. Ten pints later for the team at large and twenty pints later for Moss, the team was again summoned to the team bus. Moss was asked if the team should stay for one more drink. He shook his head. When questioned why he was opposed to the idea, Moss replied, 'No I don't. To be sure, I don't want to be making a pig of myself.'

TIGHT TACTICS

Moss featured in a story former Irish manager Paul McNaughton recalled for me:

'We were playing against France in 1980 but we lost 19–18. The backs were playing well and we got a bit of confidence and we decided to run the ball from our own 25. It was unheard of in England, let alone Ireland, to do this at the time. The Irish fans were completely perplexed at this sudden outpouring of adventure to see the ball going through hands across the pitch. Then the ball hit Rodney O'Donnell on the shoulder and France got possession and scored a try. All the backs were terrified we'd be dropped for the next match because we'd run the ball! The next time we got a scrum Ollie Campbell asked us which move we wanted to play. As one we all said: "Boot the f**king ball into touch as far up the pitch as possible!"

'Roll the clock forward ten years and we were playing in a Golden Oldies match in Bermuda for Ireland against America under lights. The back line included Mick Quinn, Freddie McLennan, Terry Kennedy and myself. Donal Spring was the captain but he got sick so Pa Whelan took his place as skipper. When he gave us our tactical talk, it was as if we been caught in a time warp because his tactical instruction was simply: "We're going to keep the ball tight." The backs all looked at each other. I knew the others were thinking the exact same thing as me: "For f**k's sake we're nearly forty. We're playing America. Let's run the f**king ball at last." Moss Keane was our number 8. At the first scrum Pa said: "Okay Mossie, you take the ball on." Mossie made a break but one of the Americans nearly cut him in half. The Americans had very little skill but they were ferocious tacklers. At the second scrum Pa said: "Okay Mossie, you take the ball on." Again Mossie made the break and this time one of the Americans nearly killed him with a tackle. The third time we got a scrum Pa said: "Okay let the ball out to the backs." I'll never forget Mick Quinn screeching the immortal words in at him: "Hold on to the f**king ball. Ye wanted it. So keep it f**king tight!"'

UP NORTH

Since his retirement Mick Quinn has gone to become known as one of the great raconteurs of Irish rugby. He is so good that is often hard to distinguish between fact and fiction when he speaks. A month after Moss Keane published his autobiography Mick met Ollie Campbell and convinced Ollie that the book had sold 70,000 copies in the first week. If that were the case, it would have been the biggest selling Irish book ever!

Quinny is also a great mimic and 'did' Moss Keane better than Moss himself! I could fill this book just with Quinn's stories of Moss but the following are my favourites:

'When the troubles in the North were at their height, Lansdowne played a match in Belfast. After the match the lads stopped for a case of beer in an off-licence because the drink was so much cheaper up there, which would set them up nicely for the train journey home. One evening, though, there was a bomb scare which ruled out travelling by train and after a long delay a bus arrived. The problem was that there was no room on the bus for Moss, Rory Moroney and I. Moss had already disposed of a couple of his beers and was not too happy with the prospect of having to wait even longer. He marched on to the bus and said: "Excuse me, this bus is going to crash." At first nobody moved but then a little old man got up and walked up timidly to the towering figure of Moss and said: "Excuse me sir, but where did you say this bus was going to?"'

THE AULD ENEMY

In 1974 Ireland faced England at Twickenham. Although they were underdogs Ireland won 26–21. Before the game the Irish players were running onto the pitch when they were stopped in the tunnel by an official in a blazer who had the archetypal RAF moustache. He said, 'Tally-ho boys. Tally ho. The BBC cameras are not ready for you yet.' The Irish lads were just itching to get on the pitch and found the waiting a pain, particularly when they were joined in the tunnel by the English team. The English were led by their captain, John Pullin, who was shouting at his team about Waterloo. The Irish players couldn't understand what Waterloo had to do with them. The English players looked bigger and stronger than their Irish counterparts. As they were always on television, they were all huge stars and had mega names like David Duckham and Andy Ripley. The Irish players were studiously trying to avoid eye contact with them as they planned to rough them up a bit on the pitch. However, Tony Neary went over and tapped Moss on the shoulder and said, 'Moss, best of luck. May the best team win.'

Keane growled back, 'I f**king hope not!'

A MEMORY LAPSE

Moss was interviewed for the *Irish Independent* by the late Sean Diffley in the 1970s. The meeting took place in a hostelry in Rathgar. There was a significant level of liquid refreshment consumed, so much so that Diffo rang Moss the next day to ask: 'What was it that we were talking about yesterday?'

79

SUPERSTITIOUS MINDS

Rodney O'Donnell in Australia

Ireland's tour of Australia in 1979 provided one particularly amusing memory of former Ireland captain Johnny Moloney:

'I was sharing a room with Terry Kennedy at one stage. Rodney O'Donnell was rooming with Mike Gibson. I can't think of a greater contrast of personalities unless you put Tony O'Reilly rooming with Moss Keane! Mike was very dedicated, prepared meticulously and normally went to bed by ten. Rodney was very laid-back and an early night for him would be midnight. He went to Australia as a twenty-two-year-old St Mary's fullback, an uncapped unknown, and returned as a hero.

'Rodney's middle name could have been "Superstition". He had a huge fear of anything connected with the number thirteen. On tour not only did he refuse to stay in a room numbered thirteen, or 213, or a room on the thirteenth floor but he would not even stay in a room in which the numbers added up to thirteen, like 274.

'When he believed in something there could be no deviation. He always insisted on being the last man on the team bus and would patiently wait for everyone to assemble on to the bus regardless of the climatic conditions. He refused to walk over a line. On a stone pavement he would make the most bizarre movements to avoid treading on a line. Such an event could only trigger tragedies of apocalyptic proportions. With all this practice some of his fellow players said he could have been world champion at hopscotch.

'A Friday the thirteenth fell on the Lions tour in 1980. Ollie Campbell and John Robbie rose at 6.30 a.m. that morning and with taping made lines right across the lobby outside O'Donnell's room and pasted the number thirteen all over the lobby and the elevator. As a result Rodney was afraid to leave the room for the entire day.

'He had an interesting theory about the psychology of the rugby ball. When an opponent had kicked a goal against his team he felt much better if the ball came down in such a way that he was able to throw it back over the crossbar, his theory being that the next time, the ball was either unsure where to go, or would lose the habit of travelling in the right direction.

'Yet another ritual was preparing to tog out before games. He had to put on his togs in such a way that the material did not touch his skin on the way up. Should such a calamity occur he would begin the whole process again – and if necessary again and again until he got it exactly right. The second part of this operation was that he would never button up his togs until he was running onto the field.

'He was preoccupied with exactitudes to the point that he went around every room adjusting pictures so that they hung straight on the walls. This tendency was dramatically illustrated on Ireland's tour to Australia in 1979. In the middle of Noel Murphy's team talk, he jumped up, to the astonishment of all present, to adjust the position of the telephone.

'One of his most famous idiosyncrasies was his desire to get into bed each night without touching the bottom sheet. The task had to be executed with military like precision. If he failed the first time he tried, he kept trying, until he got it exactly right. Only then did he allow himself to relax.

'Rodney dropped into our room for a chat one night on that Australian tour and later we were joined by Paul McNaughton. Paul asked Rodney who was he rooming with. When he answered "Mike Gibson", Paul pretended to be very sympathetic, which made Rodney a tiny bit uncomfortable because Paul had shared with Gibo the week before. He told him that when he went back into the room, he would discover that the sheets and blankets on his bed would be folded neatly, halfway back, the light would be left on in the bathroom and the bathroom door would be left slightly ajar. Then when he went into bed, he would be asleep about half an hour when Gibo would jump on top of him in the bed. Rodney was very sceptical but a couple of hours later, when he went back to his room, it was just as Paul described: the light on in the toilet, the bathroom door slightly ajar and the covers folded back on the bed. The next morning he came down for his breakfast like a zombie. He told us he hadn't slept a wink all night because he was waiting for Gibo to jump on top of him!'

80

TALES OF THE UNEXPECTED

Trevor Brennan Saves the Day

Irish rugby has produced many tales of the unexpected.

Trevor Brennan is one of the great rugby characters. He is larger than life and made a massive impact when he moved to play rugby in France.

Girvan Dempsey recalls one moment when Brennan shocked his Leinster teammates:

'Trevor was responsible for my funniest moment in rugby. It was one of my first starts for Leinster and we were playing Treviso on a pre-season tour in Italy. After we flew into the airport and collected our bags, our manager at the time, Jim Glennon, came in to tell us there would be a delay because there was a difficulty with Dean Oswald's passport and that the problem was compounded by the fact that there was a language problem. Trevor immediately piped up: "I'll sort it out for you. I know the lingo."

'We were all stunned because Trevor was not known for his linguistic skills. When we turned to him and asked him when he learned to speak Italian he coolly replied: "I worked in Luigi's chip shop one summer!"'

A TOUCH OF CLASS

Former Leinster manager and rugby raconteur Ken Ging tells a classic Brennan story:

'One day Sir Anthony O'Reilly was driving home in his brand-new Rolls Royce. He was smiling because it was the most magnificent model. He pulls up beside a Mini car at a traffic light, with a black cloud of smoke trailing from the exhaust and black tape on the windows. Trevor Brennan gets out from the mini and walks up to O'Reilly and signals to him to roll down the windows. The Lions legend duly does so and Trevor asks, "Do you have a telephone in there, Anto?"

'O'Reilly replied, "I have."

'"Do you have a TV and a DVD player?"

'"I do and before you ask, I've also got a fully stocked cocktail bar."

'"Have you a bed?"

'"I haven't a bed."

'Trevor replies, "I've a bed in my car" and walked off.

'This really got to O'Reilly. The following day he instructed his personal assistant to get a four-poster bed in his car. A few minutes later the secretary returned and explained to O'Reilly that this would cost a fortune. O'Reilly snapped back angrily, "I don't care. Just get me that bed."

'Two weeks later O'Reilly was driving home and feeling really proud of his state-of-the-art bed, with beautiful satin sheets. Then he got dejected because he thought he would never see Trevor again to show him his new prize possession. He pulled up in Tesco's to buy his groceries and to his great delight he spotted Trevor's Mini in the car park. He walked over and knocked at the window. Two minutes later Trevor pulls down the window and said, "Ah, Anto, it's yourself."'

O'Reilly was nearly jumping for joy. "Trevor, Trevor, let me show you the great new bed I have installed in my car."

Brennan shook his head and looked at him scornfully. "Do you mean to tell me you dragged me out of the shower just to show me a bed!"

THE STREETS OF DUBLIN

The most famous Trevor tale goes back to the day he was walking down Dublin City Centre, when he saw a man dead on the street. He pulled out his mobile phone and rang the gardai. He told the guard the situation and the boy in blue replied, "Okay you're there in Exchequer Street. Spell Exchequer Street."

Trevor started, "Exc, no Exh, no . . ."

He paused and said, "Hang on a second. I'm just going to drag him round to Dame Street and I'll ring you back then.'"

MILLER'S CROSSING

Munster faced Leinster in the inaugural Celtic League final in Lansdowne Road. Eric Miller was sent off after only twenty minutes in the game but Leinster won the final nonetheless. In the Leinster dressing room afterwards Eric was distraught. Sensing his pain, his teammates rallied and one by one went to console him. Finally it was Trevor's turn. He grabbed a pale-faced Miller roughly by the shoulders and said: 'If we lost the game you wouldn't be safe in Tora-fu**king-Bora!'

TARZAN BOY

Warren Gatland tells the story of how one day Trevor Brennan came to him in training and said he was feeling a bit tired and wondered if he had any suggestions. Gatland replied, 'Take four or five bananas and that should help.'

The next morning Trevor went up to apologise profusely. 'Gats, I'm sorry I could only manage twenty-nine bananas.'

Gatland shook his head as he said, 'Trevor I said four or five bananas not forty-five!'

THE BYRNE-ING ISSUE:

Many Irish players have great service to their province over many years. Shane Byrne was one such example.

The former Leinster manager Ken Ging gave a speech at the testimonial dinner to mark Byrne's 100th Leinster Cap. He told the story of two elderly Americans who were finally discovered and against all odds found to be alive in a disused Japanese POW camp having been captured during World War II. They first asked, 'How is President Roosevelt?'

'Oh, he died a long time ago.'

'And how is Stalin?'

'Oh, he died a long time ago?'

'Please tell us that Winston Churchill is still alive and well.'

'Alas, I'm afraid he died as well.'

'Tell us, is Shane Byrne still playing for Leinster?'

ISN'T IT IRONIC

Eric Miller's international career began when he was invited to a training camp with the Irish squad in the Algarve towards the end of Murray Kidd's reign. It rained for the week!

IT'S GOT TO BE PERFECT

The opening line to the fourth film in the Star Wars series was: 'In every generation a new hero is born.' The line could have been written for John Eales. The former Australian captain's nickname is 'Nobody' as in 'nobody's perfect'. Mind you Eales has often pointed out that nobody has ever called him 'Nobody' to his face.

You can only achieve a limited amount in rugby by coaching. It's really a question of natural ability. Eales was gifted with extraordinary levels of natural ability. A powerhouse in the scrum, he was one of the few forwards who was adept with kicking penalties and conversions – like 'the Panther' from Aberavon, Allan Martin (who toured with the Lions to South Africa in 1980 and kicked five penalties and three conversions in his thirty-four appearances for Wales), or John Muldoon (who famously scored a conversion against Leinster in his final home game for Connacht in 2018).

In 1996 Eales toured Ireland with Australia. There was one heart-stopping moment for him on the tour. He was having his breakfast at the team hotel in Dublin when a message came over the intercom for Eales to contact reception urgently. The message was repeated two further times in tones of ever increasing urgency. Becoming concerned and suspecting a family crisis at home, he identified himself and was quickly given a telephone.

'Mr Eales.'

'Yes.'

'This is your 8 a.m. wake up call . . .'

81

CAPTAIN FANTASTIC

Willie Duggan Captains Ireland

When he burst onto the Irish team Hugo MacNeill was in awe of Willie Duggan. In 1985, following Duggan's retirement, their relationship was more like that between two equals. Hugo promised to get Willie tickets for the Scotland match. He was sharing a room with Brian Spillane and the phone rang the night before the match. Hugo answered with the words, 'The Spillane-MacNeill suite.' Immediately he heard Willie respond, 'You might as well be sleeping together, you spend so much time together on the pitch!'

LONG LIFE
Like Moss Keane, Duggan lived by the adage that moderate drinkers live longer and it served them right.

CAPTAIN FANTASTIC?
Duggan was an Irish national institution. A man with little enthusiasm for training, his most celebrated comment was, 'Training takes the edge off my game.' Duggan was one of a

rare group of players who always made a point of bringing a pack of cigarettes with him onto the training field. Asked once in a radio interview if this was a major problem for him fitness-wise he took the broadcaster by surprise by saying that it was a positive advantage: 'Sure if it was not for the fags I would be offside all day long.'

CHESTY

There was an inherent contradiction in Duggan's preparation for matches. He always had a cigarette five minutes before going out on the pitch, then he took out a jar of Vicks and rubbed it on his chest. To put it at its kindest, he had an unconventional approach!

HOT STUFF

Willie turned up for training with the Irish squad and when he was told to warm up he replied, 'I don't need to. I had the heater on in the car.'

TIRED AND EMOTIONAL

Willie was finding it difficult to train with his club team, Black-rock in Dublin. It was agreed, at Irish hooker John Cantrell's suggestion, that one Sunday the entire squad would go down to Kilkenny Rugby Club to facilitate Willie because he lived there. That morning they were all there apart from guess who? Willie! Somebody had to go and wake him because he had slept it out.

UNORTHODOX

Donal Lenihan told me of his admiration for Willie Duggan:

'The best Irish forward I ever played with was Willie Duggan. He was the Scarlet Pimpernel of Irish rugby because he was so hard to find for training! Having said that, he wouldn't have survived in international rugby so long without training. Willie took his captaincy manual from a different world. His speeches were not comparable with anything I'd ever heard before or since.

'One of my clearest memories of Willie's captaincy is of the morning after the Scotland game in 1984: the papers all had a picture of Duggan with his arm around Tony Ward and speaking to him. It was just before Wardy was taking a penalty. It appeared that Willie was acting the real father figure but, knowing him as I do, my guess was he was saying: "If you miss this penalty, I'll kick you all the way to Kilkenny!"'

82

AMAZING GRACE

Tom Grace Captains Ireland

Tom Grace had a very different approach to the Irish captaincy than Duggan.

When Grace played rugby, he had jet black hair and a Beatles haircut so it came as an enormous shock to him when his hair went grey. He was up in Donegal before one of the international matches with his family. RTÉ were showing some footage of tries from previous seasons. When they started to show a few of Grace's, his wife rushed out to call his son, Conor, who was six at the time, to see his dad in his prime. When Conor came in, she pointed to the television excitedly and showed Grace in full flight. Conor just shook his head and said, 'No it's not him. My dad has grey hair.' Then he just turned on his heels and ran out to play soccer.

SUDS

One of the captains of the UCD side Grace played on was Peter Sutherland – who became a giant in the business and economic world after he became European Commissioner in the 1980s. 'Suds' put his own stamp on the captaincy. The night before the Cup matches the UCD players met in his house in Monkstown. A walk on Dun Laoghaire pier became part of the ritual. For the first match they had sandwiches, tea, coffee and light drinks. As their Cup run progressed the refreshments became ever more lavish. The night before the semi-final they had a totally fabulous dinner with all kinds of delicacies. Then Suds gave his speech. The food was incredibly memorable. The speech was not. The next day UCD lost narrowly . . . 28–3!

TESTING TIMES

Mick Quinn has a particular memory of Tom Grace:

'Mike Gibson had a great temperament. The only time I ever saw him rattled was on the tour to New Zealand in 1976. We were really up against it in some of the matches. I remember Tom Grace saying at breakfast, "Quinner, do you think we'll get out of the place before they realise we're afraid of them?" We laughed at the time but I wonder!

'Barry McGann did not share the general concern. He was playing at out-half that day and was kicking everything – and I mean everything. At one stage Mike Gibson yelled for a pass but Barry said, "Listen Mike when I meet a player who can run as fast as I can kick it then I'll think about passing it!"'

WAITING

Barry is less charitable when it comes to English rugby. One of his favourite questions is: 'What do you call an Englishman holding a bottle of champagne after a Six Nations game?'

'Waiter.'

JOHNNY COME LATELY

Tom Grace was succeeded as Irish captain by his clubmate Johnny Moloney. Johnny was a very single-minded player. In a schoolboy match he was charging through for a try when a despairing dive by his marker robbed him of his shorts. True to form he raced through for the try in his underpants before worrying about getting new togs.

83

INTERNATIONAL RELATIONS

Mick Quinn Makes Friends

Mick Quinn had a great affection for the late Ray Gravell:

'Ray, like a lot of the Welsh players, was really nationalistic. Once before an international when I was sub, I went into the toilet and I heard Ray in the next cubicle singing arias about the welcome in the hills in Wales. I told him that the only reason they welcomed us in the hills was that they were too mean to invite us into their homes! There's a limit to the amount of Ray's singing I can take so I asked him to give it a rest but he went on and on. To shut him up I filled a bucket of cold water and threw it over him in the cubicle. I fled because he came out like a raging bull and I said nothing about the incident in our dressing room. When the Welsh team came out some of our lads remarked that Ray must have gone through an awfully heavy warm-up because the sweat was rolling off him.'

FRIENDS FROM FAR AWAY
Through his involvement with the Wolfhounds, Quinn continued to have plenty of contact with the giants of international rugby:

'I met J.P.R. Williams one day at the end of 1990. It was the time Wales had gone thirteen international matches without winning. He's always beating the nationalist drum going on about the rugby in the valleys in Wales and how central it is to Welsh life. It was nice, in a way, to see him eating humble pie so I asked him what his most fervent wish for Welsh rugby was in 1991. He answered: "I hope that Wales win a match." He then asked me what my most fervent wish for Irish rugby was for that year. I said: "For Ireland to win the Triple Crown, the Grand Slam and the World Cup." He said: "Ah come on Mick, be serious." All I said to him was: "You f**ing started it."'

BARING IT ALL

An English international caused one of Quinn's most embarrassing moments:

'The former English international Gareth Chilcott earns a fortune from making speeches. I played him once in a golf match during the Lions' tour of New Zealand. At one stage my ball trickled into a pond. I could see it and asked him to hold my hand as I leaned over to retrieve it. He said he would but deliberately let me go and I toppled in. I had to take off all my clothes and try and squeeze the water out of them, much to the bemusement of the women who were playing on the other greens!'

WITH A LITTLE HELP FROM MY FRIENDS

Quinn developed a closer friendship than he envisaged with a legend of South African rugby:

'At one stage Willie John McBride and I were invited there to play for a World XV against the Springboks. I was interviewed on South African TV and asked what I thought of the main contenders for the number 10 shirt with the Springboks and if any out-half had impressed me. I mentioned that I had been taken by this new kid called Naas Botha, who I had seen play on television. The next day I was training when this fella came over to me and I recognised him as Botha. He wanted to thank me for my compliments.

'Naas was a hugely controversial figure in South Africa. They either loved him or hated him. We got on very well and I subsequently invited him to come over and get some experience in Lansdowne. I thought nothing more about it until some months later I got a phone call at home. It was Naas. He said he would like to take up my offer of hospitality. I told him that would be welcome and asked him when would he be travelling over. Then he told me: "Well Mr Quinn, I'm ringing you from a place called O'Connell Street in Dublin!" He brought his brother, Darius, with him, who since became a Dutch Reformed Minister. He used to organise prayer meetings in my house!'

HOW NOT TO MAKE FRIENDS

While Quinn's gregarious personality has won him many friends in rugby, it has not always helped his career to advance:

'In general I have great memories of playing with Leinster. One of the people I played with was Brian O'Driscoll's dad, Frank. Like Brian he was a great tackler. I played my final match for Leinster in the Sports Ground in Galway in 1984 when we were going for the Championship. It was an awful day with the wind and the rain which made it impossible for me to run the ball. There was only a handful of people in the stand, one of whom was Mick Cuddy, "the Cud", former Irish and Leinster selector. The only thing I could hear was a constant chorus from "the Cud" of "Run the bloody ball, Leinster". I got so fed up I shouted up at him, "Cuddy, shut your fu*k*n mouth." He was furious and roared down at me, "That's the last time you'll play for Leinster!"'

BORING

Quinn enjoys the humour in other sports:

'One player I always admired was Manchester United's Denis Irwin. I attended Irwin's testimonial dinner. Jack Charlton brought the house town there with his unconventional tribute to Denis. Jack said, "Denis was the consummate professional; the best fullback to play for Manchester United; the best full-back to play for the Republic of Ireland; he was always our most consistent player; he never made mistakes; he never gave the ball away; he was always on time for training; always first on the bus for training, he never let you down nor never once caused a problem. What a boring, f**king bast**d!"'

QUINNSWORTH

Quinn claims the credit for Mike Gibson's great displays for Ireland. Mick always blessed himself with Lourdes water before matches and splashed some on Gibson's legs when he wasn't looking, and Gibo went out and played like a genius.

Quinn was such a prankster that any time he passed on a message people got suspicious. At one stage he came into the dressing room before a match against Wales and said to Tony Ward, 'There's a strange-looking auld fella out there who wants a word with you.' Knowing Quinn's reputation Ward was very apprehensive and also wanted to prepare for the match. He told Quinn not to be annoying him or a more colourful variation of it. Eventually he agreed to go out but with some trepidation. Who was there simply just to shake his hand and say how much he admired him as a player? The former leader of the Labour Party Neil Kinnock.

GRIZZLY ALEX

They don't come much tougher than Alex 'Grizz' Wyllie. The former All Black coach was not a man to mess with on the pitch as Ireland's fly-half Mick Quinn discovered to his cost on Ireland's New Zealand tour in 1976. Ireland were losing 15–3 to Canterbury. Quinn was sub. From his point of view everything was going great. When you are a sub, you do not really want things to be going well for the team because if it does how else are you going to get your place back? Fullback Larry Moloney broke his arm, so Tony Ensor replaced him. Wallace McMaster got injured and with a sinking in his heart Quinn realised he would have to play on the wing. It was his first time ever to play in that position. He was petrified and wished he was wearing brown shorts!

As he walked on 'Grizz' Wyllie came over to him and said: 'You've come a long way to die son.' When Quinn was in school his coach had always drilled into him the belief that he should never let anybody intimidate him. At that stage he made the biggest mistake of his life. He said to Wyllie: 'Listen pal, if my dog had a face like yours, I would shave his arse and get him to walk backwards.' Every chance Wyllie got after that he clobbered Quinn. Even when the ball was somewhere else he kept coming at Quinn. When the Irish man said the ball is over there, Wyllie answered: 'I couldn't give a f**k where the ball is. I'm going to kill you.'

NICKNAMES

Perhaps Quinn's most enduring legacy to the rugby landscape is the number of players he has given nicknames to:

'I called former international scrum-half Tony Doyle "Gandhi" because there was more meat in a cheese sandwich. I called the Wesley player Dave Priestman "Vicarman" because I told him it was ridiculous for a Protestant to be called priest. I call Brendan Mullin "Bugs Bunny" because of his smile. I also christened Harry Steele "Stainless" for obvious reasons and Jean-Pierre Rives, now a noted sculptor, and the living proof that you don't have to be big to be a world-class forward, "Je t'aime" because he had such charm with women. I called my Lansdowne clubmate Rory Moroney "the Reverend Moroney" because he spent two years in the priesthood.'

84

DEAR JOHN

John Robbie Settles in South Africa

Ollie Campbell would probably be seen as the crown prince of his generation of Irish rugby. Mick Quinn is more likely to be seen as the clown prince. Yet he has a serious side:

'I would like to think I have an eye for a young player of promise. The first time I saw John Robbie play was when he played for High School. I went over to him after the match and said, "You'll play for Ireland." Years later I won £100 for him. I was playing a club match and there was a guy slagging me all through the match saying I was useless. We got a penalty fifteen yards inside our half and ten yards in from the touch-line. I had the wind behind me and John bet a pound at a hundred to one that I would score – and I did.'

UNIVERSITY CHALLENGE

Robbie went on to study at Cambridge University, where he was elected skipper of the rugby team ahead of Eddie Butler, who was destined to become one of the legends of Welsh rugby. Robbie was a bit taken aback by the side's preparation for the glamour fixture against Oxford. A few days before the big name they had a nuts and port dinner and toasted Oxford in the traditional way. They stood and said G.D.B.O. – God Damn Bloody Oxford. Robbie scored 17 points in the game, including a spectacular try. He jokes that his one regret was that he missed out on Alastair Hignell's record for a varsity game. He had instructed the team to run a penalty from in front of the posts at one stage but had he known he was just two off the record he would have kicked it.

LAUGHTER IS THE BEST MEDICINE

Robbie retains many funny memories from his time with the Lions in 1980:

'At one stage I went fishing with Ollie Campbell in Durban. Ollie got as sick as a dog and was hurling his guts overboard. He also got caught a whopper of a fish, a Barracuda. As he was feeling so ill, he asked one of the crew to help him row in the fish. He was promptly told: "The rule of this boat is that you pull in your own fish." At the best of times Ollie looks pale but that day he looked whiter than a sheet!

'But the funniest moment, I think, came after the third Test in Port Elizabeth. The Lions had gone into the game two down, and so it was the decider. In shocking weather we lost 12–10, and thereby the series. The Lions were very disappointed – it was a game that had been won everywhere but on the scoreboard.

'At one stage, quite near the end, we were all called into a special meeting. Syd Millar addressed us and asked if we were unhappy, as he had read reports to that effect. We all said we were having a whale of time. He then asked us if we would all return to tour South Africa if selected. Ironically enough, I was the only player who indicated that I would have to think about it; everyone else said they would. In fact Peter Morgan, the young Welsh utility player who had played in only a few games on the tour, brought the house down by saying that he'd love to come back again as next time they might let him have a game!'

DRIVE SAFELY

John Robbie retains a funny memory of Noel Murphy from his time as Lions manager in 1980:

'Jean-Pierre Rives, the celebrated French flanker, was there as well at the end of the tour. I was in Pretoria with Noel Murphy at some function or other, and we got a lift back with some bloke in a sports car who was taking Jean-Pierre back to Johannesburg. We got hopelessly lost, and I recall that, as we sped at breakneck speed down a back road, we could see a fork ahead. "Go left," said Noel to the driver. "Please go right," said I. "Please go fuckeeng slower!" screamed Rives, who could speak little English, from the back seat. The driver, a South African, was laughing so much he nearly crashed.'

WATCH IT

Robbie had a memorable moment after the third Test in Port Elizabeth. The Lions had gone into the game two down, and so it was the decider. In shocking weather the Lions lost 12–10, and thereby the series. The Lions were very disappointed – it was a game that had been won everywhere but on the scoreboard. Still, there was no sulking. In the best tradition the Lions decided to bury their sorrows and so a monumental p*ss-up was held. A few equally drunk South African fans had got into the hotel's off-limits area, and a bit of a skirmish developed. At one stage the Lions manager Jack Matthews chucked a couple of the intruders down the stairs from the floor. He picked up a watch off the ground and flung it down after the guys, with a cry of "And take your blasted watch with you!" Then he saw his bare wrist: in the excitement he had flung his own watch down the stairs.

MIXED FORTUNES

After the tour Robbie decided to stay on in South Africa and further his rugby career there:

'When I moved to South Africa I discovered that one of the benefits of being a high-profile sportsman in South Africa was sponsorship. I was given a car at a time when I was dropped by Transvaal. The panel on the door read: "Opel supports John Robbie." Some wit suggested that the lower panel should read: "Transvaal doesn't."'

HOMEWARD BOUND

On his rare trips back to Ireland, Robbie enjoys the opportunity of seeing the Irish team play if it presents itself. He doesn't always get the reception he expects:

'I left Ireland in 1981 after Ireland were whitewashed! In '82 Ireland won the Triple Crown and in '83 the Championship. I timed my first trip home to Ireland in '84 to coincide with Ireland's Five Nations game against Wales. Ireland were white-washed again that season. I had missed out on two glorious years for Ireland and came home to see them losing again, an experience I was all too familiar with from my playing days. After the Welsh game I was still in the stand as the crowd was thinning. I heard a voice shouting, "Robbie, Robbie". I looked around until I found the owner of this voice. When I eventually met this stranger's eye he said: "John Robbie, I'm addressing you." I was very flattered to be recognised and gave him the royal wave. After all the drama, though, he took the wind out of my sails when he said: "You're some f**king good luck charm!"'

85

THE LION KING

The Legend of Willie John

The most successful British Lions team of all time was that which toured South Africa in 1974. Their overall record in their twenty-two matches read: won 21, drawn 1, lost 0, points for 729, points against 207. After their 12–3 victory in the First Test, skipper Willie John McBride warned his fellow forwards to expect a bruising encounter: 'You have not seen anything yet. They will throw everything at you, even the kitchen sink.'

THE NUMBERS GAME

One night on the '74 Lions tour a group of players were partying and disturbed the other guests in their hotel in the middle of the night. An undiplomatic war broke out. The tiny hotel manager tried to keep the peace. Two scantily clad players were parading around the corridors and he roared at them to get back into their rooms. Not liking his attitude they told him with all due lack of politeness what to do with himself. The manager's threat to ring the police was met with no reaction. At this point along came Willie John McBride. The manager thought his problems were solved at the sight of the Lions captain arriving. When McBride seemed to be ignoring the matter, the manager repeated his threat to call the police. Willie John called him forward with a tilt of his head. The manager breathed a sigh of relief. His threat had worked. He was in for a big disappointment as McBride bent down to him and whispered, 'How many will there be?'

ONE POLICEMAN AND HIS DOG

Willie John went back to the party. Some time later a group of riot police arrived with their dogs. Again Willie John intervened decisively. He went down to the coffee machine and bought some milk and gave it to the dogs and then invited the police to join the party. They did and had the night of their lives.

When the Lions won the series in 1974 a magnificent party was staged in the hotel. The festive spirit got a little out of hand and every fire extinguisher and water hose in the hotel was set off. The problem was that nobody thought to turn them off. The result was that the next morning the hotel could have done with the services of Noah's Ark. The touring manager was summoned the next morning to explain the actions of his team. He had gone to bed early and had no idea what had happened until he discovered himself thigh deep in water. He half-walked, half-swam up to Willie John's room and prepared to knock on the door only to discover that the door had been a casualty of the flood. To his astonishment, McBride was calmly sitting on his bed, puffing contentedly on his pipe, as it bobbed around on the water. The manager lost control and launched into a vicious tirade. Finally, Willie John replied, 'Alan, can I ask you one question?'

'What?'

'Is there anybody dead?'

CLEAN CUT

Not surprisingly, there is much folklore about Willie John. One of the stories told about him goes back to the Lions tour to South Africa in 1974 when he went into a diner that looked as though it had seen better days with Andy Irvine. As they slid into a booth, Irvine wiped some crumbs from the seat. Then he took a napkin and wiped some mustard from the table. The waitress, in a dirty uniform, came over and asked if they wanted some menus.

'No, thanks,' said Andy, 'I'll just have a cup of black coffee.'

'I'll have a black coffee, too,' Willie John said. 'And please make sure the cup is clean.'

The waitress shot him a nasty look. She turned and marched off to the kitchen. Two minutes later, she was back.

'Two cups of black coffee,' she announced. 'Which of you wanted the clean cup?'

86

WORD PERFECT

A Speech for All Seasons

There are good public speakers, there are great public speakers and there's Tony O'Reilly. He sometimes begins by invoking the spoofer's promise: 'My word is my bond . . . until I get a better offer.'

After listening to O'Reilly give a lengthy speech at his alma mater, the then Taoiseach, Bertie Ahern, said: 'I'd like to congratulate Belvedere College on the great job dey did in teaching Tony O'Reilly to speak so well. A pity dey didn't teach him to stop!'

Such is O'Reilly's flair with words, it is difficult to imagine that he was once out-quipped – but miracles do happen. England beat Ireland 20–0. As he walked off the pitch O'Reilly turned to Tom Reid and said: '20–0! That was dreadful!'

Reid responded, 'Sure weren't we lucky to get the nil!'

HUSBANDS AND WIVES
O'Reilly is one of the greatest raconteurs world rugby has ever produced. When Eamon de Valera was in his final few years as

Irish president, he was virtually blind. But he was persuaded to attend one of Ireland's home internationals. Watching the game in the stands, Tony O'Reilly was unhappy with some of the referee's decisions. When he was asked afterwards to comment on the match he said, 'Dev saw more of it than the referee.'

He once told the story of an unnamed Irish international whose wife arrived home from work early one day and found her husband in bed with another woman. 'That's it!' she shouted. 'I'm leaving and I'm not coming back!'

'Wait, honey,' the Irish international pleaded, 'can't you at least let me explain?'

'Fine, let's hear your story,' the wife replied.

'Well, I was driving home when I saw this poor young lady sitting at the side of the road, barefoot, torn clothes, covered in mud and sobbing. I immediately took pity on her and asked if she would like to get cleaned up. She got into the car and I brought her home. After she took a shower, I gave her a pair of the underwear that doesn't fit you anymore, the dress that I bought you last year that you never wore, the pair of shoes you bought but never used and even gave her some of the turkey you had in the refrigerator but didn't serve me. Then I showed her to the door and she thanked me. As she was walking down the step, she turned around and asked me, "Is there anything else your wife doesn't use anymore?"'

Another of the stories attributed to O'Reilly was about the Irish international who was having an affair with an Italian woman. One night she confided in him that she was pregnant. Not wanting to ruin his reputation or his marriage, he paid her a large sum of money if she would go to Italy to have the child. If she stayed in Italy, he would also provide child support until the child turned eighteen. She agreed but wondered how he would know when the baby was born. To keep it discreet, he told her to send him a postcard and write 'Spaghetti' on the back. He would then arrange for child support. One day, almost nine months later, he came home to his confused wife, Martina (not her real name). 'Darling,' she said, 'you received a very strange postcard today.'

'Oh, just give it to me and I'll explain it later,' he said.

Martina obeyed, and watched as the Irish international read the card, turned white and fainted.

On the card was written, 'Spaghetti, Spaghetti, Spaghetti. Two with meatballs, one without.'

EYE-CATCHING

One of the many tributes paid to A.J.F. O'Reilly down through the years was: 'Never have you satisfied so many women in the one day.' This is not what it seems. The source was Irene Johnson rejoicing at his generous donation towards the running of the 1994 Women's Hockey World Cup.

O'Reilly gained a reputation as a lover of wine, women and song. Many stories are told about his exploits. They often score low on veracity but high on entertainment value. One of the many stories told about him goes back to his time on the Lions tour to South Africa. One day O'Reilly thought it was raining and put his hand out the window to check. As he did so, a glass eye fell into his hand. He looked up to see where it came from in time to see a young woman looking down.

'Is this yours?' he asked.

She said, 'Yes, could you bring it up?' and the Irish star agreed.

On arrival she was profuse in her thanks and offered O'Reilly a drink. As she was very attractive, he agreed. Shortly afterwards she said, 'I'm about to have dinner. There's plenty, would you like to join me?'

He readily accepted her offer and both enjoyed a lovely meal. As the evening was drawing to a close the lady said, 'I've had a marvellous evening. Would you like to stay the night?'

O'Reilly hesitated then said, 'Do you act like this with every man you meet?'

'No,' she replied, 'only those who catch my eye.'

DEEP THROAT

O'Reilly could have been a film star. The late Noel Purcell recommended him to Al Corfino, the casting director of the film *Ben-Hur*, for the role that was eventually played by Charlton Heston. O'Reilly's physique made him ideal for the scenes in the galleys. Purcell arranged for a meeting between the director and O'Reilly but the rugby player never showed up. The story of O'Reilly's possible role in the film made headlines in places as far away as South Africa.

Having made his name on a global scale on two Lions tours, it is not surprising that O'Reilly has a special affection for rugby tours. On a European tour the Australians were informed that the police had received a complaint saying that one of their players retaliated after being spat at by an English supporter. When the management asked the police spokeswoman what the player should do in those circumstances in the future they were told, 'If someone spits at him, he'll just have to swallow it.'

FROM RUSSIA WITH LOVE

A Russian team touring England asked in broken English for protection at the chemist shop in Heathrow Airport. Security officials were called and they were taken away for interrogation. It was some time before it dawned on the interrogators that the Russians had, in fact, been looking for condoms.

KISS ME QUICK

An Australian club team were on tour in England. Unusually each of the players brought their wives or girlfriends or both. The hooker's wife asked him to kiss her somewhere dirty. He drove her to Soho.

FEELING SHEEPISH

A club team from Kent went on hold to the Scottish Highlands. They were staying in a very quiet town and asked the hotel barman if it was possible for them to get some women for the night. 'Nothing like that here,' said the barman. 'You want to go out and find yourself a nice sheep.' The guests did so. The problem was that they ended up spending the night in jail. Returning to the hotel the next day, they said to the barman, 'Fine advice that was – telling us to get a nice sheep.'

87

BUM DEAL

O'Gara's Game

Ronan O'Gara has a lovely turn of phrase. He once said to me: 'As a Kerry man told me, walk easy when the jug is full.'

O'Gara brought a new dimension to rugby tours on the 2001 Lions tour. Usually, punishment at the players' court means drinking an evil alcoholic concoction of something that will have the poor unfortunate retching and the rest of the squad in gales of laughter. Another perennial favourite is 'the Circle of Fire' challenge where toilet paper is rolled up tight and lit with a match, and the player in question has to clench it between his bum cheek and run the whole way round the room before the flame reaches their skin.

O'Gara devised a new game with the quaint title of 'Red Arse'. His idea was that there would be one bat at each end of the table and the players had to keep a rally going while running around the table and taking it in turns to return the ball. Mess up and you were eliminated. He then added: 'Oh, and by the way, the loser gets a whack on the backside with the bat by every other player.'

BEHIND EVERY GREAT MAN

O'Gara remarked: 'Convincing your mates to join you on the Lions tour is the easy bit. Now comes the hard bit: convincing your wives to let you go.'

EVERYBODY LOVES GOOD NEIGHBOURS

O'Gara's first coaching job saw him as kicking coach to Dan Carter, the world's leading player at the time. Carter shared stories with Rog of the great rivalry that exists between Australia and New Zealand. One of his favourite stories is about the suspicious Australian who hired a private eye to check on the movements of his wife. In addition to a written report, the husband wanted a video of his wife's activities. A week later, the detective returned with a film. They sat down together and proceeded to watch it. Although the quality was less than professional, the man saw his wife meeting another man. He saw the two of them strolling arm in arm and laughing in the park. He saw them enjoying themselves at an outdoor café. He saw them dancing in a dimly lit nightclub and much more erotic adventures in a hotel afterwards. He saw them take part in a dozen activities with utter glee. 'I just can't believe this,' said the distraught husband.

'What's not to believe?' the detective said. 'It's right up there on the screen.'

The husband replied, 'I simply can't believe my wife would disgrace me by wearing an All Black jersey in public.'

THE PRICE IS NOT RIGHT

O'Gara has advertised a number of products. During the Celtic Tiger it was commonplace for stars of the Irish rugby team to be offered small fortunes for making personal appearances. During the height of the boom a young lady was given a budget of two thousand euro to promote the opening of a pharmacy in Cork. She decided to spend the entire sum on getting a top name in Irish rugby to open the pharmacy. When she got his number, she rang him and explained what she wanted him to and the fee she would pay him. The conversation unfolded as follows: 'What did you say your name was again?'

'Mary.' (The name has been changed.)

'Well, it's like this, Mary. I wouldn't turn over in the bed for two thousand euro.'

TAKING IT ON THE CHIN

For Ronan O'Gara, 2006 was a year to remember. As if a second Triple Crown triumph and a Heineken Cup win was not enough, he met his perfect match in July when he married his long-time love, Jessica. Unusually for a Cork man, on that day Limerick rugby fans were happy to sing 'There Is an Aisle' for Ronan.

The sweetness of the Heineken Cup win was magnified for Paul O'Connell by the fact that there had been so many disappointments on the journey:

'I picked up a shoulder injury playing for Munster in the run-up to the Heineken semi-final against Castres. The morning of the match I had to do a fitness test. That is a test I will never forget because my shoulder was standing up well and I was hitting a tackle bag which Declan Kidney was holding. The problem was that I hit it so hard, at one stage I knocked out one of Declan's teeth! He was due to do a TV interview three quarters of an hour later, so he had to go the dentist to get it stuck back in.'

88

LEAVE IT TO MR O'BRIEN

Des O'Brien Meets the President

One of the nicest people this scribe has ever encountered was the late Des O'Brien. Des was not the sort of a man for histrionics. So when he managed the Lions team on the 1966 tour he did not panic when the Welsh centre Ken Jones went up the mountains to shoot deer with some local men, even though he got no permission from anyone to do so. When Jones was missing for a few days, Des turned a deaf ear to those who suggested he call the police assuring them that Jones would be fine. The night before the next match was due Jones coolly strolled into the restaurant where the team were having their dinner. Des never blinked and gently asked, 'Nice to see you, Ken. Tell me, will you be joining us for the game tomorrow?'

SIZE MATTERS?

Des O'Brien went on to become Irish captain, after touring with the Lions. Before an international the president of Ireland, Seán T. O'Kelly, the first Irish president to attend a rugby international, was being introduced to the teams. He was a man who was, let's say, small in stature. The match was being played in October, so the grass was long. As captain Des was introduced to him first. He said, 'God Bless you, Des. I hope you have a good game.' Then O'Brien heard a booming voice in the crowd, 'Hey Des, would you ever get the grass cut so we'd bloody well be able to see the president!'

THAT'LL CLINCH IT

Des believed that one of the great characters of Irish rugby was Dr Jammie Clinch. When he was a medical student in Trinity College, Dublin he was sitting on the rail outside when an American tourist emerged from her first visit to the College and spoke to him. 'It's a big place, I've been three hours going through it,' she said. Jammie replied, 'Ma'am, I've been here for seven years and I'm not through it yet!'

In his medical examination Clinch was shown a bone and asked what it was.

'A femur,' he replied.

'Right or left?'

'I'm not doing Honours,' he answered.

THE SPY WHO CAME IN FROM THE COLD

Possibly one of the most famous 'backroom' characters in Irish rugby was UCD and Leinster's Ned Thornton. One of the stories told about Ned is about the day that he went to General Costello's funeral. There was a huge crowd outside as well as inside the church. The carriage came out with the coffin draped in the tricolour, with a hat and a stick on it. The troops sounded the death march and everybody was very solemn. Ned was standing beside Blackrock's Dan McCarthy at the time and turned around to him and said, 'I see he only got the one cap!'

Given that he is such a larger-than-life character, former Leinster manager Ken Ging naturally enjoyed the company of Ned Thornton. One of his favourite stories goes back to the time Ned went with Leinster to Bath. Leinster lost the match and two of the Bath officials went over to console Ned and Ken. They said all the right things, like how unlucky Leinster were and asked what the Leinster contingent thought of the Bath players. The Leinster duo expressed their great admiration for John Hall, a great back-row forward. One of the Bath officials said, 'He's a shepherd, you know."

Quick as a flash Ned replied, 'And he's in the British army.'

There followed a pantomime-like scene. 'Oh no he is not.' 'Oh yes he is.' Such was Ned's conviction that the Bath selectors became convinced that he was right.

Then Ned said, 'He's an undercover agent in the British army – part of an elite squad – he's what's known as a shepherd's spy!"

89

ALL CREATURES GREAT AND SMALL

The Legend of Deero

Apart from Moss Keane, Ireland has seldom a more loved player by his peers than Shay Deering, as Tony Ward recalls:

'I just loved Shay and it was such a sadness when I heard that he passed away. Not just the rugby community but the world at large is a much poorer place without him.'

Shay had a keen sense of humour. He described the scene when one of his Garryowen teammates got married in the late 1970s. He laid down the following rules: 'I'll be home when I want and at what time I want – and I don't expect any hassle from you. I expect a great dinner to be on the table unless I tell you that I won't be home for dinner. I'll go playing rugby, training, hunting, fishing, boozing and card-playing when I want with my teammates and don't you give me a hard time about it. Those are my rules. Any comments?'

His new bride said, 'No, that's fine with me. Just understand that there will be sex here at seven o'clock every night ... whether you're here or not.'

At a party to mark his wedding anniversary, Shay was asked to give his friends a brief account of the benefits of marriage. Deero replied, 'Well, I've learned that marriage is the best teacher of all. It teaches you loyalty, forbearance, meekness, self-restraint, forgiveness – and a great many other qualities you wouldn't have needed if you'd stayed single.'

HAPPY DAYS

Shay always enjoyed a good laugh with his fellow players. The size of the waistline of former Irish fly-half Barry McGann was the subject of many a quip during his playing days. Shay joked that Barry joined an exclusive gym and spent about four hundred quid on it. He did not lose a pound. He did not realise that you have to show up to lose weight.

LEGAL EAGLE

Former Irish fullback and subsequently leader of the Irish Labour Party Dick Spring was initially a lawyer by profession. Deering went to him in a professional capacity and stated, 'I would like to make a will but I don't know exactly how to go about it.'

Spring said, 'No problem, leave it all to me.'

Deero looked upset as he said, 'Well, I knew you were going to take the biggest slice, but I'd like to leave a little to my children, too.'

PROFESSIONAL COURTESY

Shay enjoyed a joke about lawyers at Spring's expense.

An engineer dies and reports to hell.

Pretty soon, the engineer gets dissatisfied with the level of comfort in hell and starts designing and building improvements. After a while, they've got air conditioning and flush toilets and escalators, and the engineer becomes hugely popular. One day God calls the devil up on the telephone and says with a sneer, 'So, how's it going down there in hell?'

The devil replied, 'Things are going great. We've got air conditioning and flush toilets and escalators, and who knows what this engineer will come up with next.'

God replied, 'What??? You've got an engineer? That's a mistake – he should never have gotten down there; send him up here.'

The devil said, 'No way. I like having an engineer on the staff, and I'm keeping him.'

God said, 'Send him back up here or I'll sue.'

Satan laughed uproariously and replied, 'Yeah, sure. And just where are you going to get a lawyer?'

ALL CREATURES GREAT AND SMALL

As a vet, based in Mullingar, Deero had a passionate interest in animal welfare. At one stage he met a rugby player from, of all places, Mexico. He explained to Shay that rugby was a tiny minority sport in, Mexico but that the number one sport was bullfighting.

The horrified Shay said, 'Isn't that revolting.'

'No,' the Mexican replied, 'revolting is our number two sport.'

DOG GONE

One of Shay's favourite stories was about the dog who went into a hardware store and said, 'I'd like a job please.'

The hardware store owner said, 'We don't hire dogs, why don't you go join the circus?'

The dog replied, 'Well, what would the circus want with a plumber?'

A client took his Rottweiler to Shay.

'My dog's cross-eyed, is there anything you can do for him?'

'Well,' said Deero, 'let's have a look at him.'

So he picked the dog up and examined his eyes, then checked his teeth. Finally he said, 'I'm going to have to put him down.'

'What? Because he's cross-eyed?'

'No, because he's bloody heavy.'

90

BACKHANDER

Munster Are Robbed

'The hand of God and the hand of Diego' is one of the most famous incidents of ethical dimensions in world sport. This was the explanation given by Diego Maradona of Argentina after he deflected the ball with his hand over the advancing England goalkeeper Peter Shilton in the 1986 World Cup. His goal helped Argentina to victory and they went on to take the World Cup.

The most talked about 'ethical incident' in rugby occurred in the final moments of the Heineken Cup final in 2002. Munster were trailing Leicester and were driving hard for their opponents' line when they were awarded a set scrum some five metres out from goal. It was crucial to win this ball and set up a final drive for possible victory. As the Munster scrum-half was about to put the ball into the scrum, Neil Back's infamous 'hand-of-God' backhander knocked the ball from Peter Stringer's grasp into the Leicester scrum and the ball was lost to Leicester. The referee had taken up a position opposite the incoming ball and did not see the incident.

The controversy spawned a new joke:

Q: What's the difference between Tim Henman and Neil Back?

A: Neil Back is much better with his backhand.

CHEATING

Neil Back's infamous 'backhander' left a bitter taste. One Munster fan was heard to remark: 'The Leicester Tigers should be renamed the Leicester Cheetahs.'

They also told the story about Back himself. In this account Back went on a ski trip but was knocked unconscious by the chair lift. He called his insurance company from the hospital, but it refused to cover his injury.

'Why is this injury not covered?' he asked.

'You got hit on the head by a chairlift,' the insurance rep said. 'That makes you an idiot, and we consider that a pre-existing condition.'

91

BON VOYAGE

Moss Keane Tours Australia

When Ireland toured Australia in 1979 Moss Keane came to the attention of the immigration desk at Sydney. Nobody was sure what started off a heated argument between Moss and one of the officials, which culminated in the official asking sharply, 'Do you have any previous convictions?'

Moss replied disdainfully, 'I didn't know it was compulsory any more to have a conviction to enter Australia.'

A MATTER OF PRINCIPLE

Even after his retirement Jim Glennon, to his own surprise, continued to grace the world's playing fields. When he finished playing in 1988 he got the most unexpected invitations to tour as the Golden Oldies idea was really taking off. He got a phone call from Moss Keane in June of that year inquiring if he was free for the last weekend in August. When Jim said he was, Moss told him to keep it free. Jim forgot all about it until the last Wednesday in August when he got another call from Moss. Moss told him that he had been invited to play in an exhibition match across the water for a Lions' Golden Oldies side against a junior team and, although he had been given the plane ticket, was unable to travel. He was going to ring the organiser and tell him he could not make it but that he would be meeting Jim later that day and would attempt to persuade him to travel.

Shortly afterwards Glennon got a phone call from a panic-stricken secretary, apologising profusely for the short notice, but wondering would he be willing to play instead of Moss. Jim 'reluctantly' agreed. On the plane over he was joined by Phil Orr, Willie Duggan and Fergus Slattery. It was a fabulous weekend. Glennon was the only 'non-Lion' on the team. His partner in the second row was Allan Martin of Wales. After the match the pair were chatting in the bath when Martin asked him out of the blue, 'What about Stockholm?' He went on to explain that there was a Golden Oldies match there the following weekend, Thursday to Monday, but he couldn't travel. 'Would you be interested?' When Glennon said yes, Allan told Jim just to leave it with him. On the Monday Jim rang Moss to thank him for the wonderful weekend and asked him why he had left it so late to tell them he couldn't make it. Moss answered, 'Because I didn't want some hoor from England to take my place.'

Two days later Jim got a phone call from a different panic-stricken secretary, apologising profusely for the short notice, but wondering would he be willing to play instead of Allan. This time Jim made him sweat a bit more and told him he was not sure if he would be able to make it because he had other commitments but he rang him back less than an hour later and agreed to the trip. On the plane over he was again joined by Orr, Duggan and Slattery. Also on the trip were J.P.R. Williams and Jim Renwick, among others. It was an absolutely fabulous weekend. On the Tuesday morning Jim rang to thank Allan for putting it his way. When he asked him why he had left it so late to tell them he couldn't make it he replied, 'Because I didn't want some hoor from England to take my place!'

A FINAL MESSAGE

Almost until his last breath Moss retained a deep love of Munster rugby. Hours before he died, he was visited by his old friend from Lansdowne, Mick Quinn, who had the privilege of spending ten minutes on his own with one of the most loved figures in Irish sport. Moss was very ill at the time but as Quinny was leaving he promised him he would drive down to Portarlington to see him again the following day. Moss beckoned him close and with a waving finger said, 'Ye bast**ds from Leinster beat us again last Saturday.'

My favourite Moss story comes from the late, much missed, Dermot Morgan, long before his role in *Father Ted*. Dermot told the story of Moss strolling purposefully into the pub one night and, on seeing all his mates, said to them, "Would you mind if I stayed on my own tonight, I've only enough money for eight pints!"

92

TOP OF THE PROPS

Phil O'Callaghan Tours with Ireland

Like Moss Keane, Phil O'Callaghan was one of the great characters of the game. He toured three times with Irish parties, to Australia in 1967, to Argentina in 1970 and to New Zealand and Fiji in 1976. Apart from his fire on the pitch he was also noted for his quick wit. The most oft quoted story about him is the story of the day a referee penalised him and said, 'You're boring[1], O'Callaghan.' Philo's instinctive retort was, 'Well, you're not so entertaining yourself, ref.' The referee penalised him a further ten yards.

THE FEAR FACTOR
Philo is famed for his experiences playing for Dolphin. One goes back to a match played on a bitterly cold November day. He was lifting one of his forwards Eoghan Moriarty in the line-out. The

---

[1] The term used to describe the way a prop-forward drives in at an illegal angle into an opposing prop-forward.

big man shouted down at him, 'Philo let me down. My hands are frozen.'

The Old Wesley and Leinster player Bobby Macken joined Dolphin for a season. The following year he went back to Dublin. When he next played against Dolphin, Philo was standing on the wing as usual when Macken came charging towards him but, to O'Callaghan's surprise, he tapped the ball into touch. Philo asked him, 'Are you afraid of me Bobby?'

'No, but I'm afraid of running into your mouth!' he replied.

SOLIDARITY

One of Philo's strongest memories is of an incident involving Barry McGann:

'The night before an Irish squad session McGann, Shay Deering and I and a couple of others had frequented a few pubs. In fact we were even thrown out of one of them! The squad session the next day started with some laps around the pitch. Shortly after we started off I heard Barry shout at me, "Cal don't leave me." I dropped back with him and we were lapped once or twice. The cruel irony of the situation was that after the session he was selected and I was dropped!'

GONE FISHING

There was a lot of surprise that O'Callaghan was selected to tour with Ireland to New Zealand in 1976 but he played a very significant role on that tour. He earned his cap on merit. He could be described as 'the traditional Irish rugby tourist'. When Ireland was being intimidated on the pitch he was not found wanting.

Ireland had other great characters in that squad, none more so than Brendan Foley, whose late son Axel became a star with

Munster and Ireland. At one stage on that tour Foley came down to the foyer of the hotel which had a big fountain. He went in to the middle of it to do some fishing. He didn't catch anything! After that he was known as 'Foley never caught a fish'.

93

TOM AND MURPHY

Tom Kiernan Goes Shopping

Cork Constitution has provided Irish rugby legends down through the years, including Tom Kiernan and Noel Murphy. They have entered rugby folklore in a story from the day the two former famous internationals were on a trip to England and as they passed a shop and saw a notice on the window which read 'Trousers £2. Shirts £1.50.' Tom and Noel were thrilled. They decided they would make a killing and buy them cheaply in England and sell them off at proper price back home in Ireland. They decided to play it cool and speak in English accents. When they went in they calmly walked up to the counter and said to the manager, 'We'll buy all the trousers and shirts you have.'

The manager looked at them with astonishment. Despite their feigned accents he asked, 'Excuse me, gentlemen, are you both from Cork?'

Noel and Tom asked in unison, 'How did you know?'

'Oh, call it an inspired guess. You probably didn't notice but this is actually a dry cleaner's!'

LOST IN TRANSLATION

Tom Kiernan was renowned for his quickness of thought. Hence his nickname 'the Grey Fox'. This was probably best typified on the 1968 Lions tour when the young Gareth Edwards was getting irate with the decisions of the referee. He went so far as to call him 'a cheating f**ker'. The ref told Edwards he was sending him off for bad language. Captain Kiernan intervened and asked him what the problem was. With more than a hint of impatience the ref remarked acidly, 'Your scrum-half called me a f**ker and I'm sending him off.'

Kiernan soothingly calmed him down. 'He certainly wasn't. He was talking Welsh to his out-half partner.'

The referee was immediately placated and rescinded his decision and Edwards continued to play on. And who was his out-half? None other than Mike Gibson, who didn't speak a word of Welsh.

94

SNAKES ALIVE

Irish International Makes an Impression

Some sports personalities are in the business of self-denial. Rob Henderson is refreshingly candid. He has his fair share of rugby stories but his favourites deal with the exploits of one former Irish international:

'My favourite character is Ken O'Connell, the former Irish international. His nickname is "the Legend" but you would have to know him to understand why. He gained his legendary status in a different way to Brian O'Driscoll! He went off to India or Thailand to find himself.

'We played together with London-Irish. At one stage we were playing in the European Conference. We were all there getting ready to travel to Bordeaux. We were getting kitted out and were all there with our kit bags as if we were heading to Monaco. We looked a million dollars. Just as we were ready to leave someone shouted, "Where's Ken?" Half an hour later he shows up with Malcolm O'Kelly. For once, miraculously, Mal had all his gear and luggage. Somebody must have dressed him!

'Ken turned up wearing a T-shirt and shorts. His T-shirt had a picture of a fella wearing shorts and a T-shirt but with his "manhood" sticking out. His only luggage was a kitbag which was the size of a big ice-cream tub. I said, "Ken, what are you carrying mate?"

He replied, "I've got all I need. I've got my boots, my gumshield and my heart." With that he was off to get the plane. That's Ken boy. That's why he's a legend.

'I will never forget my first introduction to Ken. Before he played his first game for London-Irish he wandered into the changing-room with his togs around his ankles. He looked down at his private parts and said to me, "I bet you thought Saint Patrick chased all the snakes out of Ireland."'

95

UNDERSTATED

Moss Keane Has a Party

Moss Keane toured with the Lions in New Zealand in 1977. After their second Test victory the Lions threw the party to beat all parties in the team hotel. It was soon discovered that one of their players was missing. According to legend when everyone else expressed concern about him Moss said he knew where the missing person was – next door with his girlfriend. Moss was dispatched to bring the guilty party back – though given strict instructions not to break down any doors. (His nickname on that tour was 'Rent-a-Storm' so the decree seemed more than justified.) The rest of the squad listened to a slight flurry next door and moments later Moss came in the door with the missing player under his arm, completely naked and squirming like a fish on a hook. Under the other arm he held the player's girlfriend in a similar state of undress and embarrassment. Moss in his best Kerry accent boomed out: 'To be sure, did you be wanting the two of them?'

In fairness Moss did try to keep the players intellectually stimulated on the tour. As he finished his last drink Moss called for silence in the bar and asked a question: who played soccer for Scotland and cricket for England? Everyone was left scratching their heads and no one could figure out the answer. Finally, just before he walked out the door, Moss answered his own question, 'Denis Law and Ian Botham!'

TABLE MANNERS

Moss made his debut with the Irish team in 1974. It was a culture shock for him on many levels. After training on a squad session on a Sunday morning the team would retreat to the Saddle Room in the Shelbourne Hotel. There was a set meal: roast beef, a seasonal-vegetable selection and a baked potato done in tinfoil. Barry McGann correctly guessed that Moss would not have experienced anything like this before. He told the rest of the squad not to touch their food until Moss started eating. Moss was totally flummoxed by the tinfoil. He turned it over and poked at it from every angle but to no avail. He looked around for guidance from his teammates but they had not touched a scrap. Exasperated, he took up the tinfoil in his hand and threw it over his shoulder, saying, 'Where I come from we don't eat Easter eggs with roast beef.'

FATHER AND SON

Moss's father was watching his son playing in Lansdowne Road and confessed to a fellow fan, 'I don't know too much about the rules of rugby.'

His friend said, 'Don't worry, your son knows even less.'

KEEPING EVERYBODY HAPPY

Tony Ward and Mick Quinn once both got 18 points in a final trial for Ireland but Quinn felt he had outplayed Ward on the day and was feeling pretty good. Later that night Moss Keane came up to Quinn at the reception and told him that he was the best out-half he had ever played with. Quinn was pretty chuffed with his compliment and told him so. Shortly after he was going to the toilet and saw Mossie talking to somebody but he couldn't make out who it was at first. As he passed them by, he realised it was Wardy and he heard Mossie tell him he was without doubt the finest out-half ever to play for Ireland. Quinn gave him a kick in the backside for his dishonesty. Mossie followed him into the toilet, put his arm around him and said, 'Don't worry, Scout. I was only being diplomatic.'

A DOG'S LIFE

Moss once was asked to give an after-dinner speech at very short notice. He began by saying that he felt like a dog surrounded by four trees – he did not have a leg to stand on.

CHRISTMAS PREPARATIONS

Moss was picking through the frozen turkeys at the local super-market but he could not find one big enough for the family. He asked a passing assistant, 'Do these turkeys get any bigger?'

The assistant replied, 'I'm afraid not, they're dead.'

96

MEDICALLY BEWILDERING

Ken Kennedy's Lions Tour

Mick Doyle was one of the many players who paid homage to the late great Ken Kennedy:

'The great thing about my rugby career was that it gave me the opportunity to meet so many great characters like Ken Kennedy. He had a great irreverence. I would describe him as a macho David Norris.'

SAFETY FIRST

Ken Kennedy was a top doctor as well as a top hooker. According to folklore when he was asked during a gynaecology lecture, 'When is the safe period?'

He replied, 'Half-time when Ireland play Wales in Cardiff Arms Park.'

A MEDICAL MIRACLE

Ken Kennedy had a dramatic introduction to his involvement on the Lions' tour to South Africa in 1974. Although he was travelling as a player, it was Kennedy's medical skills which were first called for when Bobby Windsor was taken ill with food poisoning. He was so ill that he was taken to the back of the plane and told to suck ice-cubes to help him cool down. As team doctor Kennedy came to take his temperature without knowing about the ice-cubes. When he looked at the thermometer he shouted out, 'Jaysus, Bobby you died twenty-four hours ago!'

Inevitably when talking of front rows the famous Pontypool front-row of Charlie Faulkner, Bobby Windsor and Graham Price, celebrated in song and folklore by Max Boyce loomed large for Kennedy. The camaraderie between front-row players is amazing, especially between the Pontypool gang. It is a strange fact of rugby life that people in the same positions on the field tend to pal around together. It was said that Windsor's tactic with novice opponents was to bite them on the ear early in the match and say, 'Behave yourself, son, and nothing will happen to this ear of yours.'

Windsor was one of the game's great raconteurs. One of his favourite stories was about a Welsh Valleys rugby club on tour in America. On coming back from a night on the town, two of the players could not find their rooms. They decided to check for their teammates by looking through the keyholes. At one stage they came on an astonishing sight. There in her birthday suit was a Marilyn Monroe lookalike. Close by was a man who was chanting out with great conviction: 'Your face is so beautiful that I will have it painted in gold. Your breasts are so magnificent that I will have them painted in silver. Your legs are so shapely that I will have them painted in platinum.'

Outside the two Welsh men were getting very aroused and began jostling each other for the right of the keyhole. The man inside, hearing the racket, shouted out, 'Who the hell is out there?'

The two Welsh men replied, 'We're two painters from Pontypool.'

EGG-ACTLY 1

Bobby Windsor had two culinary moments on that Lions tour. At one stage he said to a waiter, 'I want one egg boiled for exactly 26 seconds and I want another one boiled for 25 minutes 14 seconds. And I want three slices of toast which are pale gold on one side and burned pure black on the other.'

Waiter: 'But sir. That's simply not possible. We can't go to all the trouble to fill an order like that.'

Windsor: 'Oh yes you can, sonny boy. That's exactly what you dished up to me yesterday!'

EGG-ACTLY 2

Waiter: What kind of omelette would you like?

Bobby Windsor: 'One with eggs in it.'

97

MORE SEX PLEASE. WE'RE BRITISH AND IRISH

Moss and Willie go on Tour

As captain of the Lions team that toured New Zealand in 1977, the late, great Phil Bennett needed players willing to shed blood for the cause. He found one in Willie Duggan.

During one match Willie was so battered and bloodied that he went off for stitches just before half-time. When the rest of the team came into the dressing room they saw him sitting there with a fag in one hand and a bottle of beer in the other as they stitched up his face.

'Bad luck, Willie. Well played,' the Lions captain, Bennett, said.

'What do you mean?' Willie demanded. 'As soon as the f**ker sorts my face out I'll be back on.'

On the tour Willie played for Lions against a Maori team in a very physical contest. At one stage he was trapped at the bottom of a ruck when a few players kicked him on his head. True to form he got up and carried on. After the game Bennett asked him if he remembered the pounding on his head. His reply was vintage Dugganesque: 'I do. I heard it.'

SAFE SEX

Media reports often blow events on tour out of proportion. In 1977 during the Lions tour to New Zealand the British media were full of stories about the Lions team having wild sex parties involving dozens of local women picked up around the town. This was a time when 'safe sex' meant a padded headboard on the bed. Bobby Windsor was furious. When he read reports of the game and its aftermath he demanded to know where the orgies were taking place and why he had not been invited!

Bobby was less than impressed by some of the food on offer at an official reception. He made his feelings known to the chef: 'It's not often you get the soup and the wine at the same temperature.'

When the Lions stopped off at a roadside café during a long coach drive Windsor complained to Phil Bennett: 'I went into the kitchen here and, do you know, there isn't a single blue-bottle in there. They're all married with kids.'

Windsor was even more irate when he tasted the food. He asked the chef, 'What do you do about salmonella?'

The chef replied, 'I fry it in a little batter.'

In the team hotel Bobby one morning was not satisfied about some of the food. At one stage he called over the waiter and said, 'These eggs are awful.'

The waiter casually replied, 'Don't blame me. I only laid the table.'

Later that evening Windsor had another encounter with the same waiter. Bobby was early at the table for dinner but when the waiter came to take his order, he told him he wasn't ready to order until his friends arrived. The waiter sarcastically replied, 'Oh, you must be the table for two, sir.'

VIP

Not all rugby tours are pleasurable. Dissatisfaction with facilities is an occupational hazard for rugby tourists. Mick Galwey tells the story that on the Lions' tour to New Zealand in 1993 the secretary of the touring party, Bob Weighill, asked for an extra pat of butter to accompany his bread roll. He took umbrage when he was told this would not be possible. 'Do you know who I am?'

'No, sir'.

The waiter listened impassively as Mr Weighill listed his auspicious catalogue of titles. Then he softly replied, 'And do you know who I am?'

'No.'

'I'm in charge of the butter.'

98

BIG MAL

Malcolm O'Kelly's Trip

Irish rugby has produced many great characters.

There are many stories in the Irish camp about Malcolm O'Kelly's lack of organisation and his capacity for being late. The standard line was: if you are behind Mal in the airport you have missed your plane.

DEDICATED FOLLOWER OF FASHION

A particular favourite in the squad is about the time when Mal was spotted wearing a black shoe and a brown shoe. When this was discreetly pointed out to O'Kelly he shrugged his shoulders nonchalantly and said, 'Don't worry. That's the new fashion. I've another pair at home exactly like that!'

MONEY'S TOO TIGHT TO MENTION

Shane Byrne had a reputation in the squad for being 'careful with money'. Hence the joke amongst his former Irish colleagues that he installed double-glazing windows in his home so that his children would not hear the ice-cream van.

OLD VIC

There has never been a nicer or more modest player for Ireland than Victor Costello. Yet Victor was widely quoted within the squad as boasting that Bono asked him for his autograph.

I'M NEARLY FAMOUS

There is a fine line between self-confidence and arrogance. Keith Gleeson stayed on the right side of that line. That did not stop the other Irish players from recounting a tale he tells of going for a walk one night and bumping into a Stenna Sea Link! They also claim that at the moment he is writing a book called *Famous People Who Know Me*.

SIMPLY SIMON

According to rugby legend a great Munster out-half was called to a premature death. He was met at the gates of heaven by St Peter. St Peter apologised profusely for bringing the rugby player to his eternal reward at such a young age but explained that the celestial rugby cup final was taking place and, as a manager of one of the teams, he needed a star player. The out-half was whisked immediately to the stadium and marvelled at the facilities. They were literally out of this world. Such was the excitement of the occasion that the recently deceased forgot about his death and played the game of his eternal life. With just two minutes to go, St Peter's side were leading by 19 points when the giant Munster out-half noticed an athletic sub coming onto the opposition side and, in an accent that was immediately identifiable as Cork, giving instructions to his side. The new arrival got the ball four times and scored 4 tries – each more stunning than the other. He did not bother with the conversions but had the game restarted immediately and his team won by a point.

After the game St Peter rushed on to console his dejected star player. The ex-Munster player asked, 'Tell me, when did Simon Zebo die?'

'That's not Simon Zebo. That's God. He just thinks he's Simon Zebo!'

99

A STITCH IN TIME

Ireland Tour Fiji

There is a great book to be written about Ireland's tour to Fiji and New Zealand in 1976.

It did almost end in tragedy, though. Moss Keane almost drowned. He went for a swim and when he got into trouble and frantically gestured for help – all his fellow Irish players assumed that he just was waving at them!

On that tour Jimmy Davidson was called in to the Irish side as a replacement. He was so happy to be selected that he jumped for joy when he got on the team bus for the first time. He jumped so high that he smashed his head against the roof and needed six stitches.

For his first game on the tour the Irish were worried about things getting out of hand on the pitch. At one stage there was a melee in the ruck and Pa Whelan mistakenly stamped Davidson on the head. Initially the Irish lads thought one of the New Zealand guys had done it and there was bedlam for two minutes. When order was restored the first thing the Irish players heard was Davidson shouting at his own teammate who had been responsible for the injury: 'You fu**king idiot Whelan.' After the game Davidson needed multiple stitches.

THE YOUNG ONE

John Robbie was the youngest player in the Irish party and looked it. On one boat trip during the tour, some New Zealander glanced at him and remarked in all seriousness that it was nice of the New Zealand rugby union to allow the Irish manager to bring his son along on tour.

That tour concluded with a match against Fiji, which is an intimidating place to play in. Ireland defeated their hosts 8–0. There were heavy areas of the pitch, so much so that frogs were jumping on the playing surface during the match.

Normally, there are shouts of joy after an Irish team is announced. The Fiji game was no exception. However, so humid was the climate that this time all the hurrahs came from the players not selected. They were much more interested in looking out on the most beautiful ocean in the world than watching the match. The Fijians were lovely people but there was a bit of an incident after the game between an Irish player and one of theirs. When asked about the resolution of the incident the Irish player (who shall remain nameless) in all earnestness said, 'I gave him a black eye!'

MONEY

The Irish team travelled throughout the island in an old bus with no windows. John Robbie got a bit drunk after the game. He had told the team about the craze at the time of 'lobbing moons' – pulling one's trousers down, bending over and displaying the bare backside to all and sundry. The trick was to choose the time and the place with the most care to get the greatest effect. The Fijian bus without windows was too much of a temptation, and so Robbie lobbed a moon. The locals were totally amazed. Suddenly the Irish players heard an anguished scream. It was Robbie shouting, 'My God, I've lobbed my wallet.' It had fallen out the window and Christmas had come early for some lucky local.

100

WHAT'S THE NAME OF THE GAME?

Tony Ward's Question of Sport

One of Tony Ward's favourite television appearances dates back to his guest role in 1979 on *A Question of Sport* – the BBC's premier sporting quiz programme. Ward was on Emlyn Hughes team and Liam Brady was on Gareth Edwards's side. Ward was to see Coleman speak at first hand when David Coleman asked Ward's fellow contestant Liam Brady, 'In what sport is a kamen used?' Brady was very surprised to discover that the answer was *hurling*. Coleman had mispronounced 'camán?' as 'kamen'.

KEEPING UP WITH THE COMPETITION
It is the not the only time Ward has been confused. He once asked a totally unfit Willie Duggan what he was doing stamping on the ground when playing in a summer friendly. Willie replied, 'I'm stamping that bloody snail which has been following me around since the match started!'

IT WAS NOT LOVELY AND FAIR
As coach Mick Doyle conceded subsequently, Ireland made a major blunder in the build-up to the inaugural World Cup in

1987 by trying to wrap up their players in cotton wool and not allowing them to play any club matches after March, whereas the Welsh players were involved in club rugby right up to the first half of May. Ireland looked very battle-weary in that opening match in Wellington while Wales were sharp and incisive and ran out comfortable winners with 13–6.

The match is as much remembered for an incident before the game as for the action on the field. Tony Ward watched the events unfold before his eyes with a unique mixture of incredulity and horror.

'I will never forget the version of "The Rose of Tralee" which the band played before the game instead of the Irish National Anthem. It was horrendous. I love James Last's version of that song but this was excruciatingly painful and embarrassing to us all.'

After the defeat to Wales changes were inevitable for the second game – a 46–19 victory over Canada. Tony Ward was recalled at out-half in place of Paul Dean – who came in for a lot of criticism for not using the strong wind in Wellington against the Welsh.

In the press conference to announce the team Mick Doyle was asked why he had not picked Ward for the first game. Doyle replied, 'Well it's very simple. We couldn't be sure if he knew the words of "The Rose of Tralee".'

THE FINAL WHISTLE

Jack Kyle once said to me, 'I played with some great players, great teams and great coaches. We all should be grateful for the past, enthusiastic about the present and confident about the future.'

I leave my journey into Irish rugby with a smile on my face – though I feel caught between a ruck and a hard place.

We have to improve constantly or die. They've invented a new version of rugby where only people who wear glasses can play it. It's a non-contact sport.

Once you've seen one rugby joke, you've seen a maul.

I could only finish with Ireland's first-ever victory in New Zealand over the All Blacks in July.

Q: What's the difference between this morning's scrambled eggs and the All Blacks?

A: The All Blacks have just been beaten.

NEVIN

Never to Be Forgotten

The darker the night, the brighter the stars.
— Fyodor Dostoevsky, *Crime and Punishment*

This is a book to make people laugh but I am acutely mindful that it comes out on the tenth anniversary of one of the darkest days in the history of Irish rugby.

Nevin Spence was a talented centre with the Ulster rugby team. At just twenty-two years of age he was on the cusp of making the Irish team. The rugby world was his oyster. But on 15 September 2012 tragedy struck and he lost his life.

In the worst farming accident in over twenty years in Ulster, Nevin was taken from the family he adored in an attempt to rescue a beloved dog after it had fallen into a slurry tank on the family farm in Hillsborough, County Down. His father Noel (aged fifty-eight), and his brother Graham (thirty) also died while trying to rescue each other from the slurry tank. Such were the bonds of family love that Nevin's sister Emma also courageously put her life on the line in an effort to rescue her father and brothers before being overcome by the poisonous fumes and waking up in the recovery position.

While Nevin may have been a full-time rugby player, he loved farming just as much. At night-time he milked the cows and the joke was that his best workouts would be standing out in the yard.

Nevin created a monument more lasting than bronze,
More lofty than the royal structure of the pyramids,
One that neither the corroding rain
Nor the ungovernable North Wind can destroy,
Nor the countless series of the years, nor the flight of time.

His light shone too bright to ever be extinguished from our memories.

ACKNOWLEDGEMENTS

My special thanks to the great Tony Ward for writing the foreword.

I also wish to express my deepest gratitude to Donal Lenihan, Ollie Campbell, Philip McKinley and Emma Spence for their assistance.

My profound thanks to the many players, past and present, who generously shared their stories and thoughts with me and who made this book possible.

A very particular thanks for many kindnesses to Joe Schmidt.

Thanks to Simon Hess, Campbell Brown and all at Black & White for their help.

The world's nicest man, Nigel Macmillan, had a momentous year with a big birthday, a huge promotion and an important academic and professional qualification. May the rugby gods smile down on him.

The birth of Cara Moore in January was like the most splendid sun that brought dazzling rays of light and warmth for the Dobey and Moore families.

Irish rugby fans had a merry Sixmas in February 2022 when Ireland began their Six Nations campaign with a big win over Wales. However, for music fans an even bigger event the same week came when Gareth O'Callaghan flew in the face of adversity and made a triumphant return to radio on Classic Hits 4 FM. Gareth continues to be an inspiration for all rugby seasons. *Marcet sine adversario virtus.*

My thanks to Kevin McDermott of Shannonside/Northern Sound for his ongoing support for my books.

My deep gratitude also to Dave O'Connell for his practical assistance down the years and for keeping the West awake.